THE PLAYFORD BALL
103 Early Country Dances 1651–1820
As Interpreted by Cecil Sharp and His Followers

Kate Van Winkle Keller and Genevieve Shimer

A copublication of
A Cappella Books
and
The Country Dance and Song Society

©1990 The Country Dance and Song Society

ISBN 1-55652-091-3
LC# 90-81710

A Cappella Books
an imprint of
Chicago Review Press

Editorial offices:
P.O. Box 380
Pennington, NJ 08534

Business offices:
814 North Franklin Street
Chicago, IL 60610

Music engraving by Laurie Andres
Cover design by Main Street Design
Interior Design, type, and mechanicals by Kate Van Winkle Keller

On the cover: The engraving on the cover is from the title page of the fourth volume of Thompson's *Compleat Collection of 200 Favorite Country Dances*, published in London in 1780 by Saml., Ann, and Peter Thompson. By permission of the British Library.

About the Country Dance and Song Society: Founded in 1915, the Country Dance and Song Society (CDSS) is an association of people and groups interested in traditional, historical, and contemporary English and American country dance, folk song, and instrumental music. The Society has over 100 member groups and 2600 individual members, located primarily in the U.S. and Canada. CDSS currently operates summer dance camps in Massachussetts and West Virginia with sessions for adults and families. The sales department of our national headquarters features recordings, books, videos, and other materials, all of which are available by mail order. The Society provides a referral service with information about events as well as advice on programming and organization. Members receive our bimonthly newsletter, *CDSS News*, our annual magazine, *Country Dance and Song*, a members list and group directory; discounts on purchases from the sales catalog; and priority admission to our summer programs. For more information about our membership, programs, or for a sales catalog, please contact: Country Dance and Song Society, 17 New South Street, Northampton, Massachusetts 01060, (413)584-9913.
The publication of *The Playford Ball* coincides with the 75th anniversary of CDSS and is published thanks to generous contributions to our Publications Fund.

TABLE OF CONTENTS

THE PLAYFORD BALL

Enter Nicholas and Jenkin, Jack Slime, Roger Brickbat,
with Country Wenches, and two or three musicians.

Jenk: Come Nick, take you Joan Miniver to trace withal, Jack Slime, traverse you with Cicely Milkpail; I will take Jane Trubkin, and Roger Brickbat shall have Isabel Motley, and now that they are busy in the parlor, come strike up, we'll have a crash here in the yard.

Nick: My humour is not compendious: dancing I possess not, though I can foot it; yet since I am fallen into the hands of Cicely Milkpail, I assent.

Jack: Truly Nick, though we were never brought up like serving courtiers, yet we have been brought up with serving creatures, - aye, and Gods creatures, too, for we have been brought up to serve sheep, oxen, horses, hogs, and such like; and though we be but country fellows, it may be in the way of dancing, we can do the horse-trick as well as serving-men.

Roger: Aye, and the cross-point too.

Jenk: Oh Slime! Oh Brickbat! Do not you know that comparisons are odious? Now, we are odious ourselves too, therefore there are no comparisons to be made betwixt us.

Nick: I am sudden and not superfluous! I am quarrelsome, and not seditious! I am peaceable, and not contentious! I am brief, and not compendious.

Slime: Foot it quickly! If the musick overcome not my melancholy, I shall quarrel, and if they sudden do not strike up, I shall presently strike thee down.

Jenk: No quarreling for Gods sake! Truly, if you do, I shall set a knave between ye.

Slime: I come to dance, not to quarrel. Come, what shall it be? *Rogero?*

Jenk: *Rogero?* No, we will dance *The Beginning of the World.*

Cicely: I love no dance so well, as *John come kiss me now.*

Nick: I, that have ere now deserved a Cushion, call for the *Cushion-Dance.*

Roger: For my part I like nothing so well as *Tom Tyler.*

Jenk: No, we'll have *The Hunting of the Fox.*

Slime: *The Hay, The Hay,* there's nothing like *The Hay.*

Nick: I have said, I do say, and I will say again...

Jenk: Every man agree to have it as Nick says.

All: Content.

Nick: It hath been, it now is, and it shall be...

Cicely: What Master Nicholas? What?

Nick: *Put on your Smock a Monday.*

Jenk: So the dance will come cleanly off! Come, for Gods sake, agree of something. If you like not that, put it to the musicians, or let me speak for all, and we'll have *Sellengers Round.*

All: That! That! That!

Nick: Now I am resolved thus it shall be. First take hands, then take you to your heels.

Jenk: Why? Would you have us run away?

Nick: No, but I would have you shake your heels. Music, strike up!

from Thomas Heywood's play A Woman Killed with Kindness (1607), I:ii

*Woodcut from **English Dance and Song**, 31/3 (Autumn 1969): 105*

ACKNOWLEDGEMENTS

The authors are grateful to the following institutions and individuals for permission to reproduce items in their collections.

In the United Kingdom, Bath Reference Library, Bodleian Library, British Library, Central Library of Dundee, Manchester Public Libraries, Mitchell Library of Glasgow, and Vaughan Williams Memorial Library of the English Folk Dance and Song Society; in the United States, Brown University, Colonial Williamsburg Foundation, Essex Institute of Salem, Massachusetts, Forbes Library of Northampton, Massachusetts, Harvard University, the Huntington Library of San Marino, California, Lewis-Walpole Library of Farmington, Connecticut, Library of Congress, and Yale University; Individuals and publishers, Boydell and Brewer, Da Capo Press, Dance Horizons, Dover Publications, Folklore Associates, Dr. William M. Litchman, and Dorothy Poucher.

Many individuals have helped make this book a reality and we are very grateful for their contributions. Our special thanks to Malcolm Taylor, Jacqueline Schwab, Ed Wilfert, Joan Sussler, Christine Helwig, John Chapman, and Grace Feldman.

We are deeply indebted to Brad Foster, Helene and Arthur Cornelius, and Sue Salmons who helped us with the dance instructions. George Fogg and Cyril Hendrickson offered many useful suggestions, and Marshall Barron made valuable corrections to the music. We are particularly grateful for Laurie Andres' skillful engraving of the music and his thoughtful suggestions for tune versions and chording.

Our thanks to the staff of the Folger Shakespeare Library who retrieved and reshelved many precious books for us as we tracked down elusive historical clues.

Finally our thanks to Jack Shimer and Bob Keller for their editing help and their support.

THE LEGACY OF CECIL SHARP

"Parson's Farewell" in 1922

Quiet, easy motion in a simple, unaffected manner. This illustration from Cecil Sharp's *Country Dance Book, Part 6* (London: 1922, opposite page 23) shows the quintessential Sharp-style hey for four.

The woodcut opposite is from a ballad sheet in the Pepys collection, volume 3, 47.

Courtesy of Boydell & Brewer

THE LEGACY OF CECIL SHARP

This is a collection of English country dances originally from the seventeenth and eighteenth centuries. They represent the core of the rich tradition of early English country dancing as it was reinterpreted by Cecil J. Sharp and others who have carried on his legacy. Fundamental repertory for the Country Dance and Song Society for seventy-five years, these dances usually highlight annual "Playford Balls" held in many communities, events named in honor of John Playford, compiler of the earliest source of many of the dances.

Born in London in 1859, Cecil Sharp was educated at Cambridge and began a career in music as an organist and teacher. He soon noticed a strange phenomenon in his work. In the spirit of nationalism which swept Europe toward the end of the nineteenth century, many countries were reviving native song and dance. But not England. There, music education was based on German music.

Folk dances from Scandinavia and songs from France and Germany formed much of the repertory. The English were thought not to have a traditional music or dance of sufficient quality to teach. Although the study of English literary ballads was highly valued the world over, vernacular music, and particularly the country dances which were a creation of the English people themselves, were not known at all, even to Sharp.

A chance meeting in 1899 with a small group of traditional dancers changed the picture entirely. Cecil Sharp's discovery of England's rich heritage of dance was an important moment in dance history. Recognizing the significance and value of traditional arts for musical, social and educational purposes, and discovering that the English had virtually lost their own inheritance, he devoted the remainder of his life to their preservation and propagation. His work led to a vigorous revival of English ceremonial, ritual, and country dance.

The Folk Music Revival

Sharp and his family were spending Christmas of 1899 with his wife's mother, who was then living in Headington, about a mile east of Oxford. On Boxing Day, a group of men from the village came along the drive and formed up in front of the house. A musician struck up an invigorating tune and six "men dressed in white, decorated with ribbons, with pads of small latten-bells strapped to their shins, carrying coloured sticks and white handkerchiefs" danced a morris dance, while another, dressed as a fool, capered around them. Sharp was stunned! Here was real English folk dance, and music too, and no one knew about it! It opened his eyes, piqued his curiosity, and presented a challenge to every skill he had. Later he was to say that that day was the beginning of the folk music revival in England. (Karpeles, *Cecil Sharp,* 25)

He immediately collected five tunes from the concertina player, William Kimber, and when he was able, went out to search for more. The fruits were two-fold. Firstly, he found a vibrant, living tradition of folk song and remnants of morris, sword, and country dance in rural England. Secondly, when he turned to historical resources to amplify the living traditions, although he found little information on the morris and sword dance, he discovered a wealth of material on the country dance in printed and manuscript sources. He also learned that these social dances had a solid and thoroughly English heritage.

There were thousands of similar dances in publications dating from John Playford's *English Dancing Master* (London: 1651) to Thomas Wilson's encyclopedic *Complete System of English Country Dancing* (London: 1820). His response to these finds was an evangelical program of interpretation, teaching, the preparation of demonstration teams, and publications to make the newly discovered material available to others.

During World War I, Sharp made four trips to America, spending a total of nearly three years here. Initially, he came to develop dance and music interludes for Shakespearean tercentenary festivals, but soon he was travelling throughout the country collecting traditional songs, tunes, and dances, training leaders, and presenting lectures and workshops to promote folk song and all three types of dance. In the process he firmly established the American branch of the English Folk Dance Society which was to become the Country Dance and Song Society.

English Country Dance

A common misunderstanding about English country dance is that "English" means "Playford." This latter term is often used loosely to designate a certain style of country dance in much the same way that in England the word "Hoover" is applied to any type of vacuum cleaner, or as in this country "Xerox" is synonymous with "photocopy."

There are two distinct types of English country dance, one is the traditional dance of the people, the other the so-called "Playford-type" or revival dances which are based on interpretations of dances published many years before, in the style first used by Cecil Sharp.

Among the English dances popular today, "Morpeth Rant" is a traditional longways dance with boisterous north-country stepping. It was collected in Northumberland by Sharp's assistant and disciple, Maud Karpeles, and published in *Twelve Traditional Country Dances* (London: 1931). It is a true folk or community dance. These were the kinds of dances that Cecil Sharp found in rural areas when he first went out to collect dances native to the English people and published in his first *Country Dance Book* (London: 1909). They may be compared with New England contras or Appalachian square dances. They have definite regional flavor both in formations, steps, and style of music. The repertoire is limited and the dances rarely taught, since the people dancing have done them all their lives. These group dances in longways, square and circle formations had been popular for generations but by the beginning of the twentieth century they had been eclipsed by popular couple dances such as waltzes, polkas, schottisches, two-steps, and other round dances. Only remnants remained in isolated villages.

Cecil Sharp
November 22, 1859 - June 23, 1924

from Douglas Kennedy, *Sixty Years of Folk* (London: 1971), 19.

"Heartsease" is one of Cecil Sharp's own reconstructions from John Playford's *The English Dancing Master*, which was published in London in 1651. It is a controlled lilting dance for two couples. "The Hole in the Wall" is a flowing duple minor longways dance set to a beautiful hornpipe by Purcell. It was interpreted in 1929 by Douglas Kennedy, from a printed original of 1696. "The Fandango," an elegant set dance for three couples, was created in 1931 by a follower of Sharp and inspired by a longways country dance published in 1774. While each of these dances was created anew from an older model, today they are all danced in the same smooth, flowing style that Sharp developed in the first decade of this century.

The History of Country Dance

Country dancing was first mentioned as a specific type of social dance in England in the middle of the sixteenth century when Elizabeth I was queen. She enjoyed watching the ladies of her court dancing "country dances," although she herself preferred the galliard, volta, and other more demanding couple dances. Although none of the country dance choreographies from this early period have survived, a few dances in the first edition of Playford's collection of seventy-five years later have forms and movements which may be similar to those danced in Elizabeth's court and are, in turn, strongly derivative of earlier Italian *balli*.

Unlike the couple dances, in which the steps are most important, country dances are created from a vocabulary of often symmetrical floor tracks along which the dancers move with or around one another. While a galliard or a volta is best viewed from ground level, the country dance is most dramatic from above. The weavings and turnings create a kaleidoscopic effect on the floor and the steps used are secondary to the figures, and vary with changing fashion.

Country dances appear to always have been regarded as a pleasing alternative to the formal dances which required great skill in performance. Two distinguishing characteristics are that the country dance is a group dance in which there is interaction between two or more couples and it is a democratic dance in that the couples often change positions in the set and take turns leading the figures. Only in a culture in which the absolute power of the king had been tempered by the demands of democracy could such a dance form flourish. And flourish it did! From 1650 to 1850 it was a significant medium of social expression for rising bourgeois society. The English country dance was eventually exported to most of the countries of Europe and to America.

Both forms of social dance continued to exist side by side. Voltas and galliards were replaced by minuets and allemandes, which in turn gave way to waltzes and polkas, while the country dances themselves went through a gradual evolution. The earliest country dances were dances for sets of two, three, or four couples in round, square, or longways formations, a few of the latter for "as many as will." By the mid-eighteenth century most of the set dances had vanished from the ballroom, and only longways dances for an indefinite number of couples were danced. By 1800, square set cotillions were in the ascendancy, and soon the longways country dances were but a lingering memory. Near the end of the nineteenth century, "a nostalgic public began to look with favor on things 'old-world,' and various efforts were made to revive the 'old country dances'...attempts more romantic than truly historic." (Dean-Smith, *Playford's English Dancing Master*, xix) The time was ripe for serious musicologists and dance historians to study the early country dance.

John Playford

The earliest source, and therefore the most interesting to Sharp, had been compiled in 1651 by John Playford, music publisher, bookseller, clerk to the Temple Church, and vicar-choral of St. Paul's Cathedral in seventeenth-century London. Born in Norwich in 1623, he came to London in 1639 and served a seven-year apprenticeship to John Benson. He then became a member of the Yeomanry of the Stationer's Company in 1647 and opened his own shop in the porch of the Temple Church.

The times were tumultuous in the London of his day: King Charles I was under arrest and soon to be beheaded; the dissenters held power; the populace was scattered and confused. Although they were still wealthier and more powerful, the upper classes had lost forever their unquestioned hold over society. Political unrest and periodic outbreaks of plague and fire encouraged all to seek refuge, education, and leisure within their homes or away from the city. Business opportunities abounded for anyone who managed to survive and stayed in town. Never was a time more ripe for a do-it-yourself book on social dancing.

John Playford was such a survivor. On November 7, 1650, he registered with the authorities that he intended to publish the "English Dancing Master." He produced his ground-breaking volume the following year, tactfully dedicating it to the young heirs of the upper middle class and nobility who attended the several law schools in London. His book contained the music and verbal instructions for 105 country dances. Its acceptance was immediate, a second edition appeared the next year and a third in 1665, the year of the great plague! Fire struck London in 1666, yet by 1670 Playford published a fourth edition.

Shortly before James II came to the throne, Henry Playford assumed responsibility for his ailing father's business in 1684 and a seventh edition, double in size, was in preparation. Edition followed edition, dances were dropped and new ones added as fads and fashion changed. John Young took over the series in 1706, and in 1710 compiled a second volume which reached four editions, first with 200 dances, later expanded to 360. He issued a third volume shortly afterward, adding another 200 dances to the canon. He continued to release editions of the first volume, which peaked at 358

John Playford
1623-1686

from Cecil Sharp, *Country Dance Book, Part 6* (London: 1922), frontispiece.

dances in its final edition published around 1728 at the beginning of the reign of George II.

The word "English" had been dropped after the first edition, and "The Dancing Master" became a commercial phrase which was borrowed by later compilers. John Playford died in 1686, but the legacy of *The Dancing Master* lived on. So great was his contribution that his name is now synonymous with social dancing of his time, particularly as it was interpreted by Cecil Sharp.

But it is a misunderstanding to think that "Playford" dances are the only true English country dances. While John Playford was musically sophisticated and published and sold music and dance books, he was not a dancing master. In addition, although *The English Dancing Master* was unique in its time, it opened the door for many similar publications which contained similar dances, books by contemporary dancing masters such as Thomas Bray and Nathaniel Kynaston, and by publisher competitors like John Walsh and Daniel Wright.

Although we dance "The Fandango" in Sharp's style, for instance, it is not a "Playford" dance but was published by Charles and Samuel Thompson, whose firm was founded in the 1750's, long after *The Dancing Master* had disappeared from book-store shelves. Nevertheless, to the vast majority of dancers, "Playford" conveys the image of the second type of English country dance, the historical revival which Sharp created, as distinct from the traditional, which he collected.

Sharp meets Playford

When Cecil Sharp began to study the Playford editions, he found more questions than answers. He was

"Gathering Peascods"
In 1930 Maud Karpeles and Elsie Avril (violin) came from England for the classes at the summer school held at Amherst, Massachusetts. The dance style of this demonstration near Draper Hall was carefully modeled on Sharp's teachings.

a musician, not a dancer, and had no training in dance research. A glance at the illustrations in this book of pages from *The Dancing Master* will quickly show the kind of problem he encountered and the solutions he chose. The directions for performing the dances were terse and frequently obscure. Much of the early music was unbarred. Since they were intended purely as reminders to dancers who were familiar with steps and figures, no mention was made of the steps or the style in which dances were to be performed. When Playford's first edition was published, only simple forms of dance notation existed. Sharp studied Arbeau's *Orchesographie* (Langres: 1588), and borrowed his idea of indicating the timing of steps by showing them alongside the notes in the melody with which they coincide. He used this method in his earliest books on the ceremonial morris and sword dances he had collected.

Sharp also studied Feuillet's *Recuëil de Contredances* (Paris: 1706), a complex system of diagrams and symbols applied to some of the dances published in later editions of *The Dancing Master*, which John Essex had translated into English in 1710 (see page 36). But Sharp was more interested in the earlier dances, dances which preceded the new dance techniques of the French court which Feuillet documented. He was convinced that the earlier dances were the purest examples of the country dance as a form.

Sharp's Methodology

In *The Country Dance Book, Part 1* (London: Novello and Company, 1909) Sharp described the dances he had collected from country folk in Warwickshire, Derbyshire, Devon, Somerset, and Surrey. They included "Brighton Camp," "Galopede," "Speed the Plough," "Pop goes the Weasel," "Three Meet," and others. With "Jenny Pluck Pears" in *The Country Dance Book, Part 2* (1911) he began a tradition that continues today, an ambitious attempt to take the abbreviated verbal descrip-

tions of complex historical dance choreographies and make them understandable and enjoyable for a new generation of dancers. He knew that it was most important that they be fun to dance, or they would be relegated to the library shelf once again.

In working out old country dances which he found in books, Sharp did not try to interpret them for historical purposes. He saw them as lost folk dances which, with some modification for modern dress and deportment, could be enjoyed just as much as they had been many years before. Although he tried to keep as close to the original as possible in his reconstructions, he leaned heavily on the movements and style of the traditional dances he had collected.

Assessing his sources he developed a concept of origins. He became convinced that as long as the country dance was regarded as "a refreshing contrast to the more formal and conventional dance of polite society...it suffered little or no injury... But when, as time went on, it challenged, on it own merits, the supremacy of the drawing-room dances, the dance was at once subjected to an enervating influence which, paralyzing its powers of resistance, ultimately led to its corruption." (*CDB* 2, 9)

Sharp returned constantly to this theme and interpreted the dances on the basis that, above all, they should retain a simplicity of movement. He came to certain conclusions about the steps that might have been used, drawing from his experience with the traditional dancers he had observed and consulting dance manuals of the eighteenth and nineteenth centuries. He felt that with the exception of the minuet, all the steps, walking, running, skipping, slipping, and double hop, were performed in Playford's time in much the same way that his traditional dancers used them.

With regard to the figures, Sharp said that with the exception of the side, the set, and the honour, he had been able to connect nearly all of them with similar evolutions in morris or sword dances; he cited in particular the whole-poussette, whole-gip, back-to-back, cross over, and of course, "at once the most engaging and the most varied and intricate of all the figures of the set-dance," - the hey.

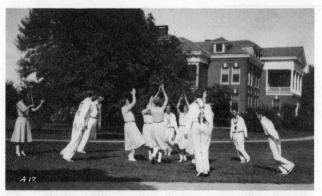

Sharp's favorite figure, the hey, is still the most popular. Henry William Bunbury's humourous print of 1798 catches the dancers in the abandon of full flight.

Problems of Interpretation

In *The Dancing Master*, Playford described "set" and "turn single," but did not define the "side." This was the one figure that Sharp felt uneasy about. At first he thought it could be interpreted in more than one way. Limited in time by the urgency of his mission, he invented a movement in which the dancers pass, then turn to face one another. Returning to "this very troublesome figure" in 1922, he suggested that, if, "instead of turning, the dancers were to 'fall back to places' along their own tracks, the Side would then be identical with the Morris figure of Half-hands, or Half-gip. And this, I suspect, may prove to be the correct interpretation." (*CDB* 6, 10-11)

But by then his dance interpretations were entrenched both in England and in America, and he found to his dismay that he could not convince his followers to change the figure. It was not until the 1970's, when Pat Shaw presented his reconstructions from Feuillet and Essex and demonstrated the accuracy

The Vicar of Wakefield: The Dance
Thomas Rowlandson depicted Mr. Thornhill's country ball, "by moonlight...to two fiddles, with a pipe and tabor," in his illustration of Oliver Goldsmith's tale (1766).

Courtesy of the Yale Center for British Art, Paul Mellon Collection.

of Sharp's early observation, that the dance public was willing to consider the "side" as a shoulder-to-shoulder movement (see page 116).

While modern researchers interested in pure reconstruction can begin with Sharp's interpretations, the original dance instructions should be reexamined if authenticity is important. Contrary to Sharp's impression, these dances were not of the common folk, but were rather a cultivated art which had grown from earlier traditional and imported forms. Some schooled steps and step-sequences probably would have been used, and different interpretations of some of the figures should be made. Even during their own lifetime, changing cultural contexts and aesthetic goals affected performance from the original texts.

The Comforts of Bath: The Ball
Thomas Rowlandson captured the awesome space of the Assembly Room at Bath, the full band and organ on a dais and tiers of spectators, all focused on the floor where a country dance is in progress.

Courtesy of the Yale Center for British Art, Paul Mellon Collection

Certainly the evolution of the dances themselves in succeeding editions of *The Dancing Master* shows that the old forms, the set dances for varying numbers of couples, were superseded by the longways dances. These changes reflected the new social environment of public dancing assemblies attended by both nobility and rising middle classes. The old forms like "Step Stately" or "Chelsea Reach" were probably always danced by an instructed elite, and "Gathering Peascods," "Rufty Tufty," and "Sellenger's Round" may well reflect dances closer to the village green.

Throughout the period we find reference to country dance as an opportunity for more relaxed and light-hearted dancing. It should always be remembered, however, that the point of comparison was the highly structured couple dances which employed strict step-sequences and narrowly defined movements. While the country dance allowed far more individual freedom in performance, it still was deeply integrated into cultivated dance practices of its time, and performance qualities were closely tied to the aesthetic goals of the dancers at the moment of the dancing.

Country Dance in Literature

Most descriptions of country dancing show it to be a form which was enjoyed by the dancers, and used by many layers of society.

John Hippisley's ballad opera, "Flora, or Hob in the Well," (1729) has an entire scene devoted to a rural country dance in which the dancers mess up the figures. Hob steps in and tries to straighten things out:

Set to now, William--Ah, rarely done! In, Mary. Ah, dainty Mary! turn her about John--...Look, Ralph should ha' cast off. And while John had turn'd Mary about, Thomas should ha' led up Nan, and Joan met Ralph at the bottom agen. Meanwhile, John should have sided with Mary, and then Mary should back to back with Ralph, and then Thomas had come in again in his own place. And so all had been right. --Come, begin again...

Charles Dickens must have known such dancing parties and describes a thoroughly believable nineteenth-century Mr. Pickwick at Dingley Dell about to take part in the dancing. Having shed his gaiters, he stood at the head of the line waiting eagerly for the dancing to begin and then

...away went Mr. Pickwick--hands across--down the middle to the very end of the room, and half-way up the chimney, back again to the door--loud stamp on the ground--ready for the next couple--off again--all the figure over again once more--another stamp to beat out the time--next couple, and the next, and the next again--never was such a going! (*The Pickwick Papers*, 1836)

Thomas Hardy's description of the dance in *Under the Greenwood Tree* (1872) reflects a similar feeling.

Threading the couples one by one they reached the bottom, when there arose in Dick's mind a minor misery lest the tune should end before they could work their way to the top again, and have anew the same exciting run down through.

In the light of the above descriptions, even Sharp's approach to the style of movement for country dancing may seem overly formal, suggesting more decorum than is necessary. The country dance, he said, "is a mannered dance, gentle and gracious, formal in a simple straightforward way, but above all gay and sociable." (*CDB* 2, 61)

It is important to remember that he was writing for the physical education instructors, teachers, and other influential figures of the 1910's. It was on these disciples that he depended to spread the enthusiasm and information about the newly discovered traditions of English dance and song. He viewed his role and theirs as a sacred trust, "to take these arts of folk song and dance from a small body of the peasantry and to pass them on to the whole nation as accurately and as reverently as possible." (Karpeles, 87)

Fiddle

Country Dance Music

As he interpreted them, certain of Sharp's dances are comparatively quiet and subdued in style. In these the gaiety is toned down to a decorous suavity, and they are almost little ballets. The formal "Oranges and Lemons," dramatic "Step Stately," and luxurious "Lull Me Beyond Thee" are among these. Between them and the free-hearted "The Queen's Jig," "Lilli Burlero," and "Jack's Maggot" are many that are emotionally intermediate in type.

The difference often is not the figure or the step, but the music. The music and the dance of "Jenny Pluck Pears" is a good example of both aspects. The formal honors and changes are danced to lyrical music in triple time, while the second figure is skipped to a lively jig. Even within the confines of court dress and aesthetic movement choices of its own period, this dance would have had a dual quality.

When Sharp substituted tunes, the difference can be even more telling. Dancing "Step Stately" as Sharp reconstructed it to the tune of "Jack Pudding" is an entirely different dance than "Step Stately" to its own music. Sharp's dance has a theatrical sweep which is almost unique among his work. It is critical that the dancer feel these temperamental differences and reflect them in his manner and style, no matter what tradition he is dancing.

In his preface to *CDB*, Sharp said, "The dance is but the interpretation or translation, in terms of bodily action, of the music upon which it is woven, just as the melody of the song is primarily the expression of the text. Music moreover is the predominant partner of the union; there can be no dance without music." (2, 61-62)

If one asks country dancers what first attracted them to the English dances, a great number will reply "the music!" Many of the tunes in Playford's early collections were old songs as well as dances. Sharp was struck by the number of English folk airs in *The Dancing Master*. He noted modifications as the tunes in later editions were modernized to current tastes and he noticed the new tunes by leading composers of England's golden age of music which were added as the years went by. He found it "impossible to examine the dances of the later editions without being impressed by the beauty...of the tunes they contain." (*CDB* 2, 25)

He pointed out that, in his opinion and for his purposes, the best tunes were not always connected with good dances, while superior dances often had inferior tunes. In his first book of reconstructions, he decided to use the tunes associated with the dances but said he might act differently in the future. (*CDB* 2, 27) In later collections he freely substituted what he considered to be better tunes to create dances which would be more acceptable to his public.

Margaret Dean-Smith comments that "in the matter of the tunes Sharp's work was less masterly and his judgement less well-founded, for there is more opinion in Sharp's dicta than in historical fact." (*Playford's English Dancing Master*, xix) Nevertheless it is hard to fault his evaluation of *The Dancing Master* as a "veritable treasure-house of precious material...the largest and, in some respects, the most authoritative collection of seventeenth century instrumental folk-tunes that we possess." (*CDB* 2, 27)

Followers of Sharp

Cecil Sharp's *Country Dance Books* contain only dances reconstructed from or inspired by those in *The English Dancing Master* of 1651 and succeeding editions of *The Dancing Master*. Since 1922 a number of choreographers have produced dances in his style which is now a strong tradition in England and in America. As the old books become more easily accessible through modern technology of microfilm and photocopy, many dance leaders are searching them for interesting new dances and tunes to use.

Douglas and Helen Kennedy first followed Sharp's lead by presenting thirty new dances from two late editions of *The Dancing Master*. In the *Country Dance Book, New Series,* they gave us the immortal "The Hole in the Wall," the boisterous "A Trip to Paris" and the lush "Draper's Maggot."

Then W. S. Porter, and Arthur and Marjorie Heffer teamed up to produce *The Apted Book of Country Dances* for which they used dances published between 1774 and 1780, reinterpreted in Sharp's "Playford" style. We have their effort to thank for "The Fandango," "The Shrewsbury Lasses," and "The Dressed Ship."

In his *Fallibroome Collections* Bernard J. Bentley went back to late editions of *The Dancing Master*, and recreated "Zephyrs and Flora," "Drapers Gardens," and "Chelmsford Assembly," among others. Pat Shaw gave us "Prince William," Frank Van Cleef found "Well Hall," and A. Simons interpreted "The Northdown Waltz."

The trend continues today as dance leaders around the world are inspired by the beautiful dance style which Sharp created. While some are looking back to the old books to reinterpret the dances more authentically, many are adding newly composed and newly interpreted dances to the "Sharp-Playford" repertoire, dances which quickly become a comfortable and welcome part of the recreational social dance tradition.

METHODOLOGY

A country dancer today has many dances from which to choose. Some contemporary "Playford-style" dances are delightful, some are not. Time will prove which of them will have lasting value. But Sharp's great dances like "Newcastle" or "Parson's Farewell" are perfect matches of melody with movement and will remain forever on the list of favorite English country dances.

Choosing one hundred and three dances from the vast repertory of English country dance is, inevitably, subjective. We tried to choose classics, truly wonderful dances with timeless qualities. Some are quite new and some have lasted for seventy-five years and are still favorites. Some of the dances immensely popular in the twenties have now disappeared completely. "Sweet Kate," for instance, was frequently on early programs and today seems a rather silly dance! Others, like "Kemp's Jig" and "The Whish" were popular in the thirties and forties, but have been superseded by new dances like "Joy after Sorrow" and "Miss Sayers' Allemand."

Although there were none in Sharp's books, we have included some country dances set to waltz tunes. It was not until the 1940's that "liberties were taken" and daring musicians introduced nineteenth-century waltz tunes for old country dances originally set to triple-time tunes. These have become particular favorites with today's dancers.

Some of the versions we have selected may surprise local dancers and leaders. The tradition of English country dancing is very much of a living and an oral one. Dances are learned in classes, workshops, parties, and from Playford Ball programs, and then joyfully carried away to be shared with others. Without the support of a definitive description, dance is one of the most difficult arts to document and remember. While they may not even match published descriptions of quite recent vintage, the versions presented here are, to the best of our knowledge, those in widest use among the Country Dance and Song Society community today.

In preparing this book a major challenge has been to create an accurate glossary of terms and then to describe each dance within those terms. Sharp was the first to look seriously at the Playford dances in 150 years, and he created his own language to describe the movements he chose for his interpretations. Since his time, other terms have been used for some of the movements and other meanings for some of his terms have arisen. We have brought all the dances into one description system.

On the right at the top of each page appears the name of the person who reconstructed the dance and the date of its publication. Beneath is the earliest known publication of the dance on which the reconstruction was based and inclusive dates of its appearance in *The Dancing Master*. While some information is included in the notes, no attempt has been made to provide complete documentation of continued appearances in the publications of John Walsh and later compilers.

Beneath the music and the dance a brief history of the tune and dance is given, with a facsimile of the source on which the reconstruction is based. Readers should remember that, like Sharp, modern choreographers often try to retain the spirit and shape of a source dance but usually do not intend to create an authentic interpretation. The dances have been changed where necessary to make them more appealing to recreational social dancers. Among these are changes like the restructuring of longways triple minor dances into set dances for three couples, as in "The Fandango" and "Joy after Sorrow," or the addition of movements for inactive couples, such as the gypsy for the bottom couple in "The Bishop."

Tunes are presented as they are used in America, and in the case of the Sharp reconstructions, the harmonies are based chiefly on Sharp's arrangements in *Country Dance Tunes*, sets 3-8, 10-11 (London: Novello & Co.,

1911-1922). Many can be found in modern arrangements for three instruments in publications by Marshall Barron and Jack Brothwell. Almost every tune is in Peter Barnes's *English Country Dance Tunes* (Boston: 1985). Cross indexes to modern recordings and other versions of the dances and their music can be found in Peter Rogers' *Country Dance Index* (New York: 1986) and to historical sources in Keller and Rabson's *The National Tune Index* (New York: 1980) and Robert Keller's *Dance Figures Index* (Sandy Hook: 1989 and 1990).

Wright's Compleat Collection of Celebrated Country Dances both Old and New that are in Vouge, with the Newest and best Directions to each Dance y'e whole Carefully corrected Voll. 1st Price 3. 6d

Printed for I. Johnson, Musical Instrument Maker, at y'e Harp & Crown in Cheapside London.

In a design derivative of the print on the frontispiece of *The Dancing Master* from 1686 to 1721, this print may have accompanied Wright's now lost collection from the 1720's. The engraving is unusual in that it shows a large group of musicians, including a keyboard, and a refreshment stand which implies a public setting. The sizable audience of onlookers and size of the room is in stark contrast with the intimate surroundings of Midwinter and Young's design for the DM I:1728. See page 112.

Courtesy of the Vaughan Williams Memorial Library

BIBLIOGRAPHY

The dances in this book were gathered from the following sources:

Bentley, Bernard J. *English Country Dances Fallibroome Collection.* Vols. 1 (1962), 2 (1965), 3 (1968), 6 (1980). London: English Folk Dance and Song Society.

Cook, Tom. *Come Let's Be Merry.* 2nd ed. London: English Folk Dance and Song Society, 1975.

___. *Again Let's Be Merry.* London: English Folk Dance and Song Society, 1979.

Kennedy, Douglas and Helen. *Country Dance Book, New Series.* London: English Folk Dance Society, 1929.

Porter, W. S., Marjorie Heffer and Arthur B. Heffer. *The Apted book of Country Dances.* London: English Folk Dance and Song Society, [1931].

Sharp, Cecil J. *The Country Dance Book, Part 2.* London: Novello & Co., 1911. Revised in 1913. Abbreviated as *CDB.* All page references to these books (*CDB* 1-6) are to the editions published by EP Publishing in 1975 and 1976.

___. *CDB, Part 6.* London: Novello & Co., 1922.

___. *The English Country Dance Graded Series.* Vol. 3. London: Novello and Company, [c. 1951].

Sharp, Cecil J. and George Butterworth. *The Country Dance Book, Part 3.* London: Novello & Co., 1912. Revised in 1927.

___. *CDB, Part 4.* London: Novello & Co., 1916.

Shaw, Pat. *Holland as seen in the English Country Dance: 1713-1820.* London: Nederlandse Volkdans Stichting, 1960.

___. *Six Simple Country Dances from Feuillet...Essex.* [N.p.: ca. 1965].

Sheffield, Ken. *From Two Barns. Ten Country Dances.* Vol. 1. Eynsham: 1982.

Simons, A. *Kentish "Hops".* Orpington: 1961. "Second Picking," 1970, "Third Picking," 1971, "Fourth Picking," 1972.

Van Cleef, Frank C. *Twenty Four Country Dances from the Playford Editions.* West Hartford: Country Dance in Connecticut, 1982.

Woods, Pat. *Long Odds and other Dances from the Preston Collection.* London: English Folk Dance and Song Society, 1958.

Seventeenth- and Eighteenth-Century Sources

Location and/or call numbers refer to specific copies. Occasionally there is variation in the contents or pagination of editions which appear to be identical. Some books cited here are mis-identified or unidentified in the holding library's catalog.

Abbreviations:

BL   British Library, London
CW   Colonial Williamsburg Foundation
DLC   Library of Congress, Washington, D.C.
Dublin   National Library of Ireland, Dublin
Mitchell   Mitchell Library, Glasgow

Bishop, Henry. *Six New Minuets and Twelve Country Dances...1788.* London: Longman & Broderip, 1788. [BL. b.53.6]

Budd, Thomas. *For the Year 1781. Six Favorite New Minuets....* London: John Rutherford, 1781. [BL a.26.o]

___. *Twenty-fifth Book for the Year 1795.* London: Preston & Son, 1795. [BL a.9.q (3)]

Compleat [and *Second Book of the Compleat*] *Country Dancing Master.* London: Iohn Walsh and Iohn Hare, 1718 [1719]. [DLC]

Compleat Country Dancing Master. London: Iohn Walsh, 1731. [CW]

THE DANCING MASTER: (Abbreviated throughout as DM I, II or III.) For the most recent detailed information about editions, additional sheets, and locations, please see Barlow's *The Complete Country Dance Tunes,* Keller and Rabson's *The National Tune Index,* or McPherson's "The Music of the English Country Dance, 1651-1728."

An outline of the editions follows:

The English Dancing Master. London: John Playford, 1651.

The Dancing Master. Vol. 1. 2nd (1652), 3rd (1657 and 1665), 4th (1670), 5th (1675), 6th (1679 and 1682), 7th edition (1686-89). London: John Playford.

The Dancing Master. Vol. 1. 8th (1690), 9th (1695), *Second Part* (1696-1698), 10th (1698), 11th (1701), 12th edition (1703). London: Henry Playford.

The Dancing Master. Vol. 1. 13th (1706), 14th (1709), 15th (1713), 16th (1716), 17th edition (1721). London: John Young.

The Dancing Master. Vol. 1. 18th edition. London: Edward Midwinter and John Young, [ca. 1728].

The Dancing Master. Vol. 2. 1st edition. London: W. Pearson, John Cullen, John Young, Alex Levingston, [ca. 1710].

The Dancing Master. Vol. 2. 2nd (1714), 3rd (1719), 4th edition (1728). London: John Young.

The Dancing Master. Vol. 3. 2nd [only surviving] edition. London: John Young, [ca. 1726-28].

Feuillet, Raoul Auger. *Recuëil de Contredances.* Paris: 1706. Reprint. Brooklyn: Broude Brothers, 1968.

Goulding & Cos. Collection of New and Favorite Country Dances. London: Goulding, D'Almaine, Potter & Co., 1820. [Mitchell]

New Country Dancing Master...2d book. London: I. Walsh [and others, 1711]. [Perth Public Library]

...3d book. London: I. Walsh and Ioseph Hare, [1728]. [BL a.8]

Preston's Twenty Four Country Dances for the Year...1791 [to 1801]. London: Preston & Son. [Annual sets of 24 dances]

Rutherford's Compleat Collection...of the Most Celebrated Country Dances. Vol. 1. London: David Rutherford, [1756]. [Mitchell]

Thompson's Compleat Collection of 200 Favourite Country Dances. Vols 1-3. London: Charles and Samuel Thompsons, [1773]. Forbes Library. Vol. 4, London: Saml. Ann & Peter Thompson, [1780]. [BL]

Twenty Four New Country Dances for the Year 1712. London: J. Walsh and J. Hare, 1712. [Dublin, JM 5739(1)]

Twenty Four Country Dances for the Year 1765 [-1780]. London: Chas. and Samuel Thompson. [Annual sets of 24 dances]

Twenty Four New Country Dances. [Supplement to DM I:11] London: Henry Playford, 1702. [Dundee District Libraries, Wighton Coll.]

[*Two Hundred Favourite Country Dances.* Vol. 8. London: John Johnson, ca. 1753]. [BL a.9.kk]

Voigt, Augs. *A Selection of Elegant & Fashionable Country Dances.* Book 3rd. London: C. Wheatstone, [ca. 1809]. [BL b.55.a.8]

W.M. Cahusac's Annual Collection of Twenty four...for the Year 1802. London: W. M. Cahusac, [1801]. [BL a.9.f.(6)]

[*Wright's Compleat Collection.* Vol. 1. London: I. Johnson, ca. 1740]. Essex Institute, Salem, Mass.

Books Used or Cited in the Text

Ashton, John. *Social Life in the Reign of Queen Anne*. London: Chatto & Windus, 1904.

___. *Humour, Wit and Satire of the Seventeenth Century*. 1883 Reprint. New York: Dover Publications, 1970.

Barlow, Jeremy. *The Complete Country Dance Tunes from Playford's Dancing Master 1651-ca.1728*. London: Faber Music Ltd., 1985

Catchpenny Prints. New York: Dover Publications, 1970.

Chappell, William. *The Ballad Literature and Popular Music of the Olden Time*. 1859. Reprint. New York: Dover Publications, 1965.

Cook, Tom. "The Assembly" [manuscript index and analysis of English country dance, 1651-1760]. Neston, England: 1979.

Curti, Martha Margaret. "John Playford's 'Apollo's Banquet' 1670." Ph.D. diss., Rutgers University, 1977.

Dean-Smith, Margaret, ed. *Playford's English Dancing Master, 1651*. London: Schott & Co., 1957.

___. *A Guide to English Folk Song Collections 1822-1952*. Liverpool: University Press of Liverpool, 1954.

D'Urfey, Thomas. *Wit and Mirth; or, Pills to Purge Melancholy*. Vols. 1-6. 1719-1720. Reprint. New York: Folklore Library, 1959.

Highfill, Philip H., and others. *A Biographical Dictionary of Actors, Actresses, Musicians, Dancers...in London, 1660-1800*. Carbondale: Southern Illinois University Press, 1973.

Keller, Kate Van Winkle, and Carolyn Rabson. *National Tune Index: 18th-Century Secular Music*. New York: University Music Editions, 1980.

Keller, Robert M. *Dance Figures Index: American Country Dances, 1730-1810*. Sandy Hook: The Hendrickson Group, 1989.

___. *Dance Figures Index: English Country Dances published by John Walsh, 1708-1766*. Sandy Hook: The Hendrickson Group, 1990.

Marsh, Carol. "French Court Dance in England, 1706-1740: A Study of the Sources." Ph.D. diss., City University of New York, 1985.

Martin, Jennifer Kaye Lowe. "The English Dancing Master, 1660-1728: His role at court, in Society and on the Public Stage." Ph.D. diss., University of Michigan, 1977.

McPherson, William Alan. "The Music of the English Country Dance, 1651-1728: with indexes of the printed sources." Ph.D. diss., Harvard University, 1984.

Moss, Harold Gene. "Ballad-Opera Songs: A record of the ideas set to music, 1728-1733." Ph.D. diss., University of Michigan, 1969.

O'Neill, Francis, ed. *O'Neill's Music of Ireland*. Chicago: Lyon and Healy, 1903.

Pepys, Samuel. *Diary and Correspondence of Samuel Pepys*. Edited by J. Smith. 4 vols. New York: McKinlay, Stone & MacKenzie, 1924.

___. *The Pepys Ballads*. Edited by W.G. Day. 5 vols. Cambridge: D. S. Brewer, 1987.

Quarrell, W. H., ed. *London in 1710 from the Travels of Zacharias Conrad von Uffenbach*. London: Faber & Faber, 1934.

Quirey, Belinda. *May I have the Pleasure? The Story of Popular Dancing*. London: British Broadcasting Corporation, 1976.

Ralph, Richard. *Life and Works of John Weaver*. New York: Dance Horizons, 1985.

Rollins, Hyder Edward. *The Pepys Ballads*. 8 vols. Cambridge: Harvard University Press, 1929-1932.

The Roxburghe Ballads. Edited by William Chappell and J. W. Ebsworth. 8 vols. London: Ballad Society, 1871-1899.

Schwab, Jacqueline. "A Bibliography of English Country Dance Books, 1700-1830" [typescript of a project in progress.] Boston: 1988.

The Second Book of the Catch Club. London: I. Walsh, 1733. Reprint. New York: Da Capo, 1965.

Shakespeare's England. Oxford: Clarendon Press, 1916.

Simpson, Claude M. *The British Broadside Ballad and Its Music*. New Brunswick: Rutgers University Press, 1966.

Van Lennep, William, and others, eds. *The London Stage 1660-1800*. Carbondale: Southern Illinois University Press, 1960-1968.

Ward, John. "A Propos the British Broadside Ballad." *Journal of the American Musicological Society*, 20/1 (Spring 1967): 28-86.

Wells, Evelyn. "Playford Tunes and Broadside Ballads." *Journal of the English Folk Dance and Song Society*, 3/2-4 (December 1937-1939): 81-92, 195-202, 259-72.

Wheatley, Henry. *London Past and Present*. 1891. Reprint. Detroit: Singing Tree Press, 1968.

Wittman, Carl. "An Analysis of John Playford's English Dancing Master (1651)." Master's thesis, Goddard College, 1981.

The English Dancing Maſter :
OR,
Plaine and eaſie Rules for the Dancing of Country Dances, with the Tune to each Dance.

LONDON,
Printed by *Thomas Harper*, and are to be ſold by *John Playford*, at his Shop in the Inner Temple neere the Church doore. 1651.

Title page of John Playford's first collection of country dances, 1651

Courtesy of the Vaughan Williams Memorial Library

THE PLAYFORD BALL

Adfon's Saraband. *Longways for fix.*

Lead up all a D. forward and back, set and turn S. • That again ⫶ Men go a D. from your we. to the wall, come back to your we. set and turn S. ⫶ Then the we. as much ⫶ ⫶

Men go all down while the we. go up, men flip to the right hand, and we. to the left, fall even to the co. fide, set and turn S. • All this again the co. way to your places, set and turn S. ⫶

Firft cu. go down betwixt the second, they coming up, the third come up between the firft, then the second come to their places between the third, set and turn S. • All this back again to your places ⫶

Go all to the left hand crofs the Room, set and turn S. • Firft and laft on each fide meet and go back, turn each other, the second turning his own ⫶ Change all places with your own, set and turn S. ⫶ Firft cu. lead down between the reft, come with a compafs to your places, the reft following ⫶ ⫶

DM I:8 (1690): 23
Courtesy of the Vaughan Williams Memorial Library

from a 1915 dance program in Pittsburgh, Pennsylvania
Courtesy of the Country Dance and Song Society archives

The New Royal Exchange. *Longwayes for as many as will.*

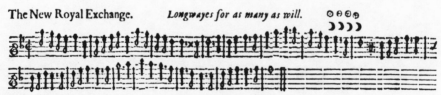

Lead up, all and fall back, That again ⫶ ⫶ Set to all your own and fall back, then arms all with your own ⫶

The two firft men take hands, and the two firft We. take hands and fall back from your own, then meet them and then change places with them and turn round fingle, the firft man and second Wo. turn back to back, and then the firft Wo. and second man turn back to back, then all four take hands behind them and go half round ⫶ Do this to all the reft ⫶

The firft and second man, and the firft and second We. take hands and fall back, then meet, and the second man take the firft Wo with his right hand and walk half round till the firft man goes into the second Wo. place, then the firft man and second Wo. change places and give their right hands to their own, and go half round, till the firft Cu. comes into the second Cu. place, and the second into the firft Cu. place, do this to all, the reft following ⫶

The firft and second man, and the firft and second Wo. fall back from your own, then meet the second man and second Wo. turn back to back. the, the firft man and Wo. change places, and the firft man take the second Wo. by both hands, and change places with them, the firft man and second man being in each others place, and the two firft We. in their own places, then the firft and second We. crofs over to their own and arms with them, do this to all, the reft following ⫶

DM I:4 (1670): 125
Courtesy of the Vaughan Williams Memorial Library

ADSON'S SARABAND
to the tune of THE NEW EXCHANGE

Longways for three couples
3 x AA BB   MM ♩ = 116

Cecil Sharp, 1912
d: DM I: 1651-1690; m: DM I: 1665-1728

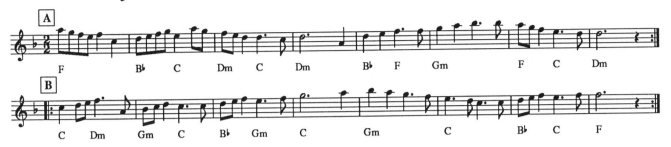

Part I

AA	1-16	Partners lead up a double and fall back a double, then all set and turn single. That again.
B1	1-4	Men face men's wall and forward a double, turn around and return a double.
	5-8	Men set to partners and turn single. {*Partners do not set.*}
B2	1-8	Women repeat B1, to women's wall.

Part II

A1	1-2	Men face down, women up: All forward a double obliquely to left, into a line up and down in the center of the set, the men below the women {*1st man & 3rd woman ending back to back.*}
	3-4	All fall back a double obliquely to opposite side, men now on women's side, women on men's.
	5-8	Partners face, set and turn single.
A2	1-8	Repeat A1, men facing up, women facing down. {*3rd man & 1st woman will be back to back at end of bar 2.*}
B1	1-4	All half-hey for three, 1st couple going down center between 2nd couple to start.
	5-8	Partners set and turn single.
B2	1-4	All half-hey again, 1st couple going up center between 2nd couple, ending in original place.
	5-8	Partners set and turn single.

Part III

A1	1-4	Men face men's wall: all forward two doubles to men's wall; then men turn to right to face partners.
	5-8	Partners set and turn single.
A2	1-4	1st and 3rd men, 1st and 3rd women, 2nd man and 2nd woman: forward a double to meet and fall back a double.
	5-8	Turn the same two-hands, ending facing partners.
B1	1-8	Partners balance back and change places (1-4), then set and turn single (5-8).
B2	1-4	1st couple take right hands and lead down center followed by 2nd and 3rd couples.
	5-8	With crossed hands, all cast **to the left** and lead up to original places, skipping.

ADSON'S SARABAND

John Adson (d. 1640) may have written the original music for the dance. English-born, he began his career in France, but eventually joined the English court band in 1625. He also played several instruments at the Blackfriar's Theatre. In 1634 he was appointed music teacher to Charles I.

Sharp substituted the tune of "The New Exchange," one of two tunes commemorating a large commercial building built in 1609 in competition to the Royal Exchange. A visitor to London in 1710 visited this building. "On 13 June, Friday morning, we had many letters to write. In the afternoon we went first to the New-Exchange, an almost square building, in the lower storey of which there are shops of all kinds where we bought various articles." (Quarrell, 30)

Because there was another tune by this name in circu-lation, this was soon renamed "The New New Exchange" (1665) and then "The New Royal Exchange" (1670).

The first verse of a song to this tune, entitled *On the Soldiers walking in the new Exchange to affront the Ladies*, is quoted by Chappell. The title betrays an intent beyond the evident meaning of the words, and the final lines sharply criticize contemporary morals in the interregnum period.

I'll go no more to the New Exchange, there is no room at all,
  It is so throng'd and crowded by the gallants of Whitehall.
But I'll go to the Old Exchange, where old things are in fashion;
  For now the Kew's become the shop of this blessed Reformation.
Come, my new Courtiers, what d'ye lack? Good consciences? If you do,
  Here's long and wide, the only wear, the straight will trouble you.

from Wit and Drollery, (1656)

References: Simpson, 353-54; Dean-Smith, 26; Chappell, 317-18; Quarrell, 30

AMARILLIS

Duple minor longways
AB AB ad lib   MM ♩ = 116

Cecil Sharp, 1911
DM I: 1670-1728

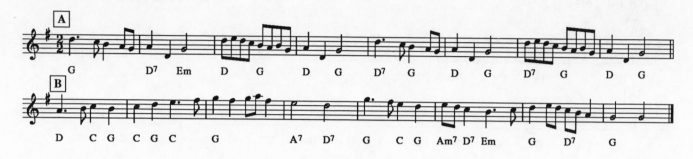

Introduction {*This part is done only at the beginning and end of the dance.*}

A   1-8   Partners lead up a double and fall back a double. That again.

B   1-4   Men set forward to partners and fall back. {*Partner does not set.*}

    5-8   Men take partners by right hand, turn them clockwise under their right arms, twice.

Part I

A   1-4   1st couple cross and move down outside into 2nd couple's place {*improper*}.
          while 2nd couple lead up center into first place.

    5-8   Repeat movement: 2nd couple cross, 1st couple lead.

B   1-2   1st corners change places.

    3-4   2nd corners change places.

    5-8   Circle four-hands once around.

Part II   {*1st couple is now progressed one place and dances with new 2nd couple.*}

A   1-4   2nd couple lead up center and, still facing up, separate with 4 slips out, man to left, woman to right.

    5-8   2nd couple fall back down outside 4 steps, face partner, forward 4 steps to place.

B   1-4   1st couple lead down center and cast up to first place.

    5-8   1st couple cast down one place, 2nd couple moving up.

"Amarillis" first appeared as one of the "select new airs" printed in an appendix (1665) to the third edition of the first volume of *The Dancing Master*, and a dance was added to the tune for subsequent editions. It probably takes its name from a pastoral song for Maria and a chorus written by John Bannister for Thomas Porter's *The Villain* (1663, ii.1). The lyric, which fits the tune only with many repeats of the phrases, begins:

> Amarillis told her swain,
>   That in love he should be plaine,
>   And not think to deceive her.
> Still he protested, on his truth,
>   That he would never leave her.

AMARILLIS

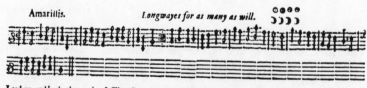

Lead up, and back, that again ∴ Then set to your own Wo. and fall back, and turn her about ∴

Cross over with your own Wo. into the second place, the second couple leading up between, the second couple doing as much ∴ The first man crossing over with the second Wo. the first Wo. crossing over with the second man, then take all hands and go quite round ⦁ Do this to the last.

The second couple lead up and slide out from your own, fall back and slide in ∴ The first man takes his Wo. by the right hand and leads into the second place, then cast off into their own place and meet, then cast off into the second place, do this to the last ⦁

References: Simpson, 17-18; Chappell, 283-84, 778

DM I:4 (1670): 137
Courtesy of the Vaughan Williams Memorial Library

APLEY HOUSE

Duple minor longways
AA BB C ad lib   MM ♩ = 120

Cecil Sharp, 1922
Twenty Four New Country Dances (Playford), 1702; DM I: 1703-1728

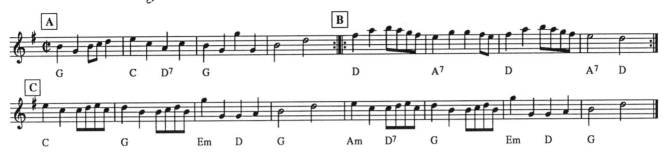

A G	C D⁷ G	**B** D	A⁷ D	A⁷ D
C C	G Em D G	Am D⁷ G	Em D	G

A1   1-4   Two men join inside hands, fall back a double, come forward a double turning single to the right.
A2   1-4   Two women the same.
B1   1-2   1st and 2nd couples right hands-across half-way.
     3-4   All face partners and turn single.
B2   1-4   2nd couple cast down one place and meet in center facing up **while** 1st couple move up center, cast down and join at ends of a line of four facing up.
C   1-4   Line of four lead up a double, fall back to reform set, all in original places but improper.
     5-8   1st couple cross and move down outside to second place **while** 2nd man lead partner up center and hand her across to place.

APLEY HOUSE

The lordship of Apley, together with the whole parish of Stockton in which it is situated, came into the possession of the family of Whitmore in the reign of Queen Elizabeth, by purchase from Sir Thomas Lucy, the celebrated prosecutor of Shakespeare. William Whitmore (d. 1648), an alderman of London, erected a mansion house on the property, which is about four and a half miles north of Bridgton and commands a view of the river Severn from its spacious terrace. His eldest son, William, succeeded him at Apley and was knighted by James I in 1620. His heir, Thomas, was created Baronet by Charles I in 1641.

In 1645, Apley House was taken by the Parliamentarians, under Sir John Price, and Sir William and Sir Thomas, along with a number of others, were taken prisoner and held for a considerable length of time. Sir Thomas was created a Knight of the Bath at the coronation of Charles II.

Two views of "Apley Park, Shropshire: the seat of Thomas Whitmore, Esq" and a brief history of the early families who lived there can be found in *Jones' Views of the Seats, Mansions, Castles, &c. of Noblemen & Gentlemen in England* (London: Jones & Co., 1829): 71.

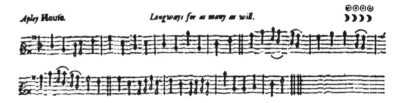

The two men take hands and fall back, and turn single; the women do the same: Hands across half round, and turn single. The second couple being in the first place, cast off, and the other couple follow and lead up abreast; the first couple cross over into the second couples place, the second couple lead up and cross over into their own places.

DM I:12 (1703): 320
Courtesy of the Vaughan Williams Memorial Library

APLEY PARK, Shropshire

Courtesy of the Print Collection,
The Lewis Walpole Library, Yale University

ARGEERS

Two couples facing
3 x AA BB   MM $\mathJ$ = 116

Cecil Sharp, 1912
DM I: 1651-1690

Part I

A1	1-4	All forward a double, take two-hands with opposite, two slips away and two back, then pass opposite quickly by right shoulder to face partner on other side of set.
	5-8	Partners turn two-hands once-and-a-half, skipping.
A2	1-4	Opposites turn two-hands once-and-a-half while traveling clockwise back to original place, skipping.
	5-8	Partners turn two-hands once around.
B1	1-4	Men change places **while** women balance back and then change places.
	5-8	Partners set and turn single.
B2	1-8	Repeat B1, women changing places first.

Part II

A1	1-4	Men lead opposite out a double, fall back a double, turn to right to face partner.
	5-8	Partners turn two-hands.
A2	1-4	Partners fall back a double with inside hands, lead forward a double.
	5-8	Partners set and turn single, ending facing opposite.
B1	1-2	All go four slips, men to right, women to left, women in front of men.
	3-4	Four slips back, women in front of men.
	5-8	Opposites turn two-hands, skipping.
B2	1-8	Women forward a double to meet, then fall back to place **while** men figure-eight around them, beginning counter-clockwise around opposite woman and passing each other right shoulder, then left on second half.

Part III

A1	1-4	Opposites poussette clockwise half-way, 1st man pushing.
	5-8	Partners set and turn single.
A2	1-8	Opposites poussette counter-clockwise, 1st man pushing, then partners set and turn single.
B1	1-4	1st man, followed by partner, cast off and go back to place **while** 2nd woman, followed by her partner, the same, all skipping.
	5-8	2nd man, followed by partner, cast off and go back to place **while** 1st woman, followed by her partner, the same, all skipping.
B2	1-4	Face opposite: all circular hey two changes, beginning with opposite, skipping.
	5-6	Face partner: turn two-hands and open into line of four, 2nd couple on left.
	7-8	Step forward and honor the Presence.

ARGEERS

"Argeers" appeared with various spellings including an alternate title, "Argiers: or, the Wedding Night" from 1670-1679 with which change the B strain was shortened by omitting bars 11-12. (See facsimile.) Sharp chose the longer version which he found in the EDM. The title may be a literary reference although as yet no convincing explanation has been found for the title. The North-African territory of Algiers was much in the news in the 1660's; see Pepys' diary entry for February 8, 1661.

References: Dean-Smith, 49

DM I:8 (1690): 18

AURETTI'S DUTCH SKIPPER

Duple minor longways
AA BB ad lib   MM ♪. = 108

Pat Shaw, 1960
Rutherford's Compleat Collection...vol. 1, 1756

A1	1-4	1st couple lead through 2nd couple and cast up to place.
	5-8	1st couple turn two-hands.
A2	1-4	2nd couple lead up through 1st couple and cast down to place.
	5-8	2nd couple turn two-hands.
B1	1-8	1st corners turn two-hands (1-4); 2nd corners turn two-hands (5-8).
B2	1-4	Partners set twice.
	5-8	All right-and-left, three changes, beginning with partner.

AURETTI'S DUTCH SKIPPER

This longways dance commemorates Anne Auretti, a French ballerina in Garrick's company whose solo hornpipes on nautical themes were popular with mid-century London audiences. She made her debut at Covent Garden in 1742 and often appeared with her sister, Janneton, in character dances and in national dances of several countries. Several other country dances and a minuet named for her appear in London-printed collections, including other figures to this same tune. Several portraits of Anne were painted, probably commissioned by wealthy theatre patrons. The beautifully detailed painting by C. Amicona, copied and published in an engraving by T. Ryley, is illustrated here. Another, in a different costume, is illustrated in Highfill, *Biographical Dictionary* (1: 176). The couplet beneath this picture suggests that Miss Auretti was involved in some sort of scandal!   References: Highfill 1: 176-77

Thompson's Compleat Collection, vol. 1 (1757): 86
Courtesy of the Forbes Library, Northampton, Massachusetts

ANNE AURETTI

"With Measure & Swiftness"
"The fair Auretti free from Blame, Received of Heaven and of Men,
The Soul of Balls, and of the dance, The Gift of Flying in Ballance."

AYE ME; or, THE SYMPHONY

Longways for 4 couples
3 x AA BB   MM ♩ = 108

Cecil Sharp, 1916
DM I: 1651-1690

Part I

A1	1-4	Partners lead up a double and fall back a double.
	5-8	Men fall back two steps (5), then women the same (6), then all forward to place, turning single to right (7-8).
A2	1-8	Repeat A1.
B1	1-4	Top and bottom couples cast to middle, then change places with partner.
	5-8	The same cast to nearest ends and change places with partner to original places (5-6), then with neighbors turn two-hands half-way, ends moving outside the set. {*Ends are now in middle.*}
B2	1-8	Repeat B1, new top and bottom couples casting.

Part II

A1	1-4	Partners slow set and honor right, then change places passing left shoulders.
	5-8	Men fall back two steps, then women the same, then all forward to place, turning single to right.
A2	1-8	Repeat A1.
B1	1-2	All face up. 1st and 3rd couples go 4 slips out away from partner **while** 2nd and 4th slip into middle.
	3-4	1st and 3rd couples fall back while 2nd and 4th couples move forward.
	5-6	1st and 3rd couples slip into middle **while** 2nd and 4th couples slip out.
	7-8	1st and 3rd couples move forward **while** 2nd and 4th couples fall back to place.
B2	1-8	All face down. Repeat B1 with 1st and 3rd couples slipping out to begin, 2nd and 4th slipping in.

Part III

A1	1-4	Partners arm right once-and-a-half.
	5-8	Men fall back two steps, then women the same, then all forward to place, turning single to right.
A2	1-8	Repeat A1, arming left once-and-a-half.
B1	1-4	Middle couples cast to the nearest ends **while** end couples forward a double to meet, pass opposite by right shoulder, then change places with partner.
	5-6	1st man with right hand, take 4th man {*in second place*} by left hand, change places, both moving forward counter-clockwise {*as in a gipsy*}, **while** 1st woman with left hand, take 4th woman by right hand, change places, both moving forward clockwise.
	7-8	Middle couples change places with partners.
B2	1-8	Repeat B1, new middle couples casting to end, new end couples meeting.

AYE ME; or, THE SYMPHONY

Dean-Smith cites concordance between this title and Giles Farnaby's "Aye me, poor hearte" (*Canzonets*, 1598, no. 15), but Farnaby's madrigal is entirely different music, possibly another setting of the same text. From 1665-1690, the title was spelled "Ay Me" in the DM. Symphony in this period means a harmony or concord, rather than a specific musical form.   Reference: Dean-Smith, 62

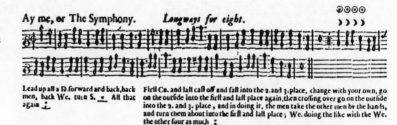

DM I:7 (1686): 28
Courtesy of the Vaughan Williams Memorial Library

BATH CARNIVAL
to the tune of KEPPEL'S DELIGHT

Triple minor longways
AA BB ad lib   MM ♩. = 112

W. S. Porter, 1931
Twenty Four Country Dances (Thompson), d: 1777; m: 1780

A   D   D   A   E   A   D   A   D   E⁷   A

E   A   E   A   E   A   E   E   A   E   A   D   E⁷   A

A1   1-8   1st couple lead out between 2nd and 3rd women and cast back to middle place,
                then lead out between 2nd and 3rd men and cast back to middle place, ending in lines with
                1st woman between 2nd couple facing down, 1st man between 3rd couple facing up.

A2   1-2   Take hands and all set.
        3-4   2nd and 3rd couples turn two-hands half-way **while** 1st couple turn two-hands three-quarters to
                end in new lines up and down the hall, all improper.
        5-8   All set again and turn partners two-hands half-way.

B1   1-8   Circle six-hands around and back, slipping.

B2   1-4   All face out and lead out a double in lines, change hands and lead back.
        5-8   Partners set and turn single.

BATH CARNIVAL and KEPPEL'S DELIGHT

Bath, the famous spa where much of Jane Austen's *Northanger Abbey* takes place, was the subject of many late eighteenth-century dances. Thomas Rowlandson's engraving of a ball in the Assembly Room is illustrated on page xi above. This title may commemorate a particularly notable pre-lenten season in 1776 or earlier.

Porter substituted a tune named in honor of Augustus, 1st Viscount Keppel (1725-1786) who accompanied George Anson on a voyage around the world in 1740-1744 and was made vice-admiral in 1770. He was courtmartialled in 1779 but the charge was dismissed as "malicious and ill-founded," prompting considerable public sympathy and probably this dance title as well.

Courtesy of the Print Collection, The Lewis Walpole Library, Yale University

ADMIRAL KEPPEL

The "Apted Book"
"Bath Carnival" is the first of several in this book based on dances found in a personal binding of collections printed in London by Charles and Samuel Thompson. A major publishing firm, the Thompsons issued annual sets of dances on engraved plates and periodically gathered these into collected volumes, sometimes rearranging them and changing the page numbers. This particular compilation contains most of the fourth volume of 1780 (comprising the annual collections: 1780, 1773-1779), followed by the collection from 1765 with pages renumbered. The first five pages are lacking and no title pages are present at all.

The book belonged to Mrs. W. G. Apted, whose father had bought the coverless book for a shilling. Porter and Heffer found it a rich inspiration for Sharp-style choreographies. The book is now at the Vaughan Williams Memorial Library.

Bath Carnival

.1ˢᵗ Cu: lead thro' between the 2ᵈ and 3ᵈ Ladies the Lady going to the top the Gentⁿ to the bottom meet in the middle and lead thro̓ the same between the 2ᵈ and 3ᵈ Gentⁿ ♫ ſet 3 & 3 top. and bottom. ſet 3 & 3 ſideways ♫ Hands 6 half. round and back again ♫ lead outſides ♫

Keppels Delight.

The 1ˢᵗ La. Sett to the 2ᵈ Gent. & turn the 3ᵈ Gent. then retreat back to her place ♫ the 1ˢᵗ Gent. Set to the 2ᵈ Lady & turn the 3ᵈ Lady & remain at bottom ♫ foot it 3 & 3 top & bottom. foot it 3 & 3 ſideways ♫ Hands 6 round ♫

Thompson's Compleat Collection, vol. 4 (1780): 7, 50
By permission of the British Library

9

THE BEGGAR BOY

Longways for three couples
3 x A BB   MM ♩. = 88

Cecil Sharp, 1911
DM I: 1651-1690

Part I

A	1-8	Partners lead up a double and fall back a double. That again.
B1	1-4	1st and 3rd men face men's wall, 1st and 3rd woman face women's wall, 2nd couple face across set. All forward a double and fall back a double.
	5-8	Men circle three-hands once around **while** women the same.
B2	1-8	Repeat B1.

Part II

A	1-8	Partners side twice.
B1	1-4	2nd couple fall back a double **while** 1st couple face down and 3rd couple face up and change places, 1st couple going between 3rd couple.
	5-8	3rd couple, now at top, turn in towards each other and circle four-hands with 2nd couple **while** 1st couple set and turn single.
B2	1-8	Repeat B1, 3rd couple again going outside and 1st couple inside.

Part III

A	1-8	Partners arm right, then left.
B1	1-4	All fall back a double, then forward a double.
	5-8	1st couple face down, others face up: all half-hey for three on sides beginning right shoulder.
B2	1-4	All face partner and fall back a double and come forward a double.
	5-8	1st couple {*at the bottom*} face up, others face down: finish the hey beginning left shoulder.

THE BEGGAR BOY

The haunting nature of this tune derives in part from its being in the Phrygian mode, which is characterized by a lowered second degree. Claude Simpson suggests that the tune name may derive from the song "The Begger-Boy of the North" (ca. 1630). The first verse follows, with a curious reference to Kent, suggesting a topical origin of southern geography, despite the title.

> From ancient pedigree, by due descent,
> I well can derive my generation;
> Throughout all Christendome, and also Kent,
> My calling is known both in terme and vacation:
> My parents old taught me to be bold,
> Ile never be daunted, whatever is spoken;
> Where e'er I come, my custome I hold,
> And cry, '*Good your worship, bestow one token!*'
> (Roxburghe 1:323-25)

From 1651-1686 the title was spelled "Begger." It was corrected for its last appearance in 1690. This tune and lyric are entirely different from an eighteenth-century ballad called "The Gaberlunzie Man" with which they have carelessly been associated.

References: Simpson, 39-40, 246-47; Dean-Smith, 8; Chappell, 269-70

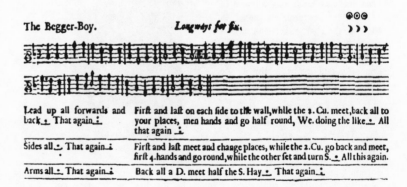

DM I:7 (1686): 30
Courtesy of the Vaughan Williams Memorial Library

THE BISHOP
to the tune of MISS DOLLAND'S DELIGHT

Triple minor longways
AA BB ad lib   MM ♩ = 108

W. S. Porter, 1931
Twenty Four Country Dances (Thompson), d: 1778; m: 1765

A	A	D	A	D	A	Bm	E⁷	A	D	A	D	B⁷	E

E⁷   A   A   E⁷   A   D   E⁷   A

A1	1-2	Starting with right foot, 1st man cast down to second place, 2nd man moving up.
	3-8	1st man set forward to 3rd woman *{who does not set}*, and turn her two-hands (5-8).
A2	1-8	1st woman the same to 3rd man, 2nd woman moving up.
B1	1-4	3rd couple, at bottom, gipsy **while** 1st couple, now in middle place, take inside hands with neighbor at top and move up center through top couple and cast down to middle place, tops acting as a pivot.
	5-8	Circle six-hands half-way around.
B2	1-4	Repeat B1, top couples pivoting **while** 2nd couple gipsy at bottom.
	5-8	Circle six-hands half-way around.

THE BISHOP

Mr. Bishop was a dancer at the Covent Garden Theatre in 1776 and 1777. He made his debut on November 23 at Covent Garden dancing a "new pastoral Dance" with a Miss Tinte, and at his benefit on April 26, 1777, he danced a minuet with one of his students.

The 1ʳᵗ Gent caſt off and turn the 3ᵈ Lady ⸫ 1ʳᵗ Lady caſt off and turn the 3ᵈ Gent: ⸫ lead thro' the top and caſt off ⸫ hands 6 quite round ⸫

Firſt Man ſet to the 2ᵈ Wo: & turn ⸫ firſt Wo do the ſame with the 2ᵈ Man ⸫ lead down 2 Cu: & caſt up one ⸫ Right & left ⸫

THE BLACK NAG

Longways for three couples
3 x A BB   MM ♩. = 116

Cecil Sharp, 1911
DM I: 1665-1716

Part I

A	1-8	Partners lead up a double and fall back a double. That again.
B1	1-2	1st couple take two-hands and move up four slips.
	3-4	2nd couple the same.
	5-6	3rd couple the same.
	7-8	All turn single right.
B2	1-8	Repeat B1, slipping back to place in reverse order, 3rd couple slipping down first.

Part II

A	1-8	Partners side twice.
B1	1-8	1st man and 3rd woman change places with 4 slip steps, leading with right shoulder and passing back-to-back.
	3-4	1st woman and 3rd man the same.
	5-6	2nd couple the same.
	7-8	All turn single right.
B2	1-8	Repeat B1 back to place.

Part III

A	1-8	Partners arm right, then left.
B1	1-8	Men hey for three, skipping: 1st man begin by passing right shoulder.
B2	1-8	Women hey as in B1, men turn single on last four beats of music.

THE BLACK NAG

With a dance and tune sharing similarities with the earlier "Millison's Jig" (DM I: 1651-1690), "Black Nagg," corrected to "Black Nag" in 1686, became "The Gallopping Nag" in 1695. When John Walsh appropriated the entire contents of the sixteenth edition of the first volume of *The Dancing Master* (1716) for his *Compleat Country Dancing Master* of 1718, the editors of *The Dancing Master* substituted a new figure with this tune in the last two editions.

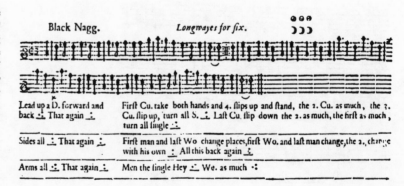

DM I:4 (1670): 53
Courtesy of the Vaughan Williams Memorial Library

Catchpenny Prints, no. 168, 115.
Courtesy of Dover Publications

THE BOATMAN

Longways for three couples
3 x AA BB   MM ♩. = 96

Cecil Sharp, 1916
DM I: 1651-1698

Part I

A1	1-4	Partners lead up a double and fall back a double.
	5-8	Partners set and turn single.
A2	1-8	Repeat A1.
B1	1-6	2nd man, passing right shoulder with 1st woman, go the track of a full hey for three with top couple, who half-hey only and end improper **while** 2nd woman, passing right shoulder with 3rd man, go the track of a full hey for three with bottom couple, who half-hey only and end improper, top and bottom couples looping back to begin a two-hand turn once around with partners **while** 2nd couple completes the hey.
	7-8	Top and bottom couples complete the two-hand turn **while** 2nd couple turn two-hands half-way. *{All are now improper.}*
B2	1-8	Repeat B1, 2nd man with bottom couple, 2nd woman with top couple, all end proper.

Part II

A1	1-8	Partners side, set and turn single.
A2	1-8	Repeat A1.
B1	1-2	2nd man circle three-hands around with top couple half-way, open to a line facing down with 2nd man in middle **while** 2nd woman the same with bottom couple, opening to a line facing up.
	3-4	Lines balance back and forward.
	5-8	2nd couple turn two-hands once-and-a-quarter **while** top and bottom couples turn two-hands once around, all ending improper.
B2	1-8	Repeat B1, 2nd man with bottom couple, 2nd woman with top couple.

Part III

A1	1-8	Partners arm right, set and turn single.
A2	1-8	Partners arm left, set and turn single.
B1	1-4	1st and 3rd men and 2nd woman circle three-hands around 2nd man.
	5-8	2nd couple turn two-hands once around.
B2	1-4	1st and 3rd women and 2nd man circle three-hands around 2nd woman.
	5-8	All turn partners two-hands.

THE BOATMAN

Allan Ramsay's song of 1728 is set to this tune.
The Bonny Scot to the Tune of, The Boat-man.
> Ye gales that gently wave the sea,
> And please the canny Boat-man,
> Bear me frae hence, or bring to me
> My brave, my bonny Scot-man.
> In haly bands we join'd our hands;
> Yet may not this discover,
> While parents rate a large estate,
> Before a faithfu' lover.

References: Dean-Smith, 8; Chappell, 270-71; *The Works of Allan Ramsay*, edited by Burns Martin and John W. Oliver (Edinburgh: Scottish Text Society, 1953), 2: 75

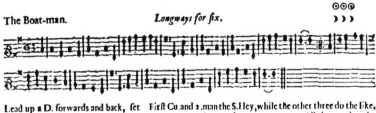

The Boat-man.   *Longways for six.*

Lead up a D. forwards and back, set and turn S. That again. Sides all, set and turn S. That again. Arms all, set and turn S. That again.

Firft Cu. and 2.man the S. Hey, while the other three do the like, come to your places and turn your own. All that again, the 2. Cu. changing their ends. The 2. man and 1. Cu. hands and go half round, while the other do the like, fall all back, then turn your own. That again, the 2. Cu. changing their ends. First and laft man and 2. wo. hands and go round, the 2. man turn his own wo. First and laft we. and 2. man hands and go round, the 2. man turn his wo.

DM I:7 (1686): 50

Courtesy of the Vaughan Williams Memorial Library

13

BROOM, THE BONNY, BONNY BROOM

Longways for four couples

12 x A   MM ♩ = 112

Cecil Sharp, 1912

DM I: 1651-1706

F   C⁷   F   Dm   B♭   F   Gm   C⁷

Part I

A1   1-4   Partners lead up a double and fall back a double.

       5-8   Top two couples face up, bottom two couples face down: 1st couple, followed by 2nd couple, cast down to middle, and lead up to places **while** 4th couple, followed by 3rd couple, cast up to middle and lead down to places.

A2   1-4   Partners lead **down** a double and fall back a double.

       5-8   Casts and leads as in A1.

A3   1-8   2nd man and 2nd woman fall back **while** 1st and 3rd couple face each other and forward a double to meet, fall back, then circle four-hands once around.

A4   1-8   3rd man and 3rd woman fall back **while** 2nd and 4th couples face, forward a double, fall back a double, then circle four-hands once around.

Part II

AA   1-16   Partners side, set and turn single. That again.

A3   1-2   Top two men turn two-hands half-way **while** top two women the same.

       3-4   Bottom two men turn two-hands half-way **while** bottom two women the same.

       5-8   Partners set and turn single.

A4   1-8   Repeat A3 back to places.

Part III

A1   1-8   Partners arm right, set and turn single.

A2   1-8   Partners arm left, set and turn single.

A3   1-2   Top couple lead up a double **while** middle two men lead out a double to men's wall, middle two women lead out a double to women's wall, and bottom couple lead down a double.

       3-4   All change hands and lead back a double.

       5-8   Circle eight-hands half-way around.

A4   1-8   Repeat A3 to places.

BROOM, THE BONNY, BONNY BROOM

The tune, "The Broom of Cowdenknows," was listed in 1632 with a ballad suggestively entitled:

The lovely northern lasse, who in the ditty here complaining shews what harme she got milking her Daddies ewes.

> O, the broome, the bonny broom,
>   The broome of Cowden Knoes.
> Faine would I be in the north Countrey,
>   To milke my daddies ewes.

The passage of one hundred years hardly affected the text as can be seen from the 1733 song on the opposite page, although the tune has been dressed up a little.

Cowdenknows was a Scottish estate and barony on the east bank of the river Leander, thirty-two miles southeast of Edinburgh, close to the English border. The broom, a shrub which blooms with spikes of small golden flowers, once grew plentifully on its hillsides but was stripped away for turnip farming in the nineteenth century.

References: Simpson, 68-71; Moss 1: 148-52; Dean-Smith, 63; Chappell, 458-61

Broom : The bonny, bonny Broom. *Longways for Eight.*

Lead up all a D. forward and back, the firſt four caſt oſt and come to your places, the laſt four do the like : Lead down, and as much : Firſt and 3. cu. meet and go back, hands and go round : The other four do as much : :

Sides all, ſet and turn S. : That again : The two firſt men hands and change places, the laſt two men change, we. doing the ſame, ſet and turn S. : All that again :

Arms all, ſet and turn S. : That again : The 2. and 3. on each ſide lead to each wall, while the firſt cu. lead up, and the laſt lead down ; change hands and meet ; hands all and half round : All that again : :

DM 1:10 (1698): 21

Courtesy of the Vaughan Williams Memorial Library

14

CHELMSFORD ASSEMBLY

Longways for three couples
3 x AA BB   MM ♩.= 116

Bernard J. Bentley, 1968
Two Hundred...Country Dances, v. 8 (Johnson), [c. 1753]

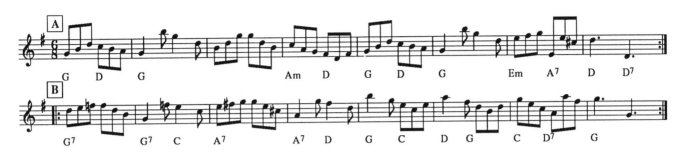

A1	1-4	1st couple cast down to middle place, 2nd couple moving up.
	5-8	1st man cast down again around 3rd man, coming into a line of three with 3rd couple facing up **while** 1st woman, turning left, cast up around 2nd woman coming into a line of three with 2nd couple, facing down.
A2	1-4	In lines across the hall, take hands and set twice.
	5-8	Each line circle three-hands once around.
B1	1-4	1st man and 1st woman cast back to middle place.
	5-8	1st couple turn two-hands and end facing 3rd couple.
B2	1-8	Top couple face each other, middles face down, bottom couple face up: all circular hey skipping, beginning passing right shoulder, first couple making an extra change to end at bottom.

Repeat dance twice more.

BROOM, THE BONNY, BONNY BROOM
{*See opposite page for dance*}

Orpheus Caledonius (London: William Thomson, 1733), 1: 10
Courtesy of Legacy Books

CHELMSFORD ASSEMBLY

Chelmsford (pronounced "Chemsfurd") is in Essex, about thirty miles northeast of London. In the eighteenth century, community assembly balls were often sponsored by public officials, dancing masters, or citizens' groups and provided an opportunity for several layers of society to meet and mingle.

Two Hundred...Country Dances, vol. 8 (1753): 49
Courtesy of the Vaughan Williams Memorial Library

15

CHELSEA REACH

Square for four couples
7 x A B   MM ♩. = 108

Cecil Sharp, 1912
DM I: 1665-1690

Part I

A1	1-8	All forward a double and fall back a double. Partners face: slow set and honor right, then left.
B1	1-4	All lead partner a double away from set and fall back a double.
	5-8	Partners face: slow set and honor right, then left.
A2	1-4	Side couples meet, turn toward partner and face out to stand back-to-back **while** head couples gipsy once around, separate, pass through corner places to face side couples, forming lines across the hall.
	5-8	Facing couples circle four-hands half-way around to face across the line (5-6), then take right hands with opposite, pull by and turn to left (7-8).
B2	1-4	The same four left hands-across, skipping.
	5-8	Partners turn two-hands once around, to end in original place.
A3	1-8	Repeat A2 but with head couples meeting, sides gipsy, lines form up and down the hall.
B3	1-8	Repeat B2.

Part II

AB1	1-16	Partners side, then slow set and honor right, then left. That again.
A2	1-2	Taking two hands, men place partners into center of set.
	3-4	Dropping hands, all change places with partner, passing right shoulder.
	5-8	Change places again, women right hands-across half-way **while** men skip counter-clockwise around the outside half-way, to meet partners in opposite place, improper.
B2	1-8	Repeat B1 to places, women putting men in the center, changing places, men left hands-across, women skipping clockwise.

Part III

A1	1-8	Partners arm right, then slow set and honor right, then left.
B1	1-8	Partners arm left, then slow set and honor right, then left.
A2	1-4	Corners take right hands, lead out a double, fall back a double, and face each other.
	5-8	Beginning with corner, all grand right-and-left four changes, skipping.
B2	1-8	Repeat A2 back to place.

CHELSEA REACH

The full title of this dance, "Buckingham House, or Chelsea Reach," commemorates the sale of an historic house in Chelsea, thought to have once been occupied by Sir Thomas More and from which he was taken to the tower in 1534.   George Villiers, second Duke of Buckingham sold the house a year before the dance appeared.   The term "reach" has two meanings. The first is simply the Chelsea stretch of the Thames which flows west to east in a straight course where sailing vessels would reach their sails before the wind, a period of relaxation for the crew. However, the date of the appearance of this dance implies that the obsolete meaning of the term probably alluded to Buckingham's political intrigues.

DM I:8 (1690): 52
Courtesy of the Vaughan Williams Memorial Library

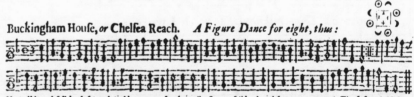

CHESTNUT; or, DOVE'S FIGARY

Longways for three couples

3 x A BB   MM ♩ = 96

Cecil Sharp, 1911
DM I: 1651-1690

Part I

A	1-8	Partners lead up a double and fall back a double. That again.
B1	1-4	All balance back, then change places with partner.
	5-8	Men circle three-hands around on women's side, **while** women the same on men's side.
B2	1-8	Repeat B1 to place.

Part II

A	1-8	Partners side twice.
B1	1-4	All balance back, then change places with partner.
	5-8	1st couple face down, 2nd and 3rd face up: Hey on sides half-way beginning right shoulder.
B2	1-8	Repeat B1 to place, 1st couple facing up and beginning hey left shoulder.

Part III

A	1-8	Partners arm right, then left.
B1	1-4	All balance back, then change places with partner.
	5-8	1st couple lead down the center to bottom place, 2nd and 3rd couple going up sides and following them down to invert the set.
B2	1-4	All balance back, then change places with partner.
	5-8	1st couple cast up to original place, followed by 2nd and 3rd couples.

CHESTNUT; or, DOVE'S FIGARY

This tune is reminiscent today of the first phrase of "God rest ye merry, gentlemen," and is a folk tune of widest distribution, the "tune of luck-visit songs, wassails, harvest suppers, may carols, and their parodies, 'chestnut' having feminine symbolism." (Dean-Smith) The second title may be explained by Deloney's ballad of 1600 on Dove's roguery with the women. Leslie Haworth proposed that the following lyric was intended for the tune and Evelyn Wells suggested that although it is an awkward fit, repeating the last words of some lines might make it work.

Welcome to towne, Tom Dove, Tom Dove,
  The merriest man alive.
Thy company stil we love, we love,
  God grant thee well to thrive.
And never will depart from thee,
  For better or worse, my joy,
For thou shalt still have our good will,
  God's blessing on my sweet Boy."

The tune and dance reappeared in the eighteenth century, without the introductions and called "Dove's Figary."

References: Simpson, 95-96; Dean-Smith, 71; Wells and Haworth correspondence, *Journal of the English Folk Dance and Song Society*, 4/3 (1942): 124.

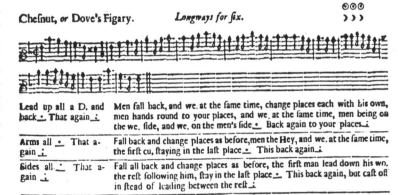

Chefnut, *or* Dove's Figary.   *Longways for fix.*

Lead up all a D. and back ⁑ That again ⁑

Arms all ⁑ That again ⁑

Sides all ⁑ That again ⁑

Men fall back, and we. at the fame time, change places each with his own, men hands round to your places, and we. at the fame time, men being on the we. fide, and we. on the men's fide ⁑ Back again to your places ⁑

Fall back and change places as before, men the Hey, and we. at the fame time, the firft cu. ftaying in the laft place ⁑ This back again ⁑

Fall all back and change places as before, the firft man lead down his wo. the reft following him, ftay in the laft place ⁑ This back again, but caft off in ftead of leading between the reft ⁑

DM I:8 (1690): 33

Courtesy of the Vaughan Williams Memorial Library

Woodcut from a ballad in the Pepys Collection entitled "The New Corant" to the tune of "Up goes aly aly." (3: 293). (See page 106 below.)

Courtesy of Boydell and Brewer.

CHILDGROVE

Duple minor longways, 1st couple improper
AA BB ad lib   MM $\downarrow$ = 112

Cecil Sharp, 1922
DM I: 1701-1728

A1	1-4	Partners side.
	5-8	Partners back-to-back.
A2	1-8	Repeat A1 with neighbor.
B1	1-4	Neighbors turn two-hands once-and-a-half, skipping, and open to face across the set.
	5-8	Partners turn two-hands.
B2	1-8	1st couple figure-eight through 2nd couple above, skipping.

{Inactive couples should change places with partner at top and bottom while waiting to re-enter the dance.}

CHILDGROVE

This appealing tune has defied efforts to unmask its meaning. Chilgrove is a very small village a few miles north of Chichester, but the connection is doubtful. The basic figures of "Childgrove" reappear with new music as "Scornfull Nancy" and "Hunting the Stagg" in several publications of John Walsh.

In Sharp's original interpretation, the first couples began the dance from their own sides in proper formation. In the 1940's the formation was made a bit more sociable by having them begin improper, a nice alteration which quickly became traditional.

CATCHPENNY PRINTS

"Dancing in a Grove" is one of eight images on a print from a series originally published over a period of about twenty years by Bowles and Carver in late eighteenth-century England. In the rich tradition of emblemata, these prints reflect both everyday life and the history of images in popular culture and folk art. Many served didactic purposes, both moral and religious; many are symbolistic rather than true reflections of the period in which they were created.

Borrowing heavily from cultivated art of the past hundred years, the print-makers who produced these sheets were eclectic and nondescriminating, with a keen understanding of the public mind. Collections of such prints were exceedingly popular and used as resources for needlework, book illustrations and woodcuts, textile and pottery decoration, and other artistic endeavors. Additional examples from this book may be seen on pages 24, 25, 42, 43, 46, 47, 55, 64, 98, 101, 103, 108, and 109.

Catchpenny Prints, 163 Popular Engravings from the Eighteenth Century Originally Published by Bowles and Carver. New York: Dover Publications, Inc, 1970, no. 43, 30.   Courtesy of Dover Publications.

First man and 2. man fide to their Partners once and go back to back. Then the wo. fide to the 2. man, and the 1. wo. to the 2. wo. at the fame time, and go back to back. Then turn fides and turn your own Partner in the 2. place. Then go the whole Figure with the 2. cu.

DM I:12 (1703): 261
Courtesy of the Vaughan Williams Memorial Library

Dancing in a Grove.

CHRISTCHURCH BELLS

Duple minor longways
A B C ad lib   MM ♩ = 116

Cecil Sharp, 1916
DM I: 1679-1728

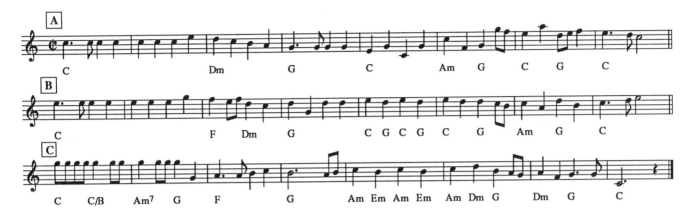

A   1-8   1st man turn 2nd woman right-hand (1-4), then turn partner left-hand (5-8).
B   1-8   2nd man turn 1st woman left-hand (1-4), then turn partner right-hand (5-8).
C   1-4   Circle four-hands once around, slipping.
     5-6   Clap hands: own, partner's right, own, partner's left
     7-8   1st couple cast off one place, 2nd couple lead up center.

CHRISTCHURCH BELLS

Some years before he became Dean of Christ Church, Oxford, Henry Aldrich (1647-1710) composed this catch, which was first published in 1673.

A dance was set to it immediately and appeared in the next edition of *The Dancing Master*. Soon political lyrics set to the tune appeared and in the early eighteenth century, the tune became associated with amorous words in several ballad operas, probably following the salacious song published by Thomas D'Urfey in *Wit and Mirth; or, Pills to Purge Melancholy*, vol. 5 (1719):252, beginning: "See how fair and fine she lies, upon her bridal bed..."

This dance, as "*Les Cloches, ou Le Carillon*," is shown complete with steps, tracks, music, and colored drawings of dancers in André Lorin's elegant manuscript made for Louis XIV in 1688. The same dance and tune, with the hand-turn replaced by a back-to-back, was printed in Raoul Feuillet's *Recüeil* (1706) as "*Le Carillon d'Oxfort*," which Pat Shaw reconstructed in 1965.

In *The Dancing Master*, the title was changed to "Christchurch Bells in Oxon" in the ninth edition (1695). In 1718, John Walsh pirated the entire contents of the sixteenth edition of volume one of *The Dancing Master*, possibly in retaliation for Young's lifting much of Walsh's *New Country Dancing Master* for his second and third volume of *The Dancing Master*. John Young then replaced the old dance with a new set of somewhat similar figures in the last two editions, dropping the introduction and keeping the longer title. Sharp dropped the introduction too, but interpreted the earlier dance.

References: Simpson, 48-49; Feuillet, *Recüeil de Contredances* (Paris: 1706): 49-54; A. Lorin, "Livre de la contredance du Roy, 1688" [MS at BN Paris]: 35-118; Moss 1: 228-31

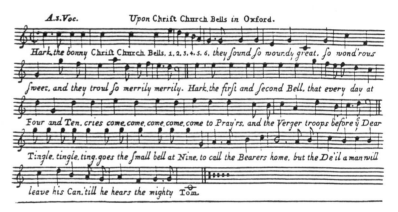

Second Book of The Catch Club (London: I Walsh, 1733): 37
Courtesy of Da Capo Press

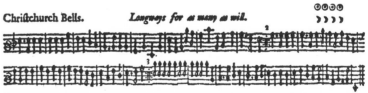

Honour to the Presence, next to your women. Lead forwards and back, that again.

First man turns right hands with the second wo. once round, and left hands with his own wo. once round. This ends the first Strain of the Tune.

Second man turns left hands with the first wo. once round, and right hands with his own once round; which ends the second Strain of the Tune.

All four take hands and go once round, then each Cu. clap hands right and left, then the first Cu. cast off into the second Cu. place, while the second Cu. lead up; which ends the third Strain.

DM I:7 (1686): 177
Courtesy of the Vaughan Williams Memorial Library

CONFESS

Longways for six, two men facing, each with two partners, one on either hand

3 x A BB   MM ♩. = 108

Cecil Sharp, 1912
DM I: 1651-1698

Em   Am   Em   B   Em   Am   Em   B

D   Em   Bm   Em   G   Am   D⁷   G   Em   Bm   Am   D   Em   Am   B⁷   Em

Part I

A	1-8	All forward a double and fall back a double. That again.
B1	1-4	Men lead both women on their left {*their own left-hand partner and right-hand partner of opposite*} out a double {*up or down the hall*}, change hands and lead back a double.
	5-8	Men turn two-hands once-and-a-half **while** women turn opposites two-hands once around.
B2	1-4	Men lead their two original partners out a double to the walls, change hands and lead back.
	5-8	All turn opposites two-hands to end in original places.

Part II

A	1-8	1st man and partners, 2nd man and partners, face 1st man's wall, balance back, then forward a double and turn around. Repeat to place.
B1	1-2	1st man and left corner woman {*on 2nd man's right*}, balance back and forward, then make an arch with right hands.
	3-8	The others circle four-hands once around 1st man, passing under arch.
B2	1-8	2nd man and left corner woman {*on 1st man's right*}, balance back and forward, then make an arch with right hands (1-2). The others circle four-hands once around 2nd man, passing under arch.

Part III

A	1-8	Repeat Part II, to 2nd man's wall.
B1	1-4	Women lead opposite woman away from set a double, change hands and lead back **while** men face out and move away from set a double, turn around and move back.
	5-8	Women circle four-hands around men who turn single right, then left.
B2	1-8	Repeat B1, but this time in bars 5-8 the women turn single right, then left, and men turn two-hands once around.

Part IV

A	1-8	All forward a double and fall back a double. That again.
B1	1-4	1st man lead woman on his left down toward his other woman's place, change hands, lead back making an arch **while** woman on his right cast up and return to place under the arch. **Meanwhile** the 2nd man lead woman on his right down a double, change hands, lead back making an arch **while** woman on his left cast up and return to place under the arch.
	5-8	Men turn the same women two-hands **while** other two women turn two-hands.
B2	1-8	Repeat B1, 1st man leading woman on his right, 2nd man the woman on his left, up a double, back and arch, the other women casting down.

CONFESS

Mr. Confesse was a court dancing master active in the early seventeenth century. The elaborate dance and modal tune were simply called "Confesse, his tune" in the table of contents of *The Dancing Master* between 1651 and 1665, but in 1670 the title became "Confess, or: The Court Lady." Claude Simpson is not convinced that ballads set to the second tune title are meant for the earlier tune.

In his pamplet, "Mr. Confesse, His Tune" (1986), Tom Cook takes up in detail the many issues surrounding the historically accurate interpretation of this unusual dance. *See dance facsimile on opposite page.*

References: Simpson, 136-37; Dean-Smith, 19; Chappell, 361

THE CORPORATION
to the tune of FETE CHAMPETRE

Longways for three couples
3 x AA BB   MM ♪. = 116

W. S. Porter, 1931
d: *Twenty Four Country Dances* (Thompson), 1777
m: *Thompson's Compleat Collection*, v. 4 (Thompson), 1780

A1	1-8	1st couple cross at top and hey on the opposite side, passing **outside** 2nd couple to begin.
A2	1-8	1st couple cross back, hey on their own side, again passing **outside** 2nd couple.
B1	1-4	1st man lead partner down center through 3rd couple, hand her across to men's side.
	5-8	1st couple, now improper, cast up to top **while** 2nd couple half figure-eight down through 3d couple to end in 2nd place improper.
B2	1-4	1st and 2nd men turn right-hand **while** 1st and 2nd women turn left-hand.
	5-6	1st and 2nd men change places with partners.
	7-8	1st couple move down outside to bottom, 2nd and 3rd couples moving up.

Repeat dance twice more.

THE CORPORATION and FETE CHAMPETRE

The "corporation" probably refers to the Corporation of the City of London. *Fêtes champêtres* were lavish outdoor entertainments, part of the "back to nature" movement of the mild-weathered, mid-eighteenth century. This tune was probably inspired by one of the most splendid of the century, the five-day party which Lord Stanley held at his country seat, The Oaks, near Epsom, Surrey, to celebrate his marriage to the daughter of the Duke of Hamilton in 1774. An elaborate masque with a great deal of dancing was composed by François Bartelemon and General John Burgoyne, and it was the centerpiece of the event. It was later expanded to the full length opera, *The Maid of the Oaks*. The event may also have inspired the musical piece called "Fete Champetre" played for a decade afterwards at the Drury Lane Theatre.

References: David Johnson, *Music and Society in Lowland Scotland in the Eighteenth Century* (London: Oxford University Press, 1972), 74; Roger Fiske, *English Theatre Music in the Eighteenth Century* (London: Oxford University Press, 1973), 380-81; *Gentleman's Magazine* (1774), 263.

The Corporation
112

Hey contrary Sides ⁓ then on your own fides ⁓ lead down the middle thro' the bottom, the 2d Cu: follow and caft up into their own places ⁓ crofs over one Cu: and right and left ⁓

CONFESS
{*See dance on opposite page.*}

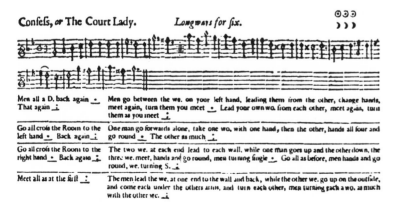

Confefs, *or* The Court Lady.   *Longways for fix.*   ☉ↃↃ ⟩⟩⟩

Men all a D. back again ⁓	Men go between the we. on your left hand, leading them from the other, change hands, meet again, turn them you meet ⁓ Lead your own wo. from each other, meet again, turn them as you meet ⁓
That again ⁓	
Go all crofs the Room to the left hand ⁓ Back again ⁓	One man go forwards alone, take one wo. with one hand, then the other, hands all four and go round ⁓ The other as much ⁓
Go all crofs the Room to the right hand ⁓ Back again ⁓	The two we. at each end lead to each wall, while one man goes up and the other down, the three we. meet, hands and go round, men turning fingle ⁓ Go all as before, men hands and go round, we. turning S. ⁓
Meet all as at the firft ⁓	The men lead the we. at one end to the wall and back, while the other we. go up on the outfide, and come each under the others arms, and turn each other, men turning each a wo. as much with the other we. ⁓

DM 1:8 (1690): 29
Courtesy of the Vaughan Williams Memorial Library

Fete Champetre
76

Turn your Part: right-hand then left ⁓ lead down the middle up again & caft off ⁓ the 1st 2d & 3d Cu. Promenade quite round ⊟ caft off one Cu. & right & left at top ⊟

Thompson's Compleat Collection, vol. 4 (1780): 56, 38
By permission of the British Library

COTTEY HOUSE

Duple minor longways
AA BB ad lib   MM ♩. = 116

Douglas and Helen Kennedy, 1929
Twenty Four New Country Dances (Playford), 1702; DM I: 1703-1728

A1	1-4	1st couple cast down to second place and cross, 2nd couple moving up on bars 3-4.
	5-8	1st man lead 2nd woman out to women's wall, change hands and lead back **while** 1st woman lead 2nd man to men's wall, change hands and lead back.
A2	1-8	Repeat A1, 2nd couple cast and cross, and two men and two women leading out and back.
B1	1-4	All clap on first beat, partners gipsy clockwise.
	5-8	All clap on first beat, partners gipsy counter-clockwise.
	9-12	Right-hand across half-way (9-10), all turn single to right (11-12).
B2	1-4	1st couple half figure-eight through 2nd couple ending in a line of four facing up, 1st couple in the middle improper.
	5-6	Line lead up a double.
	7-8	Turning towards neighbor, change hands and lead down a double, 1st couple changing sides and ending in second place on last two beats.
	9-12	All clap twice {*on first and second beats*}, then partners turn two-hands once around.

COTTEY HOUSE

Like Apley and Hunsdon, this dance probably commemorates the home of a particular person in the news, in this case someone who may have gained public notice at the beginning of the reign of Queen Anne. While the meanings of many of the dance titles are quite clear, having recognizable topical or song references, some will probably never be understood fully. Their references lie hidden in contemporary gossip, allusions, rumours, and everyday events, most of which were not recorded for posterity. Even contemporary "scandal sheets" such as the *Spectator*, the *Tatler*, and the *London Spy*, and the hundreds of poems and pamphlets which flooded from the Grub Street presses, couch allusions in discreet metaphors. Throughout the topical literature of the times, if names were mentioned at all, notable people would be referred to in print as "Lord B---ke" or "Lady M----h."

In the early part of the eighteenth century, new dances were named in one of several ways. Most frequently, the titles were devised by the choreographer, usually a local dancing master, who hoped for patronage from the nobility and gentry and tried to draw their attention by flattering them. Dances were named for them and their wives, daughters and mistresses. Another ruse was to introduce a new country dance whose title referred to a recent event or person in the news or gossip circuit.

Often titles were quite oblique, which made the author appear clever in their eyes. Literary conceits, emblems, riddles, and word puzzles were popular throughout the century. Lastly, dances were named for their music, particularly if the music was part of a recently popular theater work. This would have the same effect--to attract attention to the commercial interests of the dancing master, assembly manager, or publisher of the dance collection.

The 1. cu. caſt off and croſs over into the 2. cu. place, the 1. man and 2. wo. lead to the wall, 1. wo. and 2. man do the ſame at the ſame time. The 2. cu. do the ſame as the firſt. The 1. and 2. cu. turn back to back and clap hands; then Face about and clap hands again, Right hands a croſs half round, all 4 turn ſingle, the 1. cu. go half a figure of Eight through the 2. cu. all hands a breaſt to the top and back again, the 1. cu. lead between the 2. cu. all a breaſt down, the 1. cu. change places the while they lead down, and all four clap Hands twice, and turn their Partners half a turn into their places.

Twenty Four New Country Dances (1702): 12

DARGASON; or, SEDANY

Straight line of 4 women facing 4 men, inside couple is 1st couple.

19 x A   MM $\quad\bullet$ = 120

Cecil Sharp, 1911
DM I: 1651-1690

Part I

A1	1-4	1st couple side.
	5-6	1st couple set.
	7-8	1st couple pass by left shoulder **while** turning single, man to right, woman to left.
A2	1-8	A1 repeated by 1st man with 2nd woman **and** 1st woman with 2nd man.
A3	1-8	A1 repeated by three pairs of dancers.
A4	1-8	A1 repeated by four pairs of dancers, except that all turn single once-and-a-half to reverse direction on bars 7-8.
4 x A		On completing the fourth round, the movement is repeated, all retracing their steps. By turns, couples 4, 3, and 2 become inactive.

Part II

8 x A	Progression repeated as in Part I, with couples arming right, setting and turning single in A1-4, arming left in A5-8.

Part III

3 x A	1st couple, giving right hands, begin a progressive hey with hands, all dancers going through all positions in the set. At ends, turn and re-enter hey with same hand.

DARGASON; or, SEDANY

With two titles of Welsh derivation, both of which escape convincing explanation, this unique progressive dance is paired with a late sixteenth-century double-tonic circular tune of haunting familiarity. The title of the song below also connects the tune to Wales, Shropshire lying in the foothills on the English side of the border.

Today's ears hear strong traces of "The Irish Washerwoman" and "Skip to my Lou" in the opening measures.

Chappell quotes the first of sixteen verses set to this tune in the seventeenth century:
The Shrop-shire Wakes, or hey for Christmass, being the delightful sports of most countries, to the tune of Dargason.

Come Robin, Ralph, and little Harry, and merry Thomas to our green;
Where we shall meet with Bridget and Sary, and the finest girls that e'er were seen.
Then hey for Christmas a once year, when we have cakes, with ale and beer,
For at Christmas every day, young men and maids may dance away, &c.

References: Simpson, 165-66; Dean-Smith, 60; Fuld, 489; Chappell, 63-66; Ward, 36

DM I:3 (1665): 24
Courtesy of the Bodleian Library (pressmark: Douce P 581)

DICK'S MAGGOT

Duple minor longways
AA B ad lib   MM ♩ = 108

Cecil Sharp, 1922
Twenty Four New Country Dances (Playford), 1702; DM I: 1703-1728

A1	1	1st man change places with partner.
	2	1st couple lead down center into second place **while** 2nd couple cast up into first place.
	3-4	Partners balance back, then change places.
A2	1	2nd man change places with partner again.
	2	2nd couple lead down center into second place **while** 1st couple cast up.
	3-4	Partners back-to-back.
B	1-4	Circular hey, three changes beginning with partner, skipping, then turn to right to face partner.
		{*The third change in the hey should make a big loop, opening out the set.*}
	5-8	Partners turn two-hands twice around, skipping.

DICK'S MAGGOT

This same tune and the slightly re-worded dance figures appear in the *New Country Dancing Master 2d Book* (London: I. Walsh, [1711]) as "Duble the Cape" and a few pages later with a new tune called "Hiland Lass."

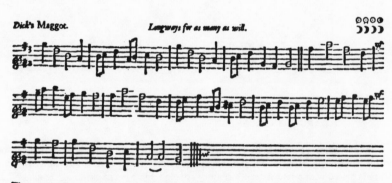

DM I:14 (1709): 332
Courtesy of the Vaughan Williams Memorial Library

Catchpenny Prints, no. 68, 55

Courtesy Dover Publications

DOVER PIER

Duple minor longways
AA BB ad lib   MM ♩ = 112

A. Simons, 1961
Preston's Twenty Four Country Dances (Preston), 1791

A1	1-4	Partners set twice.
	5-8	All right hands-across half-way and fall back into opposite place.
A2	1-8	Repeat A1 with left hands.
B1	1-4	1st couple cross, and move down outside into second place **while** 2nd couple move up.
	5-8	1st couple turn two-hands once-and-a-half.
B2	1-8	All right-and-left, four changes, beginning with partner.

DOVER PIER

The wharfs at Dover are the chief point of departure for the continent, being but twenty-one miles across the English channel to Calais in France.

Dover Pier

1st & 2d Cu: foot it & Right hands acrofs half round : foot it & left hands back again : crofs over & turn your Partner : right & left :

Preston's Twenty Four Country Dances (1791): 65
By permission of the British Library

Jolly Boatswain   Portsmouth Moll   Monfieur from Paris   Jolly Tar   Kitty Fisher   Town Bully

Catchpenny Prints, no. 180, 125

Courtesy Dover Publications

DRAPERS GARDENS
to the tune of THE MARGRAVINE'S WALTZ

Duple minor longways
AA B ad lib   MM ♩ = 120

Bernard J. Bentley, 1965
d: DM I: 1706-1728; m: *Preston's Twenty Four...*(Preston), 1799

A1	1-4	1st corners set forward and turn single to right.
	5-8	1st corners turn two-hands once around.
A2	1-8	2nd corners repeat A1.
B	1-2	Two women face and turn two-hands half-way.
	3-4	Two men the same.
	5-8	Circle four-hands half-way and fall back into lines.
	9-12	All right-and-left, two changes, beginning with partner.
	13-16	1st couple lead up through 2nd couple and cast down one place.

Waltzer au Mouchoir by H. Humphrey, January 20, 1800,
one of the earliest depictions of the waltz in England.
Courtesy of the Print Collection,
The Lewis Walpole Library, Yale University

DRAPERS GARDENS

Bentley published both tunes with this dance in 1965. "The Margravine's Waltz" has
come to be the preferred tune. See next page for background on both titles.

Note: *Each Strain twice over.*

The 1. man and 2. wo. set and turn single, then back to back and turn. The other two do the same. Then the 1. and 2. wo. change places, the other two do the same, then hands half round, and right and left half round, and lead through the bottom, then through the top, and cast off and turn.

DM I:14 (1709): 189
Courtesy of the Vaughan Williams Memorial Library

Turn your Partner with the Right hand quite
round, turn back with your Left hand, lead
down two Cu: & foot it, lead back again to
the 2d Cus place, Hands 6 half round,
Hands 6 back again.

Preston's Twenty Four Country Dances (1799): 160
Courtesy of the Vaughan Williams Memorial Library

DRAPER'S MAGGOT

Triple minor longways
AA BB ad lib   MM ♩ = 138

Douglas and Helen Kennedy, 1929
DM I: 1706-1728

A1   1-4   1st and 2nd couples circle four-hands once around.

           5-8   1st couple cast down to middle place **while** 2nd couple lead up.

A2   1-8   1st and 3rd couple right-and-left, beginning with partners.

B1   1-4   1st man turn 3rd woman two-hands **while** 1st woman the same with 2nd man.

           5-8   Partners turn two-hands.

B2   1-4   1st man turn 2nd woman two-hands **while** 1st woman the same with 3rd man.

           5-8   Partners turn two-hands.

THE DRAPERS

The Drapers, cloth merchants in London, were chartered in 1364. The gardens behind their hall in Throgmorton Street commanded a fine view of Highgate and in 1700 were commended by "the London Spy" as a fashionable promenade. They were described a few years later by a foreign visitor.

"On 10 June...we drove to the Exchange in order to speak with our Merchants...[then] we walked for a mile to the garden behind the Drappers-Hall, which is fairly large and pleasant and is open to all." (Quarrell)

Drapers Hall was used for social events as well as official business. A prelenten masquerade ball held there February 4, 1695/6 is reported in *The London Stage* (Part 1: 459).

The dance commemorating the gardens was probably originally danced with a minuet step rather than the waltz which the music inspires today. The rhythm of the opening bars is frequently found in minuets, most familiar being the "Trumpet Minuet" from Handel's *Water Music* (1715) and the minuet from the dinner scene in Mozart's *Don Giovanni* (1787).

THE WALTZ

The waltz as a gliding and turning dance for a couple in a closed face-to-face dance position first appeared in the 1750's in Germany. By the 1790's waltz tunes appeared in English books for use with country dances and for the new couple dance. The new dance provoked howls of outrage from those charged with the protection of the morals of the populace. Belinda Quirey describes the waltz as "...quite simply the greatest change in dance form and dancing manners...in history!" She points out that it exemplified the triple revolution of the later eighteenth century: political, imaginative, and material.

"From this point on, dancing became a bourgeoise activity, and aristocratic style was seen only in stage imitations, some ludicrously off-target...Waltz reflected and exemplified...these changes. That in Polite Society a man should actually put his arm round a girl when he danced with her was nothing short of scandalous...Not only indecent, but vulgar!"

Waltz introduced the change from dances which reinforced position with ceremony to dances danced for their own sake--each couple turned inward towards each other and cut off from the throng of similarly closed couples.

In the new century, the young people loved the waltz. Quirey sums up the reason for its success. "The Waltz is basically a work rhythm. It was the first work rhythm that we ever accepted above the level of folk dance...It perfectly suited the new conditions of life, socially, psychologically and materially...It both reflected the new standards, and satisfied the new needs."

Waltz was the star of the Congress of Vienna in 1814-1815. Although it had been taught and danced in England for nearly twenty years, once it was publicly danced in such surroundings, it gained respectability. The waltz was here to stay. Always ready to capitalize on new trends, Thomas Wilson quickly published *A Description of the Correct Method of Waltzing, the truly Fashionable Species of Dancing* (London: 1816) which in 113 pages [!] attempted to codify the rules of a dance which threatened his livelihood.

"The Margravine's Waltz" may have been named in honor of Lady Elizabeth Berkeley, Margravine of Brandenburg-Anspach, a composer herself. "Draper's Maggot" is a minuet country dance which today is performed with a smooth waltz movement. This dance and tune were also known as "Cupid's Guess" and the same dance with another tune was called "Mrs. Booth's Minuet."

References: Quarrell, 15; Quirey, *May I have the Pleasure*, 66-76

Draper's Maggot.   Longways for as many as will.

Note: *Each Strain twice over.*

Hands all four quite round and cast off⌐ and Right and Left with the 3. cu⌐ then the 1. man turn the 3. wo. and the 1. wo. the 2. man, and then his own Partner⌐ then the 1. man turn the 2. wo. and the 1. wo. the 3. man, and then turn Partners.⌐

DM I:14 (1709): 203

Courtesy of the Vaughan Williams Memorial Library

THE DRESSED SHIP

Duple minor longways
AA BB ad lib   MM ♩ = 116

W. S. Porter, 1931
Twenty Four Country Dances (Thompson), 1774

A1	1-8	1st man and 2nd woman set forward (1-2), fall back (3-4), turn two-hands (5-8).		
A2	1-8	1st woman and 2nd man the same.		
B1	1-4	1st couple cast down into second place, 2nd couple leading up on bars 3-4.		
	5-8	All set to partner (5-6). Men turn partners under their right arms counter-clockwise (7-8).		
B2	1-4	1st couple cast up to top, 2nd couple leading down on bars 3-4.		
	5-6	All set to partner.		
	7-8	2nd couple cast up **while** 1st couple lead down center, 1st man turning his partner under as in B1.		

THE DRESSED SHIP

A "dressed ship" displays all its flags and bunting in honor of holidays or special visitors. As the illustration suggests, in the eighteenth century this term might have been applied satirically to an overdressed lady, particularly in light of the elaborate hoops and headdresses then in fashion.

The drefs'd Ship

1st. Man fet to the 2d Wo. & turn ‖ 1st Wo. do the fame ‖ caft off 1 Cu. & Al‑ ‑lemand ‖ caft up & Allemand & lead down in the 2d Cus place ‖

Thompson's Compleat Collection, vol.4 (1780): 18
By permission of the British Museum

A Lugtail Privateer towing A Crippled Man of War into Port
(R. Sayer and J. Bennett, April, 1783)
Anne S. K. Brown Military Collection, Brown University Library

DUBLIN BAY; or, WE'LL WED AND WE'LL BED

Duple minor longways
A B ad lib   MM ♩. = 116

Bernard J. Bentley, 1962
DM II: 1710-1728

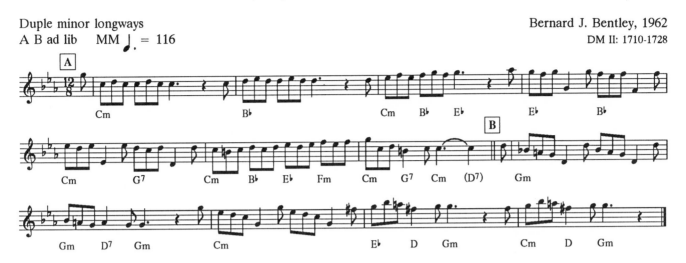

A

1   1st woman set forward diagonally to 2nd man **while** 1st man, passing his partner by right shoulder, does the same to 2nd woman.

2-3   1st woman turn 2nd man right-hand **while** 1st man turn 2nd woman right-hand, ending improper in first place.

4-5   1st couple cross by left shoulder, go down outside 2nd couple and meet between them in center, 1st man facing 2nd man, 1st woman facing 2nd woman.

6-7   All arm right **once around**, and end in line across the hall, facing down.

B

1-2   In line with hands, fall **back** a double {*up the hall*}, go forward a double {*down the hall*}.

3-4   Turning towards neighbor, change hands into a line facing up and fall **back** a double {*down the hall*} and come forward a double {*up the hall*}.

5   1st couple drop partner's hand and move up center through top couple and cast down to second place, neighbor acting as a pivot.

DUBLIN BAY; or, WE'LL WED AND WE'LL BED

Bentley's note with this dance explains its changed name: "This dance was first worked out at a Summer School in Dublin--hence the title, which I have retained as it is now well established."

The Wonders in the Sun, or the Kingdom of the Birds was premiered at the Queens Theatre in 1706, with a libretto by Thomas D'Urfey and plenty of trick staging. It was a low-brow version of the immensely popular Purcellian opera and in many ways anticipated *The Beggar's Opera*. The following dialogue in Act 1 between "Maturity" and "Sport" was set to this tune.

SHE: Oh Love if a God thou wilt be, do justice in favour of me, for yonder approaching I see, a man with a beard, who as I have heard, has often undone poor maids that have none, with sighing, and toying, and crying, and lying, and such kind of foolery.

HE: Fair maid by your leave, my heart does receive, strange pleasures to meet you here. Pray tremble not so, nor offer to go, I'll do ye no harm, I swear. I'll do ye no harm, I swear.

SHE: My mother is spinning at home, my father works hard at his loom, and we here a milking are come. Their dinner they want, pray gentlemen don't make more ado ont, nor give us affront, we're none of the town will lie down for a crown, then away, Sir, and give us room.

He: By Phoebus, by Jove, by honour, by love. I'll do ye dear sweet no harm. Y're fresh as a rose, I want one of those. Ah! how such a wife would charm, ah! how such a wife would charm.

SHE: And can you then like the old rule, be conjugal, honest and dull, and marry, and look like a fool. For I must be plain, all tricks are in vain, there's nothing can gain, the thing you'd obtain but moving, and proving, by wedding, true loving, my lesson I learnt at school.

HE: I'll do't by this hand, I've houses, I've land, estate too in good freehold. My dear, let us joyn. It all shall be thine, besides a good purse of gold.

SHE: You make me to blush, now I vow, Oh, Lord, shall I too baulk my cow, but since the late oath you have swore. Your soul shall not be, in danger of me. I'll rather agree, of two to make three. We'll wed, and we'll bed, there's no more to be said, and I'll ne'er go a milking more.

HE: I'll do't by this hand...

D'Urfey, *Wit and Mirth* 1 (1719): 100-102

We'll Wed and we'll Bed.   *Longways for as many as will.*

Note : *Each Strain is to be play'd but once over.*

The first couple change places, the first man Sett to the second woman, and the first woman to the second man, then turn Right-hands round; the first man turns his woman with his Left-hand half round, and cast off below the second couple, then cross over above the second couple and fall down between, Arms half round, back again all four of a-row, Face up the Room, then fall back and lead forwards half a turn single, Faces down the Room, fall back, lead forwards half a turn single, Faces up, cast off and to to the end.

DM II:1 (1710): 104
By permission of the Director of Manchester Public Libraries

29

THE DUKE OF KENT'S WALTZ

Duple minor longways
AA B ad lib   MM ♩ = 120

A. Simons, 1970
W.M. Cahusac's Annual Collection (Cahusac), 1801

A1   1-8   All right hands-across and left hands back.

A2   1-8   1st couple take two hands and move two waltz side-steps down center, two back,
and cast down to second place, 2nd couple leading up.

B   1-4   All take right hands with partner and balance forward, back, and change places,
men turning partners under their arms {*down the set*}.

      5-8   Repeat movement giving left hands.

      9-12   Men turn women below their partners by right-hand.

      13-16 Men turn partners left-hand.

THE DUKE OF KENT'S WALTZ

Edward Augustus, 1767-1820, was the fourth son of George III and father of Queen Victoria. He was made Duke of Kent in 1799 and was commander-in-chief of the forces in British America in 1799-1800.

During the 1790's, country dances to waltz tunes began to appear in English books. This waltz country dance commemorating the Duke was found in a coverless book at the British Library, which Jacqueline Schwab has since identified in the course of her work preparing a bibliography of published English country dances, 1700-1830.

Prince Edward

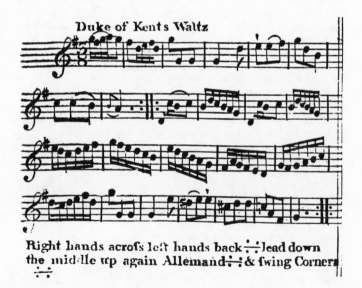

Right hands acrofs left hands back ∴ lead down the middle up again Allemand ∴ & swing Corners

W.M.Cahusac's Annual Collection (1801): 2
By permission of the British Library

EPPING FOREST

Round for three couples
3 x AA B C   MM ♩. = 96

Cecil Sharp, 1922
DM I: 1670-1690

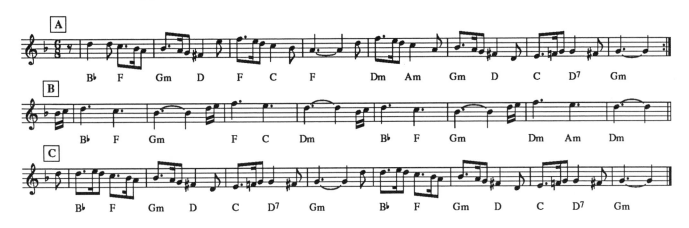

A												
B♭	F	Gm	D	F	C	F	Dm	Am	Gm	D	C	D⁷	Gm
B												
B♭	F	Gm		F	C	Dm		B♭	F	Gm	Dm	Am	Dm
C												
B♭	F	Gm	D	C	D⁷	Gm		B♭	F	Gm	D	C	D⁷	Gm

Part I

A1 1-4 Circle six-hands eight slips to left.
    5-8 Partners set and turn single.
A2 1-8 Repeat A1, slipping right.
B   1-4 Partners slow set and honor
         right, then left.
    5-8 Corners slow set and honor
         right, then left.
C   1-4 Men turn partners two-hands,
         skipping.
    5-8 Men turn corners two-hands,
         skipping.

Part II

A1 1-8 Partners side, set and turn single.
A2 1-8 Repeat A1.
BC   As in Part I.

Part III

A1 1-8 Partners arm right, set and turn
         single.
A2 1-8 Repeat A1, arming left.
BC   As in Part I.

EPPING FOREST

Sharp left the kissing out of his interpretation of this simple dance named for the ancient forest on the northern boundaries of London, a frequent resort of the citizens of the city for the pleasures of hunting.

The congestion of people, dogs and horses in Bunbury's delightful satire certainly suggests that the catch may have been slim. It is more likely that the real goal of the "Easter Hunt" was to see and be seen, and to take the fresh air, away from the coal, peat, and wood smoke of the city.

DM I:4 (1670): 89
Courtesy of the Vaughan Williams Memorial Library

The Easter Hunt at Epping Forest
Henry William Bunbury
1785

Courtesy of the Print Collection
The Lewis Walpole Library, Yale University

FAIN I WOULD

Square for eight

3 x AA BB   MM $\downarrow$. = 88

Cecil Sharp, 1912
DM I: 1651-1690

Part I

A1	1-4	Partners lead out a double, change hands and lead back a double.
	5-6	All turn corners two-hands half-way, ending in two lines on sides facing across the hall.
	7-8	All turn opposite two-hands half-way, into *square* formation.
A2	1-4	Current partners lead out from square a double, change hands, and lead back a double.
	5-6	All turn corners two-hands half-way, ending in two lines on sides.
	7-8	All turn opposites two-hands half-way to original places in square formation.
B1	1-4	Head couples forward a double to meet (1-2), fall back, side couples separate and join heads in lines across the hall.
	5-8	Head couples arm right with opposite and fall into nearest side place, improper **while** side couples arm right with opposite on end of same line and fall into nearest head place, improper.
B2	1-8	Repeat B1 with new head and side couples, ending proper, in original square formation.

Part II

A1	1-8	Partners side (1-4), then all change places as in Part I, A1 5-8.
A2	1-8	Men side with current partner, then all repeat Part I, A1 5-8.
B1	1-4	Head couples cast off and move back to place **while** sides separate and follow head neighbor.
	5-8	Head couples turn in to circle four-hands with the two who followed them.
B2	1-8	Repeat B1, side couples leading, heads following.

Part III

A1	1-8	Partners arm right (1-4), then change places as in Part I, A1 5-8.
A2	1-8	Men arm left with current partner (1-4), then change places as in Part I, A1 5-8.
B1	1-2	Head couples meet, face out and join hands.
	3-8	Head couples circle four-hands to right {*clockwise*} once around while facing out; head men fall out with opposite woman into nearest side place, improper. **Meanwhile** side couples circle four-hands counter-clockwise around them and fall into the nearest head place, improper.
B2	1-8	B1 repeated with new head couples meeting, new sides circle around them, all falling into original places.

FAIN I WOULD

In the dance facsimile opposite note the last sentence in the first part, and the unusual placement of the symbols of the men and women. Having lost London to Cromwell, Charles I convened a royalist parliament in Oxford in 1644. A supporter of Charles I, John Playford continued a royalist at heart and again served as printer to the king at the restoration of Charles II.

From 1670-1690, the title of the dance was "Parthenia, or: Fain I would," and it should be distinguished from "Parthenia. A Dance" which later came to be called "The Jovial Beggars" (DM I: 1665, 1701-1728).

W. B. Olson recently discovered an early song to this tune entitled "The King's Complaint, Or, Fain I Would," discussed it in the *Folk Song Journal*, and presented the entire text. The first verse, given on the opposite page, serves to identify it as a topical song from the interregnum period.

References: Simpson, 209-11; Dean-Smith, 40; Olson, *Folk Song Journal* (1980): 63-64; Chappell, 91-92

The King's Complaint

Fain I would, if I could,
By any meanes obteine,
Leave of my best Masters,
To sit with them againe.
But my blest Parliment
Will never give consent,
They say tis such a thinge,
For the worst of them's a Kinge.
Wee will rule still,
In spight of Cavalieres.
O brave house of Comons,
O brave House of Peeres.
Religion you have pull'd downe,
And soe you have the crowne,
My laws & Kingdome too.
I thinke the Devill's in you.
Else you'll not endure,
Such a constant flood,
All of childrens teares,
And theire dead Fathers blood...

Parthenia, *or* Fain I would.   *A Figure Dance for eight, thus :*

Lead all out, lead all in again, 1. man and 4 wo. the 1. wo. and 2. man change places by both hands, the other doing the like, then the 1. man and 1. wo. the 2. and 4. wo. change by both hands, the other 4. doing the like • then each man hands with the wo. on his left hand, lead out and in as before, changing places, back as before _i_

The 1. and 3. cu. meet, the 2. and 4. falling back, the 1. and 3. cu. fall back four abreaſt, the 2. man and 4. wo. with the 1. cu. the 4. man and 3. wo. with the 3. the 1. man and 3. wo. the 3. man and 1. wo. Arms and fall into the 4. and 2. places, whilſt the 2. man and 4. wo. the 4. man and 2. wo. arms behind and fall into the 1. and 3. places • The other as much _i_ As in *Oxford*.

Sides and change places as before • Sides again and change places, back again :'

The 1. and 3. cu. caſt off, and come into your places all again, the 4. wo. following the 1. man, the 2. man the 1. wo. the 2. wo. the 3. man, the 4. man the 3. wo. the uppermoſt and lowermoſt 4 hands round to your places • The 2. and 4. cu. caſt off, and the other follow to your places four and tour of each ſide, hands round to your places.

Arms and change as you ſided • That again to your places :'

The 1. and 3. cu. meet, turn back to back, the other four hands about them, and go round to the right and fall into each others places, the 2 and 4. wo. into the 1. place, the 4. man and 2. wo. into the 3. place, the 1. man and 3. wo. to the 4. place, the 3. man and 1. wo. to the 2. place • Other four as much :'

DM I:8 (1690): 51
Courtesy of the Vaughan Williams Memorial Library

THE FAIR QUAKER OF DEAL

This dance (see next page) was probably named as much for Hester Santlow as for Charles Shadwell's play, which was produced in 1710. A visitor to London attended a performance.

"On 13 June...in the evening we saw an extremely live[ly?] comedy: 'The Fair Quacker of Deal,' an uncommonly curious play, in which English Quakers and Quakeresses are represented most naturally. The female who played the chief part, that of a Quaker, is a person well known throughout England, called Mistress Sandlow. She is universally admired for her beauty, matchless figures and the unusual elegance of her dancing and acting...Between every act they introduced several dances for variety... [she] danced charmingly as Harlequin." (Quarrell)

Hester Santlow made her debut in 1709, and as Dorcas Zeal in *The Fair Quaker of Deal, or, The Humours of the Navy*, she won Colley Cibber's praise.

"Before this, she had only been admired as the most excellent Dancer; which, perhaps, might not a little contribute to the favorable Reception, she now met with as an Actress, in this Character, which so happily suited her Figure, and Capacity: The gentle Softness of her Voice, the compos'd Innocence of her Aspect, the Modesty of her Dress, the reserv'd Decency of her Gesture, and the Simplicity of the Sentiments, that naturally fell from her, made her seem the amiable Maid she represented." (Cibber)

In 1719 she married Barton Booth (1681-1733), a fellow actor in Betterton's company.

Reference: Quarrell, 30-31; Colley Cibber, *An Apology for the Life of Colley Cibber*, edited by by B. R. S. Fone (Ann Arbor: University of Michigan Press, [1968]), 230

HESTER SANTLOW

Harvard Theatre Collection

THE FAIR QUAKER OF DEAL

Duple minor longways
AA BB ad lib   MM ♩. = 116

A. Simons, 1970
DM II: 1710-1728

A1	1-4	1st corners set and turn single.
	5-8	1st man cast down into second place, 2nd man moving up **while** 2nd woman cast up to 1st place, 1st woman moving down.
A2	1-8	A1 repeated by 1st woman and 2nd man, 1st man moving up and 2nd woman down.
B1	1-4	1st corners meet and stand back to back, facing out, then 2nd corners the same.
	5-8	Taking hands and facing outward, set and circle four-hands to right {*clockwise*} half-way.
B2	1-4	Two men, two women lead out to opposite wall, turn and lead back to place.
	5-8	1st couple lead up, man handing his partner across in front of him, cast down to 2nd place **while** 2nd couple change places, all ending proper.

THE FAIR QUAKER OF DEAL

See previous page for a portrait and brief biography of Hester Santlow, who played the "fair Quaker" when this comedy was first produced. She apparently not only acted the lead female role, but distinguished herself dancing a breeches part as "Harlequin" in an entre-act.

The somewhat unusual dance figures reappeared twice in Walsh's *New Country Dancing Master 3d Book* (1728) with new tunes entitled "Hannibal" and "Amsbury." Miss Santlow was further honored with a country dance named for her directly, "Miss Santlow's Frolic."

A. Simons, who reconstructed this dance in 1954 wrote an interesting article on the process of interpretation and on the oral tradition which was changing his interpretation which at that point had not been published. He said that it was one of his club's favorite dances and a number of other Kentish country dance clubs were adopting it. He registered strong objection to a "vigorous balance in the modern style" which one club has substituted as "completely out of keeping!" Deal was, of course, the nearby Kentish seaside town in which the action of the play takes place. Simons also noted that his musicians used both "The Quaker's Wife" and Jimmy Shand's recording of "Cumberland Reel" (Parlophone) as alternate tunes.

References: *English Dance and Song* 24/2 (1960): 70-71

Catchpenny Prints, no. 40, 27
Courtesy of Dover Publications

Fair Quaker of Deal   *Longways for as many as will*

Note   Each Strain twice

The 1st man and 2d wo Set, turn S, the 1st cu cast off. ∺ the 2d man and 1st wo Set, turn S, the 2d cu cast off. ∺ the 1st man and 2d wo meet back to back, the 2d man and the 1st wo do the same, all four hands half round backward, ∺ the 1st cu being in the 2d cu place, lead to the wall and back again, the 1st cu lead through the 2d cu and cast off ∺.

Twenty Four New Country Dances (London: I. Walsh, 1712): 5
Courtesy of the National Library of Ireland, Dublin

THE FANDANGO

Longways set for three couples
6 x AA BB   MM ♩. = 116

W. S. Porter, 1931
Twenty Four Country Dances (Thompson), 1774

D   G A D   D A⁷ D   G A Bm Em A⁷ D

D   G   A⁷ D G D G A⁷ D A⁷ D

Part I

A1 1-4 1st couple turn right-hands.

5-8 1st couple cast down to second place, 2nd couple moving up on bars 7-8.

A2 1-4 1st couple turn left-hands.

5-8 1st couple cast down to bottom place, 3rd couple moving up on bars 7-8.

B1 1-8 All circle six-hands around clockwise and back, slipping.

B2 1-6 1st couple lead up center to top and cast down to middle place, 3rd couple moving down.

7-8 1st couple meet and turn single, man to right, woman to left.

Part II

A1 1-4 1st man turn 3rd woman two-hands **while** 1st woman turn 2nd man two-hands.

5-8 1st couple turn two-hands in center.

A2 1-4 1st man turn 2nd woman two-hands three-quarters **while** 1st woman turn 3rd man
two-hands three-quarters.

5-8 1st couple turn two-hands once-and-a-half {*skipping and increasing speed of turn*}.

B1 1-8 1st man figure-eight through 2nd couple above, passing right shoulder with 2nd woman,
while 1st woman does the same with 3rd couple below, passing 3rd man right shoulder.

B2 1-6 1st couple pass by left in center and hey for three at other end, skipping,
the 1st woman passing 2nd man left shoulder, 1st man passing 3rd woman left shoulder.

7-8 Finishing the hey, 1st couple lead down center to bottom, 3rd couple end in middle, 2nd at top.

Repeat dance twice more.

THE FANDANGO

This dance was originally a triple minor longways. No real connection to the Spanish fandango can be discerned in the music or figures. This Castilian and Andalusian courtship dance was in triple time featuring a rhythm with stress on the first and fifth beats over two bars.

Of popular origin, by the late eighteenth century it had become fashionable among the aristocracy and its popularity was partly responsible for the return of the guitar to the drawing room. An earlier version of the country dance called "The Fandango" can be found in *Twenty four Country Dances* (London: R. Bride, 1772), 33. It is unusual in that it includes performance suggestions of dynamic changes which might have been inspired by a Spanish model. In *Travels through Portugal and Spain* (London: 1775), 18, Richard Twiss described the Spanish fandango in detail. As he saw it, it was a couple dance with unique music related to the *La Folia* tune, with much stamping of the feet and "every part of the body...in motion, and thrown into all postures, frequently into very indecent ones."

The Fandango

Turn Right hands & caft off 1 Cu. turn Left hands and caft off below the 3d Cu. hands 6 round lead up the middle & caft off 1 Cu. turn corners & turn your Part: the fame at the other corners Man whole fi-_gure at bottom & Wo. at top the fame time then the Wo. hey at bottom & Man at top.

Thompson's Compleat Collection (London, 1780): 15
Courtesy of the Vaughan Williams Memorial Library

35

THE FEMALE SAYLOR

Duple minor longways
AA BB ad lib   MM ♩. = 116

Pat Shaw, 1965
Recuëil de Contredances (Feuillet), 1706

A1	1-4	1st couple lead through the couple above them and cast down to place. {*At top, lead through an imaginary couple.*}
	5-8	1st couple lead through the couple below them and cast up to place.
A2	1-4	1st couple half figure-eight through couple below.
	5-8	1st couple turn right-hands once around, ending improper and facing down.
B1	1-4	All back-to-back with neighbors.
	5-8	All turn two-hands with neighbors.
B2	1-4	Partners back-to-back.
	5-8	1st couple turn two-hands half-way and cast down one place **while** 2nd couple turn two-hands moving up center one place.

THE FEMALE SAYLOR

Pat Shaw reconstructed this dance from John Essex's 1710 translation of Feuillet's "La Matelotte" (1706) and commented that "the tune of this dance is, of course, the one to which William Morris wrote the well-known carol 'Masters in this Hall.' A note in the *Oxford Book of Carols* says that he obtained the tune from Edmund Sedding sometime before 1860 amd that Sedding obtained it from the organist of Chartres Cathedral. Here is evidence that though the tune is French, it was known in England as a country dance tune as early as 1710, nearly 150 years earlier. One wonders from the title whether the tune originally was sung to a French version of "The Handsome Cabin Boy." Feuillet himself composed this dance to it." (Shaw, *Six Simple Country Dances*, ca. 1965.)

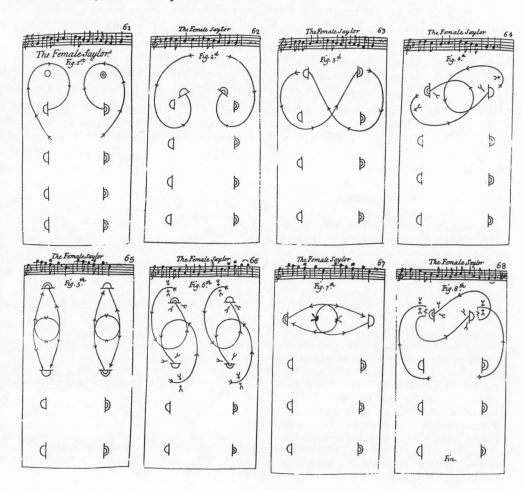

John Essex, For the Further Improvement of Dancing (London: I. Walsh & P. Randall, 1710),
Reprint, (Brooklyn: Dance Horizons, 1970): 61-68

THE FINE COMPANION

Round for four couples
3 x AA BB   MM ♩. = 108

Cecil Sharp, 1911
DM I: 1651-1690

Part I

A1   1-4   All take hands, forward a double and fall back a double.

        5-8   Partners set and turn single.

A2   1-8   Repeat A1.

B1   1-4   Men forward a double to center (1-2), women forward **while** men fall back (3-4).

        5-8   Men forward **while** women fall back, men circle four-hands once around and fall back.

B2   1-8   Repeat B1, women meeting first and making circle.

Part II

AA   Partners side, set and turn single. That again.

B1   1-4   Head couples forward a double to meet (1-2); side couples meet **while** heads fall back (3-4).

        5-8   Heads meet **while** sides fall back, and circle four-hands once around and fall back to places.

B2   1-8   Repeat B1, side couples meeting first and circling.

Part III

A1   1-8   Partners arm right, set and turn single.

A2   1-8   Partners arm left, set and turn single.

B1   1-8   Men forward to center, turn to left to face outward, and circle four-hands to right
            {*clockwise*} **while** women skip around outside, counter-clockwise to places.

B2   1-8   Repeat B1, women making ring and men skipping outside.

*Detail of a set of tiles depicting dancers, ca. 1700, found
unidentified on a greeting card.*
Courtesy of Dorothy Poucher

THE FINE COMPANION

No information has been found concerning the background of this lovely tune.
References: Dean-Smith, 31

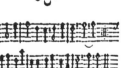

The fine Companion.   *Round for eight.*

Hands all and meet a D. back again, fet
and turn S. • That again ⦂   Men meet and go back, we. as much, men meet, hands and go round •
                              we. meet and go back, men as much; we. hands and go round ⦂

Sides all, fet and turn S.•. That again ⦂   The 2. Cu. againft each other meet and back , the other four as much.
                                 The firft four hands and go round • That again, the laft 4.beginning ⦂

Arms all, fet and turn S.•.That again ⦂   Men meet turn back to back, the we. go round about, the men to their
                                 their places •. we.meet, turn back to back, men go about the we. ⦂

DM I:4 (1670): 10
Courtesy of the Vaughan Williams Memorial Library

GATHERING PEASCODS

Round for as many as will
3 x AA BB CC   MM ♩ = 116

Cecil Sharp, 1911
DM I: 1651-1690

A   D   E   A   E⁷   A   E   A   B7

E   F#m   B7   E   A   D   A   D   A   D   A   E⁷   A

Part I

A1	1-6	All join hands and eight slips left (1-4), all turn single to right (5-6).
A2	1-6	Eight slips right (1-4), all turn single to right (5-6).
B1	1-6	Men join hands and eight slips to left back to place.
B2	1-6	Women the same.
C1	1-4	Men forward a double to center and clap on third step (1-2); women the same **while** men fall back (3-4).
	5-8	Men the same **while** women fall back (5-6); men fall back turning single to right (7-8).
C2	1-8	Repeat C1, women to center first.

Part II

AA		Partners side, then turn single right. Repeat.
B1	1-6	As in Part I, B1, but women's ring first.
B2	1-6	As in Part I, B2, men's ring.
C1	1-6	As in Part I, C1, women forward first.
C2	1-6	As in Part I, C2, men forward first.

Part III

A1	1-6	Partners arm right, then turn single right.
A2	1-6	Partners arm left, then turn single right.
BB		As in Part I, B1 and 2.
CC		As in Part I, C1 and 2.

Peas.

GATHERING PEASCODS

Set to an instrumental tune with no clear connections to a song or other source, this dance is one of the oldest in *The Dancing Master*. The first four bars of the tune are identical to "All in a Garden Green."

Peascods were, of course, peapods. In his *Observations on the Popular Antiquities of Great Britain* (London: 1849, 2: 99-100), John Brand discusses "Peascod wooing" and an old tradition of divining love affairs from pea pods.

References: Dean-Smith, 81; Chappell, 258-59

Gathering Peascods.   *Round for as many as will.*

Go all 2. doubles round, turn S. ∴ That back again ∴	Men hands, and go round in the inside, and come to your places ∴ We. as much ∴	Meet and clap hands, We. as much, while the men go back, men meet again and turn S. ∴ we. meet, men meet, while the we.go back, we. meet again and turn S. ∴
Sides, turn S. ∴ That a-gain ∴	As before, the we. going first ∴	As before, the we. meeting first ∴
Arms all, turn S. ∴ That again ∴	Men hand as at the first.	Men meet as at the first time ∴

Courtesy of the Vaughan Williams Memorial Library   *DM 1:4 (1670): 9*

THE GEUD MAN OF BALLANGIGH
to the tune of HUNT THE SQUIRREL

Duple minor longways
AA BB ad lib   MM ♩.= 120

Cecil Sharp, 1922
d: DM I: 1696-1728; m: DM I: 1709-1728

A — A — D — A — E⁷ — A — A — E⁷ — A

D — Bm — F♯m — A — C♯m — Bm — E⁷ — A

A1	1-4	1st couple lead down between 2nd couple and cast up to place.
	5-8	Two men lead out between women and cast back to place.
A2	1-4	2nd couple lead up between 1st couple and cast down to place.
	5-8	Two women lead out between men and cast back to place.
B1	1-4	1st man set forward to 2nd woman {*who does not set*}, and turn single to right, back to place.
	5-8	1st woman the same to 2nd man.
B2	1-4	Circle four-hands half-way and fall back in lines, improper and progressed.
	5-8	Partners set forward (5-6), and change places passing right shoulder (7-8).

THE GEUD MAN OF BALLANGIGH
and HUNT THE SQUIRREL

Sharp interpreted the dances of "Hunt the Squirrel" (1709) and "Geud Man" (1696) and presented them on facing pages in *CDB 6*, uncharacteristically suggesting that both were to be danced to the tune of "Hunt the Squirrel."

This recently popular tune was used for a remarkably modern sounding song written by John Gay for *Polly* (1729), his sequel to *The Beggar's Opera.*

The World is always jarring; this is pursuing t'other man's ruin, friends with friends are warring, in a false cowardly way.

Spurr'd on by emulations, tongues are engaging, calumny, raging; murthers reputations, envy keeps up the fray.

Thus, with burning hate, wounds and robs his friends.

In civil life, even man and wife squabble for selfish ends.

The title, "The Geud Man of Ballangigh," has been linked to James V of Scotland, who acceded to the throne as an infant in 1513 and died in 1542. However, there is no trace of the title, tune, or dance before 1696.

In her biography of James V, Caroline Bingham discusses the stories of his incognito wanderings, which are part of the popular history of Scotland and are very much more reminiscent of folktales than of biographical anecdotes. In the classic form of the old English tale, "The King and the Miller of Mansfield," several stories are told about James's meeting with a country-man, and identifying himself only as the "gudeman of Ballengiech [sic]"-- meaning a tenant in the hollow on the north side of Stirling Castle, his own residence. Credit for these stories may need to be given to Sir Walter Scott, nineteenth-century romantic and orchestrator of King George IV's visit to Scotland in 1822, for which many of today's "authentic" Scottish traditions were invented. In the same decade, William H. Murray developed the story into a full-length play, *Cramond Brig; or the Gudeman O'Ballangeich.* References: Moss 2:164-68; Caroline Bingham, *James V King of Scots* (London: Collins, 1971), 90-94

the 1. cu. lead down between the 2. cu. and caſt up into their places, then the 1. man take the 2. man with his right hand and lead through between the two we. and come into their own places. *This to the firſt Strain once.*

The 2. cu. lead up through the 1. cu. and caſt off into their own places, and the 1. wo. and 2. wo. lead through between the two men, and caſt off into their own places. *This to the firſt Strain twice.*

The 1. man ſet to the 2. wo. then fall back and turn S. the 1. wo. do the like to the 2. man, then all four hands half round, then ſet to your Partners and change to your own ſides.

FINIS

Second Part of the Dancing Master (1696): 24
Courtesy of the Central Library, Dundee, Scotland

Note, *Each Strain muſt be play'd twice over, to each Part of the Dance.*
Firſt Man hey on the We. Side, and the 1ſt Wo. on the Men's Side at the ſame Time: Then 1ſt Man hey on the Men's Side, and the Wo. on the We. Side, 'till they come into their own Places: Firſt Cu. croſs over and turn: Second Cu. do the ſame:

Firſt Man go the Figure of 8 on the Men's Side, his Partner follows him at the ſame Time, then ſhe ſlips into her own Place: Firſt Wo. caſt off on the Outſide of the 3d Wo. and half Figure with the 3d and 2d We. her Partner follows her at the ſame Time, then the Man ſlips into his own Place: Firſt Cu. being at the Top, the 1ſt Man change over with the 2d Wo. and the 1ſt Wo. with the 2d Man, then all four Hands half round, 1ſt Cu. being at Top, caſt off: Right and left quite round, and turn your Partner:

Compleat Country Dancing Master (1718): 16
Courtesy of the Library of Congress

39

GREENWICH PARK

Duple minor longways
AA BB ad lib   MM ♩ = 108

Cecil Sharp, 1922
DM I: 1698-1728

A F	C	F		C		F	C	F	F Gm	C

B C		F	C F	B♭	Gm		C F	Gm	C⁷	F

A1   1-8   1st couple lead up seven steps and close (1-4), change hands and lead back (5-6). Separate and go down outside to second place, 2nd couple leading up (7-8).

A2   1-8   2nd couple repeat A1.

B1   1-8   1st couple cross and move down outside below 2nd couple, into center and turn two-hands moving up center to top.

B2   1-4   All back-to-back.

  5-8   Clap hands: own, partner's right, own, partner's left;
then 1st couple cast down one place, 2nd couple moving up.

COME SWEET LASS, OR GREENWICH PARK

Jeremiah Clark's lovely song "Come Sweet Lass, or Greenwich Park" may have been among those inserted in William Mountfort's theatre piece *Greenwich Park*, published in 1691. The park itself had been laid out by Le Nôtre during the reign of Charles II.

Come sweet lass, this bonny weather, let's together,
  Come sweet lass, let's trip it on the grass:
Ev'ry where, poor Jockey seeks his dear,
  Unless you appear, he sees no beauty here.

On our Green, the loons are sporting, piping, courting;
  On our green, the blithest lads are seen;
There all day, our lasses dance and play
  And ev'ry one is gay, but I, when you're away.
                    D'Urfey, *Wit and Mirth*, 3: 217

References: Simpson, 127-29; Chappell, 600-601; Thomas F. Taylor, *Thematic Catalog of the Works of Jeremiah Clark* (Detroit: Information Coordinators, 1977), #336, 55

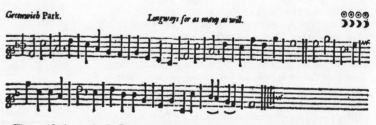

DM I: 14 (1709): 237
Courtesy of the Vaughan Williams Memorial Library

GREEN SLEEVES AND YELLOW LACE

Longways for three couples
6 x AA BB   MM ♩. = 88

Douglas and Helen Kennedy, 1929
DM I: 1721-1728

Part I

A1	1-4	1st couple set forward and cast down one place, 2nd couple moving up.
	5-8	2nd couple repeat A1, 1-4.
A2	1-8	Repeat A1.
B1	1-8	1st man, going down center, figure-eight through 3rd couple, passing 3rd woman left shoulder **while** 1st woman, following partner, figure-eight through 2nd couple, passing 2nd man right shoulder.
B2	1-8	1st couple, passing right shoulder, figure-eight at the other end, 1st man passing 2nd woman right shoulder, 1st woman passing 3rd man right shoulder.

Part II

A1	1-6	1st couple cross through center by right shoulders and circle three-hands once-and-a-half around at ends, 1st man with 3rd couple, 1st woman with 2nd couple who are now in top place.
	7-8	1st couple pass right shoulders, face other couples and join hands.
A2	1-6	Circle three-hands at ends once-and-a-half.
	7-8	1st couple pass right shoulders and end in middle place, proper.
B1	1-8	1st man hey for three with 3rd couple, passing 3rd woman left shoulder **while** 1st woman hey with 2nd couple, passing 2nd man left shoulder.
B2	1-8	1st couple pass right shoulder, hey at other ends (1-6); 1st couple cast down to bottom, 3rd couple moving up to 2nd place (7-8).

Repeat dance twice more.

GREEN SLEEVES AND YELLOW LACE

Several versions of a dance to "Green Sleeves" were published in this period. "Green Sleeves and Pudding Pies" appears in DM I: 1686-1716. Walsh borrowed it for his 1718 publication, so John Young replaced the dance figures in his 1721 edition and changed the title. It is this latter dance, with some modifications, that Sharp chose to reconstruct. Feuillet published a much simpler dance in his *Recuëil* of 1706, calling it "Les Manches Vertes," and Pat Shaw reconstructed this dance in the 1960's.

The tune "Green Sleeves" had many names in the eighteenth century, most prominent among them being "The Blacksmith" or "Which nobody can deny," the burden of that song. It was used chiefly for political rather than sentimental texts, witness Macheath's violent outburst in *The Beggar's Opera* (London: 1728):

Since laws were made for ev'ry degree,
To curb vice in others, as well as me,
I wonder we han't better company,
Upon Tyburn Tree!
But gold from law can take out the sting;
And if rich men like us were to swing,
'Twould thin the land, such numbers to string
Upon Tyburn Tree!

The dance takes its title from the first line of the third verse of a lyric collected by David Herd in the 1760's.

LVII. Green Sleeves.

Green sleeves and pudden-pyes, come tell me where my true love lyes,
  And I'll be wi' her ere she rise: Fidle a' the gither!
Hey ho! and about she goes, She's milk in her breasts, she's none in her toes,
  She's a hole in her a--. you may put in your nose, Sing: hey, boys, up go we!
Green sleeves and yellow lace, Maids, maids, come, marry apace!
  The batchleors are in a pitiful case, to fidle a' the gither.

References: Moss 4: 213-18; Ward, 44-46; Simpson, 268-78; Chappell, 227-33; Hans Hecht, ed. *Songs from David Herd's Manuscripts* (Edinburgh: 1904), 177

Green Sleeves and Yellow Lace.   *Longways for as many as will.*

Note : *Each Strain is to be play'd twice, and the Tune twice through.*

The 1. cu. fett and caft off then fett and caft off 2. cu. ‿ Then the fame to their places again ‿: The 1. Man whole figure with the 3. cu. and the Wo. with the 2. cu. ‿ Then the 1. Man whole Figure with the 2. cu. and the Wo. with the 3. cu. ‿:

Then the 1. Man hands half round with the 3. cu. and the 1. Wo. hands half round with the 2. cu. ‿ Then the 1. Wo. hands round with the 3. cu. and the Man hands round with the 2 cu. ‿ The firft Man hay with the 3. cu. and the 4. Wo. hays with the 2. cu. ‿ Then the 1. Wo. hays with the 3. cu. and the Man hays with the 2. cu.

DM 1:17 (1721): 113

41

GRIMSTOCK

Longways for three couples
3 x AA B   MM ♩= 96

Cecil Sharp, 1911
DM I: 1651-1690

Part I

A1   1-8   Partners lead up a double and fall back a double, set and turn single.
A2   1-8   Repeat A1.
B   1-8   All mirror hey: 1st couple go between 2nd couple to begin.

Part II

A1   1-8   Partners side, set and turn single.
A2   1-8   Repeat A1.
B   1-8   As in B of Part I, except the partners take both hands and slip up and down, 1st couple going under 2nd couple's arch, over 3rd couple's, etc.

Part III

A1   1-8   Partners arm right, set and turn single.
A2   1-8   Partners arm left, set and turn single.
B   1   1st couple change places, passing left shoulders. {*All of B skipping.*}
      2-4   1st couple hey for three half-way on sides.
      5   1st couple change places, passing right shoulder.
      6-8   1st couple complete the hey for three half-way on sides to original places.

Catchpenny Prints, no. 154, 101
Courtesy Dover Publications

GRIMSTOCK

    No one seems to know what this title refers to. A straight translation would be something grim or foreboding--but this belies the lilting beauty of the melody. The A strain appears titled "CLIV. Courante" in Michael Praetorius's *Terpsichore* (Wolfenbuttel: 1612).
References: Dean-Smith, 15

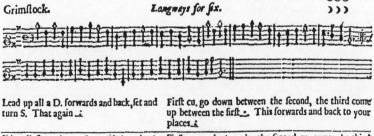

DM 1:8 (1690): 40
Courtesy of the Vaughan Williams Memorial Library

HAMBLETON'S ROUND O

Triple minor longways
A B ad lib   MM ♩ = 116

Bernard J. Bentley, 1962
DM II: 1710-1714

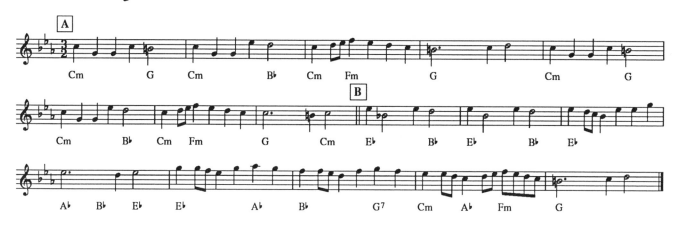

A   1-2   1st couple cast down to middle place, 2nd couple moving up.

        3-6   1st man hey for three with 3rd couple passing 3rd woman left shoulder **while** 1st woman hey with 2nd couple passing 2nd man left shoulder.

        7-8   1st couple turn two-hands in middle place.

B   1   1st woman and 2nd man change places.   {*They are in first corner positions.*}

       2   1st man and 2nd woman change places.

       3-4   Circle four-hands half-way around and turn single to right.

       5-8   Partners face: 1st and 2nd couples circular hey, four changes.

HAMBLETON'S ROUND O

Melodies like "Hamilton's Round O" and "Dargason," which seem to have no end, are termed "circular tunes." This dance may originally have had a more leisurely pace, set to this tune in 3/2 time. The same figures can be found set to a tune in 2/4 in DM III:2 as "Smiths Round O" and in a large collection by John Johnson as "Hot Grey Pease or Pipeing Phips."

The Hambleton Hills, with their fine cliffs, lie south of Durham in Yorkshire, and may be the reference intended. However, Hambleton was considered a transliteration of the name "Hamilton," so a more personal connotation is possible.

The firſt couple caſt off, the man going the Hey with the third couple, and the woman with the ſecond couple, then turn Hands in the ſecond couples place ; then the firſt woman changes place with the ſecond man, and the firſt man do the ſame with the ſecond woman, then Hands half round and turn ſingle, then Right and Left into the ſecond couples places.

Miſs Violin.

DM II:1 (1710): 105
By permission of the Director of Manchester Public Libraries

Catchpenny Prints, no. 153, 100
Courtesy Dover Publications

THE HEALTH; OR, THE MERRY WASSAIL

Longways for four couples

12 x A   MM ♩ = 112

Cecil Sharp, 1916
DM I: 1651-1690

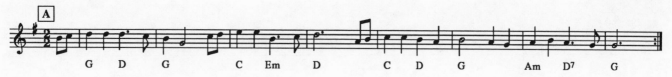

G   D   G   C   Em   D   C   D   G   Am   D⁷   G

Part I

A1	1-4	Partners lead up a double and fall back a double.
	5-8	Partners slow set and honor right, then left.
A2	1-8	Repeat A1.
A3	1-4	1st and 4th couples face, forward a double to meet, then back-to-back, **while** 2nd couple cast up to top, 3rd couple cast down to bottom of set.
	5-8	1st couple cast up to top and lead down to middle place **while** 4th couple cast down to bottom and lead up to middle place.
A4	1-8	Repeat A3, new top and bottom couples meeting, back-to-back, &c.

Part II

A1	1-4	Facing out, circle eight-hands around half-way, clockwise {*to the right*}.
	5-8	Face partner, slow set and honor right, then left.
A2	1-4	Facing out, circle eight-hands half-way counter-clockwise, back to place.
	5-8	Face partner, slow set and honor right, then left.
A3	1-4	1st and 4th couples face, forward a double to meet, then back-to-back, **while** 2nd couple cast to top, 3rd couple cast to bottom.
	5-8	1st and 4th couples circle four-hands facing out, clockwise.
A4	1-8	Repeat A3, new top and bottom couples meeting, back-to-back, etc.

Part III

A1	1-2	Partners turn two-hands half-way.
	3-4	Ends turn neighbors two-hands half-way.
	5-8	Partners slow set and honor right, then left.
A2	1-8	Repeat A1 to places.
A3	1-2	1st man and 4th woman meet and join right hands **while** 2nd man cast up to first place, 3rd woman cast down to fourth place.
	3-4	1st woman and 4th man meet and join right hands **while** 2nd woman cast up to first place, 3rd man cast down to fourth place.
	5-8	Couples in center right-hands across once around and fall back in middle places in set.
A4	1-8	Movement repeated with new head and bottom couple. {*2nd couple at top, 3rd couple at bottom*}

"Here's to thee, kind Harry"
Woodcut from Rollins, Pepys Ballads, 2: 90

THE HEALTH

In 1670, the title was expanded to "The Healths, or: The Merry Wasel." Chappell cites a song which certainly fits the title. Probably originally from a play, it has a number of specific personal references. The reference to Wickham may be a seafaring one, as that village is very near Portsmouth, a major port, particularly for military operations. The first verse follows.

> Come, faith, since I'm parting,
>   And that God knows when
> The walls of sweet Wickham I shall see again,
> Let's e'en have a frolic, and drink like tall men,
> Till heads with healths go round,
>   Till heads with healths go round.

References: Dean-Smith, 47; Chappell, 288-89

The Healths, *or* The merry Wasel.   *Longways for eight.*

Lead up a D. and back, set ⁚. That again ⁚.

Firſt Cu. and laſt meet, turn back to back, caſt off, and going on the outſide, the other four to come to your places on the inſide, the other as much ⁚.

Hands all backwards, and go half round to the right, set ⁚. That back again ⁚.

Firſt Cu. and laſt meet, turn back to back, hands backward round to your places ⁚. The other 4. as much ⁚.

Change places with your own by both hands, then 1. and 2. the 3. and 4. man change, ſo the we. doing the like, set ⁚. Change back again to your places ⁚.

Firſt and laſt Cu. meet, clap hands, hands acroſs round to your places ⁚. The other four as much ⁚. (or this laſt paſſage thus) Firſt man and laſt wo. meet and give right hands, firſt wo. and laſt man the like, then holding hands acroſs, go round to your places ⁚. The other four as much ⁚.

DM I:7 (1686): 58
Courtesy of the Vaughan Williams Memorial Library

44

HEARTSEASE

Two couples facing
3 x A BB   MM ♩. = 96

Cecil Sharp, 1916
DM I: 1651-1690

Part I

A   1-8   All forward a double and fall back a double. That again.

B1   1-4   Partners face, fall back a double and come forward a double.

        5-8   Opposites face, turn right-hand once around.

B2   1-4   Opposites face, fall back a double and forward a double.

        5-8   Partners face, turn left-hand once around.

Part II

A   1-4   Partners side.

        5-8   Opposites side.

BB   As in Part 1, B1 and 2.

Part III

A   1-4   Partners arm right.

        5-8   Opposites arm left.

BB   As in Part I, B1 and 2.

HEARTSEASE

There are two distinct tunes named "Heartsease" and considerable differences of opinion as to whether any of the known lyrics fit either of them. The earliest lyric is "a songe to the tune of hartes ease" from Thomas Richardes' play on an Italian model, called *Misogonus* (c.1560). Although it scans well, the text is arranged in short verses which would only use half the dance tune, implying that an earlier tune by this name may only have had one strain. The first and last two verses are:

>Singe care away with sport & playe,
> Pasttime is all our pleasure;
>Yf well we fare, for nought we care,
> In mearth consist our treasure.

>Let snugis lurke, & druges worke,
> We doe defie their slaverye:
>He is but a foole, yt gois to schole,
> All we delight in braverye...

>In card & dice, our comforte lies,
> In sportinge and in dauncinge,
>Our mindes to please and live at ease,
> And sometime to use prauncinge.

>With Bes and Nel we love to dwell
> In kisinge and in hakinge.
>But whope hoe hollie, with trolley lollye!
> To them weil now be walking.

Richard Dering's catch "Cries of London" (1599) is set to the A strain of the DM tune, with the following lyrics:

>A cooper I am, and have been long, and hooping is my trade.
>And married man am I to as pretty a wench, as ever God hath made.

(bars 107-115)

Hearts-ease in sixteenth century herbal culture was the little wild pansy, known today as Johnny-jump-up. It was also called "Love-in-idleness," a definition which certainly agrees with the burden of the song in *Misogonus*.

References: R. Warwick Bond, *Early Plays from the Italian* (New York: Benjamin Blom, 1967), 197-98; Ward, 46-47; Simpson, 301-302; Dean-Smith, 46; Chappell, 209-11.

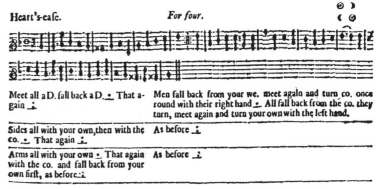

DM I:8 (1690): 19
Courtesy of the Vaughan Williams Memorial Library

45

HEY, BOYS, UP GO WE

Two couples facing

3 x A BB   MM ♩. = 116

Cecil Sharp, 1911
d & m: DM I: 1679-1728 as "Cuckolds all a Row"

Part I
A   1-8   All forward a double and fall back a double. That again.

B1   1-4   Men gipsy with opposite women, facing out, clockwise.

        5-8   Men gipsy with same women, facing in, counter-clockwise.

B2   1-8   Repeat B1 with partner.

Part II
A   1-4   Partners side.

        5-8   Opposites side.

B1   1-4   Men change places (1-2), then women change places (3-4).

        5-8   Circle four-hands once around.

B2   1-8   Repeat B1, women changing first.

Part III
A   1-4   Partners arm right.

        5-8   Opposites arm left.

B1   1-4   Men poussette opposite women half-way clockwise {*1st man push*}.

        5-8   Men cast outward to right and move back to same place, partners following.

B2   1-8   Repeat B1, continuing poussette clockwise to original place {*1st man pull*}, then cast outward to left.

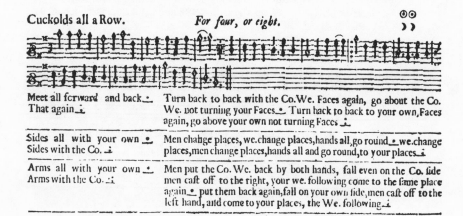

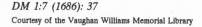

DM 1:7 (1686): 37

Courtesy of the Vaughan Williams Memorial Library

Tom Tweedle-dum Dance

Catchpenny Prints, no. 144, 92

Courtesy Dover Publications

"CUCKOLDS ALL AWRY," THE OLD DANCE OF ENGLAND!

"CUCKOLDS ALL A ROW" OR "HEY BOYS UP GO WE?"

The dance which Sharp reconstructed under the title "Hey, Boys, up go we" is "Cuckolds all a Row." Margaret Dean-Smith identified William Chappell as the source for the exchange of titles. In his brilliant but dated work on the history of English popular and national music, Chappell noted that a Cavalier song of "Hey, boys, up go we" was sung to the "Cuckolds" tune, initiating a confusion which Sharp perpetuated, when, in the interest of propriety, he gave that name to this dance and tune. "Hey, boys" is a very different dance, and its tune is distinct.

Judging from the "Hey, boys" reference in the lyric to "Green sleeves and Pudding Pies" (see page 41), Sharp might have been better advised to keep the "Cuckolds" title, as "Hey, boys" has even more suggestive content. A cuckold is the unsuspecting husband of an unfaithful wife--often signified in the visual arts by a pair of horns.

Chappell himself recognized that the two tunes were distinct and printed the following lyric to the tune of "Cuckolds all a Row."

The Cruel Shrew; or The Patient Man's Woe

Come bachelors and married men, and listen to my song.
And I will shew you plainly then, the injury and wrong
That constantly I do sustain through my unhappy life,
The which does put me to great pain, by my unquiet wife.

Roxburghe Collection, 1: 28

HEY, BOYS, UP GO WE

Claude Simpson traces the background of songs set to the "Hey, Boys" tune which was much used for political satire. "About 1641, when an intense pamphlet warfare broke out between the high-church party and the Puritans...Francis Quarles wrote a political song whose chief distinction was the concluding line of each stanza, 'and Hey then up go wee'...It pictures the systematic overthrow of institutions, an upheaval which the Puritans could be presumed to favor..."

In 1682 Thomas D'Urfey reworded Quarles's song to fit the new anti-Royalists needs. It appears with its tune in *A Collection of One Hundred and Eighty Loyal Songs* (London: Richard Butt, 1694), 6-8:

The Whigs Exaltation. To an old Tune of Forty One

Now, now the Tories all shall stoop, Religion, and the Laws,
  And Whigs on Commonwealth get up, to tap the Good Old Cause:
Tantivy-boys shall all go down, And haughty Monarchy,
  The leathern Cap shall brave the Throne, Then hey boys up go we!

When once that Antichristian Crew are crush'd and over thrown,
  We'll teach the Nobles how to bow, And keep their Gentry down.
Good manners has a bad repute, And tends to Price, we see;
  We'll therefore cry all Breeding down, And hey boys up go we!

Douglas Kennedy reconstructed the original "Hey Boys" dance to its own tune in 1929, calling it "The Way to Norwich" to distinguish it.

PEPYS AT COURT

Samuel Pepys [pronounced "Peeps"] went to Whitehall, the current residence of Charles II and his queen, on December 31, 1662, and the next morning wrote a detailed description in his diary of the party he witnessed but in which he did not participate. Pepys wrote in short hand, but it was clear enough that most of his editors arrive at virtually the same text. It is a superb description of ballroom etiquette and practice, with the rules of precedency observed with punctilious observation. It also tells something about the country dance as being more relaxed, but still a dance in which the participants were on display.

Pepys went "...into the room where the ball was to be, crammed with fine ladies, the greatest of the Court. By and by, comes the King [Charles II] and Queen, the Duke [of York, his brother and later James II] and Duchess, and all the great ones; and after seating themselves, the King takes out the Duchess of York; and the Duke, the Duchess of Buckingham; the Duke of Monmouth, my Lady Castlemaine; and so

other lords other ladies: and they danced the Brantle.

After that the King led a lady a single Coranto; and then the rest of the lords, one after another, other ladies: very noble it was, and great pleasure to see. Then to country dances; the King leading the first, which he called for, which was, says he "Cuckolds all awry," the old dance of England.

Of the ladies that danced, the Duke of Monmouth's mistress, and my Lady Castlemaine, and a daughter of Sir Harry de Vicke's, were the best. The manner was, when the King dances, all the ladies in the room, and the Queen herself, stand up: and indeed he dances rarely, and much better than the Duke of York..."

References: Moss 2: 132-37; Simpson, 145-47; 304-308 and passim; Dean-Smith, 56; Chappell, 340-42, 425-29; Barlow, 15-16 (illustrations)

Miſs Polly Mac Prance

Hey-boys up go we.   *Longways for as many as will.*   ⊕⊕⊕⊕
                                                           ))))

Honour to the Preſence, then to your women. Lead up forward and back, that again.

The firſt man take his own wo. and the ſecond by their hands, and go round till they come into their own places, the ſecond man ſtanding ſtill, then the firſt man and woman with the ſecond man do the ſame, the ſecond wo. ſtanding ſtill, then fall back and turn S. then the two men back to back, and the two we. back to back at the ſame time, then the firſt Cu. clap hands and caſt off, and the two men clap hands on their ſide, and the two we. clap hands on the other ſide, and ſo on to the next.

DM I:7 (1686): 179
Courtesy of the Vaughan Williams Memorial Library

HIT AND MISS
to the tune of DAPHNE

Two couples facing
3 x AA BB C   MM ♩. = 100

Cecil Sharp, 1916
d: DM I: 1651-1716; m: DM I: 1651-1690

Em   Bm   Em   G   D   C   Em   Em   D   C   Bm⁷

Em   Am   D   G   G   D   Em   Bm   C   Em   G   Am   D   Em

Part I

AA	1-8	All forward a double and fall back a double. That again.
B1	1-4	All forward again, men lead opposite women away from set.
B2	1-2	Changing hands, men lead same women back.
	3-4	Opposites face, take right hands with partner and fall back a double.
C	1-6	Partners face and circular hey, four changes, beginning with partner, skipping.

Part II

| AA | Partners side twice. |
| BB & C | As in Part I. |

Part III

| AA | Partners arm right, then left. |
| BB & C | As in Part I. |

HIT AND MISS and DAPHNE

Although the tune Sharp chose to substitute for this dance was well known, no explanation has been found for the name of the dance. In the fourth edition of *The Dancing Master*(1670), although the dance figures remain the same, the title was changed to "Hit or Miss" and the formation given as "longways for eight." (See illustration) In the seventeenth and eighteenth edition, the figures were replaced with a new triple minor dance, but still marked "longways for eight." "Hit or Miss" is one of the very few that John Walsh did not include when he appropriated the contents of the sixteenth edition of the DM (1716) for his *Compleat Country Dancing-Master* of 1718.

An early seventeenth-century song retells Ovid's myth of the pursuit of Daphne, who was turned into a laurel tree to prevent violation by Apollo. G. L. Bernini's spectacular sculpture of the moment of Daphne's transformation had been created in Rome in 1622-24, the subject being popular in baroque art. Apollo was also known as Phoebus and the lyric makers saw no problem in using both names within one song. Chappell printed the entire song, of which the first verse is cited here.

When Daphne from fair Phoebus did fly,
The west wind most sweetly did blow in her face.
Her silken scarf scarce shadow'd her eyes,
The God cried, O pity! and held her in chace.
Stay, Nymph, stay, Nymph, cries Apollo, tarry, and
turn thee, Sweet Nymph, stay,
Lion nor Tiger doth thee follow, turn thy fair eyes,
and look this way.
O turn, O pretty sweet, and let our red lips meet:
O pity me, Daphne! pity me. O pity me, &c.

References: Ward, 36; Simpson, 163-64; Dean-Smith, 18, 28; Chappell, 338-39

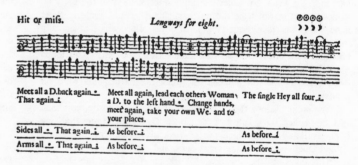

DM I:7 (1686): 47, 38

Courtesy of the Vaughan Williams Memorial Library

HOLBORN MARCH

Duple minor longways
AA B C ad lib   MM ♩ = 116

Pat Shaw, 1965
Wright's Compleat Collection, v. 1 (Johnson), 1740

A1   1-4   1st couple set, then cast down one place, 2nd couple moving up.
      5-8   All turn partners two-hands once around.
A2   1-8   Repeat A1, 2nd couple casting and 1st couple moving up.
B   1-8   1st and 2nd couples right hands-across and left back.
C   1-4   1st couple cross and move down outside to second place, 2nd couple moving up.
      5-8   1st couple half figure-eight up through 2nd couple.

HOLBORN MARCH

High Holborn is a main thoroughfare of London, the old road leading from Newgate Prison and the Tower, through the borough of Holborn to the gallows at Tyburn. The precise location of the gallows is disputed but evidence seems to point to the present site of 49 Connaugh Square, just north of Marble Arch at the end of Oxford Street. The Michelin *Green Guide* describes the scene in grisly detail.

"The gallows, first a tree, then a gibbet, was finally replaced by an iron triangle for multiple executions. From the Tower or Newgate, the condemned were drawn through the streets on hurdles to be hanged (and sometimes drawn and quartered too) before the great crowds who gathered to hear the last words, see the spectacle and enjoy the side shows. Popular victims were toasted in gin or beer as they passed."

The music of "Holborn March" consists of the same musical phrase repeated three times and might well have been played by a military band of musick or even the lone fifer depicted here, as they marched through the streets.

It is curious that the same dance and the same music appeared in 1731 entitled "Princess Amelia," in reference to a daughter of George II.

Reference: *Michelin "Green Guide" for London* (London: Michelin Tyre, 1985), 99; The dance was first printed in *English Dance and Song* 27/5 (October 1965): 153

Wright's Compleat Collection, vol. 1 (1740): 31
Courtesy of The Essex Institute, Salem, Massachusetts

"English Courage Undaunted: O Stout! You Valient Englishmen."
Woodcut from Rollins, The Pepys Ballads, 3: 38

THE HOLE IN THE WALL

Duple minor longways
AA B ad lib   MM ♩ = 88

Douglas and Helen Kennedy, 1929
DM I: 1696-1728

B♭	F	Gm	Dm	E♭	B♭	F⁷	B♭	Gm	Cm	D	D⁷

Gm Cm Gm D⁷ Gm E♭ F Gm F B♭ F Cm F⁷ B♭

A1   1-4   1st couple cast down, move around 2nd couple and lead up center to place.
A2   1-4   2nd couple cast up, move around 1st couple and lead down center to place.
B   1-2   1st corners change places, falling back on last three steps.
      3-4   2nd corners the same.
      5-6   Circle four-hands half-way around.
      7-8   1st couple cast down one place, 2nd couple moving up.

THE HOLE IN THE WALL

This lovely music was written by Henry Purcell and published in 1695 as "Air VIII Hornpipe" in the incidental music for the 1693 revival of Mrs. Aphra Behn's 1677 tragedy, *Abdelazer, or the Moor's Revenge*. It is hard to understand where the music would have fit into this violent and melodramatic play which is based on an earlier text entitled *Lust's Dominion; or, the Lascivious Queen* and includes many elements of Shakespeare's *Othello*.

The title, "The Hole in the Wall" is not relevant to the play and may reflect a different use of the melody. It might have been an interpolation in Purcell's *Fairy Queen*, which was based on Shakespeare's *A Midsummer Night's Dream* and features the Pyramis and Thisbe scene in which a "hole in the wall" is prominent. We have not been able to find a London reference for this title, although there is an old pub in Bath known as "The Hole in the Wall," the reference there said to be to the coal chute.

As a hornpipe, the music is related to French court dance tradition of the late seventeenth century, and probably would have featured the *pas de bourrée* as its principle step. Popular with folk dancers in this century, "The Hole in the Wall" has been subjected to foppish and unnecessary ornamentation with extravagant bows and pauses. No matter what tradition is chosen for performance of this dance, great skill is needed to sustain the long phrases without violating the spirit of elegant simplicity which both Kennedy's dance and the original are embued.

The 1. cu. cast off below the 2. cu. and lead up in the middle. The 2. cu. cast up and lead down the middle.
The 1. Man cross over with the 2. Wo. and the 1. Wo. with the 2. Man, so all four hands half round, and so cast off into the 2. cu. place, the rest do the like.

DM 1:17 (1721): 222
Courtesy of the Bath Reference Library

HUNSDON HOUSE   {*See opposite page*}

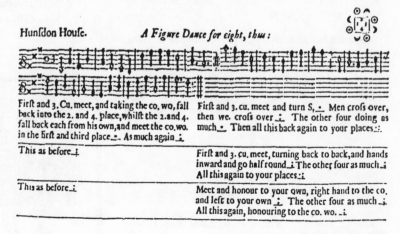

Hunsdon House.   *A Figure Dance for eight, thus:*

First and 3. Cu. meet, and taking the co. wo, fall back into the 2. and 4. place, whilst the 2. and 4. fall back each from his own, and meet the co. wo. in the first and third place. As much again.

First and 3. cu. meet and turn S. Men cross over, then we. cross over. The other four doing as much. Then all this back again to your places.

This as before.

First and 3. cu. meet, turning back to back, and hands inward and go half round. The other four as much. All this again to your places.

This as before.

Meet and honour to your own, right hand to the co. and left to your own. The other four as much. All this again, honouring to the co. wo.

DM 1:8 (1690): 50
Courtesy of the Vaughan Williams Memorial Library

50

HUNSDON HOUSE

Square for four couples
3 x AA BB   MM ♩. = 88

Cecil Sharp, 1912
DM I: 1665-1728

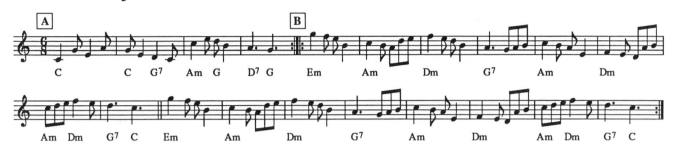

C   C G⁷ Am G D⁷ G   Em   Am   Dm   G⁷   Am   Dm

Am Dm G⁷ C   Em   Am   Dm   G⁷   Am   Dm   Am Dm G⁷ C

Part I

A1	1-2	Head couples forward a double to meet **while** side couples face partner and fall back a double.
	3-4	Taking right hands with opposites, head couples fall back to nearest side place **while** side couples meet opposites in head places.
A2	1-4	New heads meet and fall back to original side places **while** new sides face and fall back, then meet original partners in head places. {*The movement of A1 and 2 is called "grand square."*}
B1	1-4	Head couples forward a double to meet and turn single to the right, back to places.
	5-6	Head men change places.
	7-8	Head women change places.
	9-16	Side couples repeat B1 1-8.
B2	1-16	Repeat B1 to places.

Part II

AA		As in Part I above.
B1	1-4	Head couples meet, turn around {*to right*} to stand back to back.
	5-8	Circle four-hands clockwise half-way facing out, then lead out into opposite place.
	9-16	Side couples repeat B1 1-8.
B2	1-16	Repeat B1 ending in original place.

Part III

AA		As in Part I above.
B1	1-2	Head couples forward a double to meet, then face partners.
	3-4	Head couples slow set and honor partners right.
	5-8	Head couples face opposite: right-and-left, two changes, beginning with opposite.
	9-16	Side couples repeat B1 1-8.
B2	1-16	Repeat B1, except that men slow set and honor **opposite** women, partners face for right-and-left.

{*This is a slow, dignified dance.*}

HUNSDON HOUSE

This dance is often pointed out as the earliest version of the "grand square."

The Hunsdon manor in the county of Hertford was the residence of Henry Carey, fourth Lord Hunsdon, a prominent Royalist supporter in the Civil War who died three years after this dance first appeared in *The English Dancing Master*. According to Martha Curti, Hunsdon provided a refuge from the plague for Henry VIII, whose daughters Mary and Elizabeth lived there as children. Queen Elizabeth gave the manor to Henry Carey, the brother of her mother, Anne Bolyn, and created him Baron Hunsdon in 1559.

References: Curti, 400-401; *Jones' Views of the Seats, Mansions, Castles, &c. of Noblemen & Gentlemen in England* (London: Jones & Co., 1829): 139

HUNSDON HOUSE, Hertfordshire
Courtesy of the Print Collection, The Lewis Walpole Library, Yale University

HYDE PARK

Square for four couples
3 x A BB   MM ♩. = 108

Cecil Sharp, 1912
DM I: 1651-1665

Part I
A   1-4   Head couples forward a double to meet and fall back a double.

         5-8   Side couples the same.

B1   1-2   Head men face partners, balance back and forward, then take both hands.

         3-4   Head couples slip sideways to middle.

         5-8   Men face opposites, take both hands, and slip out between side couples,
                     and cast back to place.

B2   1-8   Repeat B1, side couples slipping in, &c.

Part II
A   1-8   As in Part I above.

B1   1-2   Side men face partners, take right hands, change places, then make an arch, right hands.

         3-8   Head men face partners, pass right shoulder, go outside side couples and under arches to
                     head places, improper.

B2   1-2   Movement repeated, heads changing and making arches.

         3-8   Side couples face partners, pass right shoulder, go outside, under arches, &c.

Part III
A   1-8   As in Part I above.

B1   1-8   Men pass in front of partners, behind next women, weaving in and out
                     around the set to places, skipping.

B2   1-8   Women repeat B1, passing in front of partners to start.

HYDE PARK

This short-lived dance, its title modernized by Sharp, may be associated with Shirley's popular play, *Hide Park* (1637), which contained a wedding scene with dancing. In 1668, Pepys attended a revival which included live horses brought on stage, probably for the race scene in the fourth act. He was not much impressed and considered it "a very moderate play." Hyde Park was a fashionable spot for drives and promenades. An old ballad describes the park, beginning "Of all parts of England Hide Park hath the name, for coaches and horses, and persons of fame." (Roxburghe 2: 379)

The first and last verses of a song from 1672 give a good idea of the way Londoners used and thought of this large park, as well as a biting satire of court intrigues.

A Song called Hide-Park.

The tune: Honour invites you to delight,
Come to the Court, and be all made Knights

1. Come all you noble[s], you that are neat ones,
    Hide-Park is now both fresh and green:
Come all you Gallants that are great ones,
    And are desirous to be seen:
Would you a Wife or Mistress rare?
    Here are the best of *England* fair:

Here you may chuse, also refuse, as you your judgements please to use....

6. Here come the Girls of the rich City, Aldermens daughters fair and proud,
    Their Jealous Mothers come t'invite ye, for fear they should be lost i'th'croud:
Who for their breeding are taught to dance, their birth and fortune to advance:
    And they will be as frolick and free, as you your self expect to see.

Westminster Drollery (1672): 73-75

References: Simpson, 327-28; Dean-Smith, 77; Chappell, 325-28

Courtesy of the Bodleian Library (pressmark: Douce P 581)

DM I:3 (1665): 43

52

INDIAN QUEEN

Duple minor longways
AA BB ad lib   MM ♩ = 108

Cecil Sharp, 1922
DM I: 1701-1728

A1   1-4   1st corners set forward to each other, and turn single back to place.
     5-8   The same turn two-hands once around.
A2   1-8   2nd corners repeat A1.
B1   1-8   All right-hands across and left-hands back.
B2   1-4   Partners back-to-back.
     5-8   Circular hey, three changes,
              beginning with partner.

INDIAN QUEEN

John Dryden's tragedy "The Indian Queen" was converted into an opera by Henry Purcell shortly before he died in 1695. The score includes at least one tune which was later used as a country dance, the second air, which became the "Duke of Gloucester's March" in Thomas Bray's collection of 1699.

A tune called "The New Bore [Bourrée]" appears at the very end of the ninth edition of *The Dancing Master* (1695), and in 1701 the same tune appeared with slightly changed cadences and a new dance titled "The Indian Queen." It continued through the eighteenth edition, while "The New Bore" and its dance was dropped after the twelfth edition (1703). Although it is not in Henry Purcell's score, it is possible that this tune was interpolated into the opera in later productions. It may simply have been inspired by the successful opera. We did not find this music in the published additions to the score by Daniel Purcell which are at the Folger Shakespeare Library.

Anne Bracegirdle (c. 1674-1748) was a leading London actress during the first half of the eighteenth century, playing with Betterton's company at Lincoln's Inn Fields. The mezzotint portrait of her in the role of the Mexican Queen Zempoalla is a typical example of European concepts of the appearance of natives of North and Central America and the Caribbean, and exists in several versions, all of which probably originated with a painting.

References: Simpson, 507-508

Anne Bracegirdle as THE INDIAN QUEEN
Harvard Theatre Collection

The 1. man meets and set with the 2. wo. and turn Single, and turn her ‥ The 2. cu. does the same ‥ Then all four right hands a cross half round, and left hand back again ‥ Then back to back again with your Parner, and right and left quite round.

DM I:11 (1701): 267
Dundee District Libraries, Wighton Collection

THE INSTALLATION

Longways for three couples

3 x AA BB CC DD   MM ♩. = 108

Tom Cook, 1979
Twenty Four Country Dances (Thompson), 1772

A	(D7) G	G	C	G	D	G	D	G		D	A7	D	
B	D	G Em Am D7	G Am D7	G	C D	G	C	G D7	G				
C	D7 Gm D7 Gm	Cm	D Gm	Cm F7	Bb	Eb F7	Bb						
D	Cm D7 Gm	Cm	D (Gm)	D	Gm	Cm D7	Gm						

A1   1-8   Hey on the opposite side, 1st couple crossing through the center place.

A2   1-8   Hey on own side, 1st couple crossing again.

B1   1-4   1st couple half figure-eight down through 2nd couple,

     5-8   All turn partners two-hands once around.

B2   1-8   Repeat B1, 3rd couple half figure-eight up through 2nd couple.

C1   1-4   All take hands in a circle and stepping onto right foot, step-swing right, left, right, left,
          then men face women on their right.

     5-8   Giving right hands, grand right-and-left three changes, and then face in to ring again.

C2   1-8   Repeat C1.

D1   1-8   1st couple cross and move down outside one place, 2nd couple moving up,
          then half figure-eight up through 2nd couple.

D2   1-8   Two bottom couples {*improper*}, right-and-left, five changes, beginning with partners,
          then 1st couple continue outside to bottom place, 3rd couple leading up to middle place.

Repeat dance twice more.

THE INSTALLATION

There is no particular event to which this dance title can immediately be connected. Installations are usually associated with the establishment of a bishop or of a prince of the realm into one of his titles.

Tom Cook found this dance in an unidentified collection of about 1772 and noted that this same music appeared with another dance titled "St. George's Fields," barred evenly, without the half-measure pickup found here. Both can also be found in *Thompson's Compleat Collection*, vol. 3 (London: 1773), and another "Installation" appears in volume 4 of Thompson's collection (1780).

The 1st Man Hey on the 1st Wo. fide ‖ then Hey on their own fides ‖ lead thro' the 2d Cu. caft up ‖ turn ‖ 2d Cu. lead up caft off ‖ turn ‖ foot it 4 half Right & Left ‖ the fame back again ‖ crofs over ‖ figure at top ‖ Right & Left ‖

Thompson's Complete Collection, vol. 3 (1773): 90
Courtesy of the Forbes Library, Northampton, Massachusetts

54

JACK'S MAGGOT

Duple minor longways
AA BB ad lib   MM ♩ = 116

Cecil Sharp, 1922
Twenty Four New Country Dances (Playford), 1702; DM I: 1703-1728

A1	1-8	1st man cross down the center diagonally and hey for three with the two women, passing 2nd woman right shoulder, ending in his original place.
A2	1-8	1st woman the same with the two men, passing 2nd man left shoulder.
B1	1-8	All right hands-across and left-hands back.
B2	1-2	1st corners change places.
	3-4	2nd corners the same.
	5-6	All circle four-hands half-way around.
	7-8	1st couple cast down one place, 2nd couple leading up.

Fidler   Dame Dowdy   Quack Docter   Jack of the Green   Shepherd   Shepherdess

Catchpenny Prints, no. 68, 55
Courtesy Dover Publications

JACK'S MAGGOT

Over twenty dances named for the ubiquitous "Jack" can be found in the early eighteenth century, possibly references to the Jacobites, who supported the return of the Stuarts to the throne. A variant of this dance continued in eighteenth-century country dance collections with new tunes entitled "The Rakes of Mellow" and "Jack's Meggot."

The 1. man goes the Hey with the 2. wo.╌. The 1. wo. goes the Hey with the 2. man╌: Then right-hands a-crofs, and left-hands back again╌. The 1. man changing places with the 2. wo. the 2. man changing places with the 1. wo. then hands half round and caft off╌:

DM I:14 (1709): 331
Courtesy of the Vaughan Williams Memorial Library

JACOB HALL'S JIG
to the tune of UNDER AND OVER

Duple minor longways
AA BB ad lib   MM ♩. = 120

Cecil Sharp, 1916
d: DM I: 1695-1728; m: DM I: 1652-1728

Gm	F	Bb	F	Gm7	C7	F	Dm	Gm	Dm	Bb	C	Dm	Gm

Dm		C	F	Gm7	C7	F		Gm	Dm		C	Dm	Gm

A1   1-4   1st man turn 2nd woman right-hand, then his partner left-hand.

      5-8   1st couple and 2nd woman circle three-hands counter-clockwise.

A2   1-4   2nd man turn 1st woman left-hand, then his partner right-hand.

      5-8   2nd couple and 1st woman circle three-hands clockwise.

B1   1-4   1st couple lead down center, and lead back to stand between
               2nd couple forming a line of four, all facing up.

      5-8   Line lead up a double and fall back a double, ending
               with 1st couple in 2nd place, 2nd couple in 1st place.

B2   1-4   Circle four-hands once around.

      5-8   1st couple lead through couple above and
               cast down to progressed place.

JACOB HALL
Harvard Theatre Collection

JACOB HALL'S JIG

Samuel Pepys went to Bartholomew Fair on August 29, 1668 and "there did see a ridiculous, obscene little stage-play, called Marry Andrey [Merry Andrew]; a foolish thing but seen by everybody: and so to Jacob Hall's dancing of the ropes; a thing worth seeing and mightily followed."

The following September, Pepys saw him again at the Southwark Fair. "[I went] to Jacob Hall's dance on the ropes, where I saw such action as I never saw before,...[afterwards we went] to a tavern, whither come...Jacob Hall himself, with whom I had a mind to speak, to hear whether he had ever any mischief by falls in his time. He tells me, 'Yes, many; but never to the breaking of a limb.'"

According to Pepys, to avenge herself on the King's neglecting her, Lady Castlemaine, the cast-off mistress of Charles II, fell "mightily in love" with the talented aerial acrobat and lavished him with gifts and money. By coincidence, the lyrics to the tune of "Under and Over" which Sharp chose to substitute for "Jacob Hall's Jig," are in Pepys's own collection of broadside ballads:

As I abroad was walking, I heard two lovers talking:
  One to the other spake, of loves constancie:
As ore a medow turning, upon a Summers morning:
  I heard these Lovers mourning, cause of loves cruelty.
For under and over, over and under, under and over agen,
  Quoth she, sweet heart I love thee,
  As maydens should love men.

References: Highfill, 7: 23-25; Simpson, 722-24; Rollins, 2: 208; Pepys, *Ballads*, 1: 264

"Jacob Hall's Jig," DM I:9 (1695): 182
"Under and over," DM I:4 (1670): 108
Courtesy of the Vaughan Williams Memorial Library

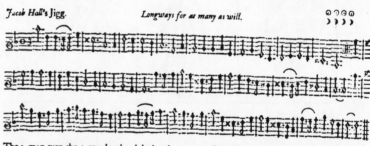

Jacob Hall's Jigg.   *Longways for as many as will.*

The 1. man turn the 2. wo. by the right hand once round, then take the 1. wo. by the left, and all three hands quite round ∴ The 2. man turn the 1. wo. by the left hand once round, then take the 2. wo. by the right, and all three hands quite round ∴ The 1. cu. lead down the middle, and then up, then all four hands abreast and lead up, the 1. cu. fall in the middle, and all four hands quite round till the 1. cu. comes into the 2. cu. place, then lead through and cast off ∴

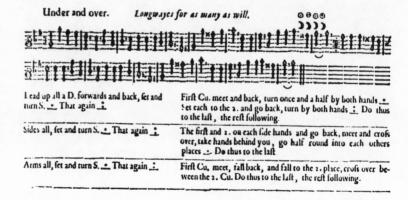

Under and over.   *Longwayes for as many as will.*

Lead up all a D. forwards and back, set and turn S. ∴ That again ∴

Sides all, set and turn S. ∴ That again ∴

Arms all, set and turn S. ∴ That again ∴

First Cu. meet and back, turn once and a half by both hands ∴ Set each to the 2. and go back, turn by both hands ∴ Do thus to the last, the rest following.

The first and 2. on each side hands and go back, meet and cross over, take hands behind you, go half round into each others places ∴ Do thus to the last

First Cu. meet, fall back, and fall to the 2. place, cross over between the 2. Cu. Do thus to the last, the rest following.

JAMAICA

Duple minor longways
AB AB ad lib   MM $\downarrow$ = 96

Cecil Sharp, 1911
DM I: 1670-1728

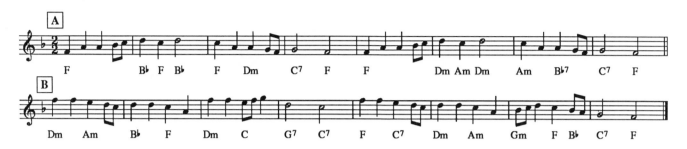

Part I

A	1-2	1st man take 1st woman by right hand, then left.
	3-4	Hands crossed, they turn half-way.
	5-8	1st man the same with 2nd woman **while** 1st woman the same with 2nd man.
B	1-8	1st couple figure-eight up through 2nd couple, skipping, and change places with partner at end.

Part II

A	1-4	With new 2nd couple below, 1st man turn 2nd woman two-hands once around.
	5-8	1st woman the same with 2nd man.
B	1-4	All turn neighbors two-hands once-and-a-half.
	5-8	All turn partners two-hands.

JAMAICA

This tune is derived from a 1656 broadside ballad entitled *Joy after Sorrow, being the Sea-mans return from Jamaica*, inspired by the recent British capture of Jamaica in the West Indies. The first verse follows:

1. There was a maid as I heard tell,
     Which fell in desperation.
   She lov'd a young man passing well,
     Which brought her in vexation:
   The young man had the maid beguil'd
     The matter so was carried,
   For he had gotten her with Child
     Before that they were married.
   Which caus'd this maid to make great moan,
     And often times to speak so,
   My belly is up and my heart is down,
     And my love is gone to Jamaica...

5. My love gave me a holand smock,
     And bid me for to weare it,
   One night 'twixt ten & eleven a clock
     I'm sure he did not teare it:
   My love gave me a feather bed,
     To lye on when I was weary,
   On which he had my maiden-head,
     When he had made me merry.
   But since dame fortune she doth frown
     This makes me sigh and speake so,
   My belly is up...

6. And since that time I am possest,
     With many griefs I tell yee,
   In head, in side in back and breast,
     But chiefly in my belly:

Oh that my love were here againe, I'm sure he would befriend me,
   And use a meanes to cure my pain, and take a course to mend me.
I sigh, I sob, and I make great moan, the reason why I doe so, &c...
     [*The sailor eventually comes home...*]
9. Good Lord what kissing there was then, with friendly kind embraces,
     Until the joyfull tears of them, ran down each others faces:
   The very night when this was done, as is for certain spoken,
     She was delivered of a Son, a fair and goodly token.
   Whereby she alters so on her tune, her fancy made her speak so,
     My heart is up and my belly is down, and my Love is come from Jamaica...

Feuillet published a version of this dance in his *Recuëil* (Paris: 1706), calling it "*La Bonne Amitie*."
References: W. B. Olson, *Folk Song Journal*, 2/4 (1973): 315-17; Moss, 2: 244-50; Simpson, 376-77; Chappell, 446-47

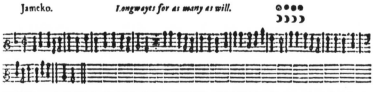

Jameko.   *Longwayes for as many as will.*

The first man take his Wo. by the right hand, then with his left, and so holding hands, change places, then do the same to the 2. Wo. the first Wo. and the 2. man do the same .:. Then fall back from your own, the first couple being in the second place, go the Figure of 8 .:. Do this to the last.

The first man take hands with the second Wo. and turn her round, the first Wo. and the 2. man do as much .:. Then the two men take hands and two Wo. take hands and turn once and a half, and then turn your own .:. Do this to the last.

DM I:4 (1670): 142

JENNY PLUCK PEARS

Round for three couples
6 x AA B   MM ♩. = 126; ♩ = 104

Cecil Sharp, 1911
DM I: 1651-1690

Am G Am Em Am G Am Em C G Am Em D Em Am

Am G Am G Am G Am⁷ D⁷ G Am G C Am G Am

Part I
A1   1-8   All circle six-hands, eight slips around clockwise (1-4), then partners set and turn single (5-8).
A2   1-8   All circle six-hands, eight slips back, then partners set and turn single.
B   1-2   1st man take partner by right hand, place her in center facing him.
     3-4   2nd man the same with his partner.
     5-6   3rd man the same.
     7-8   Partners slow set and honor right.

Part II
A1   1-8   Men skip clockwise around the women standing back to back in center.
A2   1-8   Men turn around to left and skip back to place.
B   1-6   1st man take partner by left hand, place her on his right beside him (1-2), 2nd man the same (3-4),
           3rd man the same (5-6).
     7-8   Partners slow set and honor right.

Part III
AA   1-16 Partners side, set, and turn single. That again.
B   1-8   As in part II, B, 1st woman take partner left-hand, place him in center; 2nd woman the same;
           3rd woman the same, then partners slow set and honor right.

Part IV
A1   1-8   Women skip clockwise around the men standing back to back in the center.
A2   1-8   Women turn around to left and skip back to place.
B   1-8   1st woman take partner by right hand, place him on her left; 2nd woman the same; 3rd woman the
           same; then partners slow set and honor right.

Part V
A1   1-8   Partners arm right, set and turn single.
A2   1-8   Partners arm left, set and turn single.
B   1-8   Men place partners in center as in part I.

Part VI
AAB 1-24 Men skip around, back to place and hand partners to place as in Part II.

JENNY PLUCK PEARS

This is the first dance that Sharp reconstructed from *The English Dancing Master* (1651) and is a most elegant one.   The changing meter of the tune bespeaks a sophisticated composition, but the subject matter is earthy. Margaret Dean-Smith relates the tune to a "Green Sleeves" model and adds: "No explanation can be offered for the title beyond recalling that 'Jenny' is a common type-name for a rustic sweetheart and can be as disreputable as Betty or Moll; that a pear, or pear-tree has an oblique meaning, and that the whole may have much the same sexual significance as 'Green Sleeves.'" (See page 41) Even Dean-Smith is circumspect here. The blatant sexualism of pre-nineteenth-century popular English literature was an uncomfortable aspect for scholars until very recent times.   References: Dean-Smith, 80

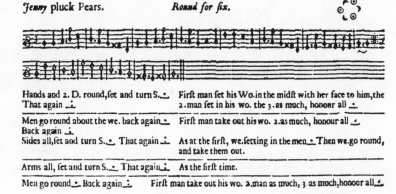

DM I:7 (1686): 7

JOY AFTER SORROW

Longways for three couples
3 x AA BB MM 𝅗𝅥 = 126

Bernard Bentley, 1980
DM II: 1719-1729

A1 1-4 With two waltz steps, 1st man move down center to bottom of set **while** 1st woman move down outside the set (1-2), and both turn single to right (3-4).

5-8 1st man move up outside to original place **while** 1st woman move up center (5-6), and both turn single to right (7-8).

A2 1-2 1st couple set forward to each other, then face down.

3-8 All mirror hey, 1st couple going between 2nd couple to begin.

B1 1-2 1st man forward a double to 2nd woman, take her left hand in his right, and both face up.

3-6 1st man lead 2nd woman up, turn half-way around as a couple, and lead down center to face 3rd couple, 2nd man moving to top on outside.

7-8 1st man and 2nd woman {*improper*} turn single, man to left, woman to right.

9-16 The same half figure-eight through the couple above and turn two-hands once around in middle place, ending proper.

B2 1-8 1st man, 2nd woman {*on his right*}, and 1st woman {*on his left*} circle three-hands clockwise, **once-and-two-thirds** around, ending with 1st couple improper in middle place.

9-16 1st couple, crossing, lead up to top place and face (9-10), honor each other (11-12) and cast down to bottom of set, the others moving up.

Repeat dance twice more.

JOY AFTER SORROW

This dance appears set to two different tunes, "Joy after Sorrow" and "Love and Beauty," both in 3/4 time, surely implying the use of a minuet step for the figures. As "Joy after Sorrow" it appeared in 1718 (DM II:3) with the music which had been printed with a contemporary song: "Joy after Sorrow...to the Duke d'Aumond's Minuet." It celebrates the 1714 arrival of George I from Hanover to fill the English throne.

Let Burgundy flow, let the glass run o'er,
    Let the glass run o'er boys,
To cure all our woe, let the glass run over the brim.
    Though Anna is gone, think of it no more,
Think of it no more, boys,
    Toast away your bumpers to him,
Tho' the feuds were so big,
    'twixt Tory and Whigg,
That the mischiefs pursuing
Prov'd almost our ruin
Like a prophet I know,
    They will be no more so,
We've a King will unite now
    Both High-Church and Low.

D'Urfey, Wit and Mirth (London: 1719), 2: 42

Joy after Sorrow.   *Longways for as many as will.*

Note, Each Strain is to be play'd twice over.

First Man go down the Middle below the 3d Wo. the 1st Wo. flip outside to meet her Partner, and turn single, the 1st Wo. flip up the Middle to the Top, her Partner flip outside the Men, both turn single ꞉. First Cu. let, go the Hey fides with the 2d and 3d Cu. The 1st Man take the 2d Wo. by her left Hand, lead her to the 3d Cu. and turn single, figure between the 1st Wo. and 2d Man and turn ꞉. Then 1st Cu. take Hands with the 2d Wo. and go round 'till you are improper in the 2d Cu. Place, crofs up the Middle to your Place, fall back one Step, and caft off ꞉.

The Second Book of the Compleat Country Dancing Master (1719): 344
Courtesy of the Library of Congress

59

JUICE OF BARLEY

Duple minor longways
A BB ad lib   MM $\bullet$ = 116

Cecil Sharp, 1916
DM I: 1686-1690

A   1-4   Partners back-to-back by right shoulder.

     5-8   Partners turn two-hands once around.

B1   1-4   Men half figure-eight between women, 1st man leading.

     5-8   All clap hands on first beat and circle four-hands once around clockwise.

B2   1-4   Women half figure-eight between men, 1st woman leading.

     5-8   All clap as in B1 and circle four-hands once around clockwise.

JUICE OF BARLEY

The history of this tune and dance is convoluted! An earlier title for this superb tune was "Stingo, or the Oyl of Barley" and it was included with a dance in DM I: 1-8 (1651-1690). The first strain of the tune shares strong family resemblance to "Bobbing Joe" (DM I: 1651-1728). Many lyrics were set to the tune, all having in common the metaphorical themes of strong ale, and of "selling barley," the feminine equivalent of "sowing wild oats."

In 1688 a "new Scotch Song" set to the tune appeared. Written by D'Urfey, it began "Could and Raw the North did blow..." With this song came a new popularity for the melody, and in 1689, Henry Playford cashed in on it, issuing a sheet with six dances, two of them to the tune: "Cold and Raw" and "Juice of Barley" (the dance Sharp reconstructed). He repeated the latter dance as "Cold and Raw" in the next edition of the DM (I:9,1695). After Walsh appropriated almost the entire contents of DM I:16 (1716) for his collection of 1718, the dance was changed for the final two editions back to the figures which had first appeared as "Cold and Raw" in 1689.

The following song set to the tune was published in 1647.

Good Ale for My Money

Be merry my friends, and list a while
  Unto a merry jest,
It may from you produce a smile,
  When you heare it exprest:
Of a young man lately married,
  Which was a boone good fellow;
This song in's head he alwaies carried,
  When drink made him mellow.
I cannot go home, nor I will not go home,
  It's 'long of the oyle of Barly,
I'le tarry all night for my delight,
  And go home in the morning early.
         Ashton, *Humour, Wit and Satire*, 276

Woodcut from Ashton, Humour, Wit and Satire, 124

Juice of Barly.   *Longways for as many as will:*

The 1. cu. go back to back with their Partners, and the 2. cu. do the same at the same time.

The 1. cu. take hands with his Partner and turn her round, the 2. cu. doing the same at the same time.

The two we. stand still, whilst the 1. man goes round about the 2. wo. into the 2. man's place, and the 2. man goes round about the 1. wo. into the 1. man's place, then all clap hands, then all four take hands and go quite round, the we. doing the like.

References: Simpson, 46-47, 687-92; Dean-Smith, 13; John Ashton, *Humour*, 276

DM 1:8 (1690): 207
Courtesy of the Vaughan Williams Memorial Library

KELSTERNE GARDENS

Longways for three couples
3 x AA BB   MM ♩ = 116

Tom Cook, 1975
DM III: 1727

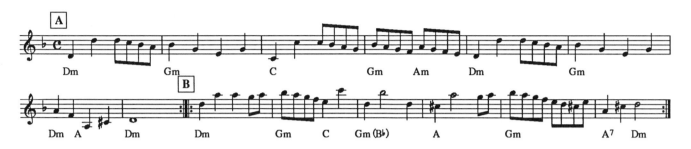

A1	1-8	All mirror hey, 1st couple going between 2nd couple to begin.
A2	1-8	1st and 2nd couple double figure-eight: 1st couple cross down through center and move up outside **while** 2nd couple cast up outside and cross through center. Continue movement until all are in original places.
B1	1-4	1st and 2nd couples circle four-hands once around.
	5-6	1st couple cast down one place **while** 2nd couple lead up.
B2	1-6	As in B1, 1st and 3rd couple circle once around, 1st couple cast down to bottom, 3rd couple leading up.

Repeat dance twice more.

Catchpenny Prints, no. 109, 74
Courtesy Dover Publications

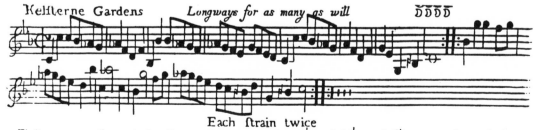

The New Country Dancing Master, 3d book (1728): 110
By permission of the British Library

61

KNOLE PARK

Duple minor longways
AA BB ad lib   MM ♩ = 112

A. Simons, 1961

d: Voight, *Selection* (Wheatstone), 1809; m: Bishop, *Six New Minuets* (L & B), 1788

A1	1-4	Circle four-hands once around.
	5-6	1st corners change places.
	7-8	2nd corners change places.
A2	1-8	Repeat A1 to place.
B1	1-8	1st couple lead down center, lead back, and cast down one place, 2nd couple moving up.
B2	1-8	Whole poussette counter-clockwise, 1st man {*in 2nd place*} pushing.

KNOLE PARK

The great park with its ancient trees and herds of deer makes a moving introduction to Knole, the vast Tudor house in Sevenoaks, Kent, owned since 1603 by the Sackville family. One of the finest houses in England, Knole still evokes the unrivaled splendour of English country house life of the baroque period.

In the late eighteenth century Knole was the setting for extravagant balls and cricket matches hosted by the batchelor third Duke of Dorset, Lord Sackville, who was Ambassador to the Court of Louis XVI. He married in 1789 and died a decade later.

Reference: H. Avery Tipping, *English Homes*, Period III, vol. 1 (London: Country Life, 1929), 222-68

KNOLE PARK, THE SOUTH ELEVATION
Courtsey of the Print Room, Lewis Walpole Library, Yale University

Voight, A Selection, bk. 3 (ca. 1809): 2
By permission of the British Library

Bishop, Six New Minuets (1788): 18
By permission of the British Library

LILLI BURLERO

Duple minor longways
A BB ad lib   MM ♩. = 108

Cecil Sharp, 1916
DM I: 1690-1728

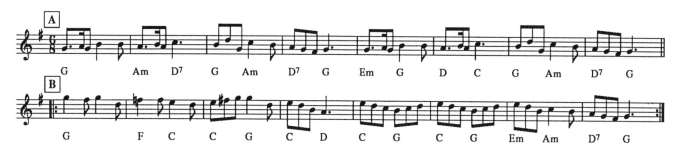

G   Am   D⁷   G   Am   D⁷   G   Em   G   D   C   G   Am   D⁷   G

G   F   C   C   G   C   D   C   G   C   G   Em   Am   D⁷   G

A   1-4   1st couple lead down through 2nd couple and cast up to place.
     5-8   2nd couple lead up through 1st couple and cast down to place.
B1   1-2   1st corners change places.
     3-4   2nd corners change places.
     5-8   All fall back a double, then come forward a double turning single to right.
B2   1-2   Partners change places, passing right shoulder.
     3-4   Neighbors change places, moving backward and passing right shoulder.
     5-8   Partners face and circular hey, three changes, skipping.

LILLI BURLERO

John Ashton gave an undocumented but interesting bit of information about this title which we have not found elsewhere, that "Lilli burlero" and "bullen a lah" were pass words used by the Irish papists in their massacre of the Protestants in 1641. (*Social History*, 19) According to Nicholas Carolan, director of the Irish Traditional Music Archive, the Irish words *Ba linn an Lá*, meaning "to us will be the day," have recently been associated with this tune title and appear to support Ashton's conjecture.

Although its attribution to Purcell is now considered doubtful, there is no question that "Lilli burlero" was the new Irish tune to which was set a biting satire against the Earl of Tyrconnell, a bigoted papist whom James II unwisely made deputy to Ireland in 1687. A very early version of the rabble-rousing statement/chorus ballad follows:

Ho! Brother Teague, dost hear the Decree,
  Lilli burlero bullen a la
Dat we shall have a new Deputie,
  Lilli burlero bullen a la
  Lero, lero, lero, lero, Lilliburlero, bullen a la
  Lero, lero, lero, lero, Lilliburlero, bullen a la

Though by my shoul it is a T[albo]t, lilli &c.
And he will cut all de English Troat, lilli &c. Lero...
  That if Dispence do come from de Pope, lilli &c.
  We'll hang Magna Charta & demselves in a rope,
    lilli... Lero...
And the good T[albo]t is made a Lord, lilli &c.
And he with brave lads is coming aboard, lilli... Lero...
  Ho! all in France have taken a swear, lilli &c.
  Dat dey will have no Protestant h[ei]r, lilli... Lero...
O but why does he stay behind, lilli &c.
Ho by my shoul 'tis a Protestant wind. lilli... Lero...
  Now T[yrconne]l is come ashore, lilli &c.
  And we shall have commissions gillore, lilli... Lero...
And he that will not go to M[a]ss, lilli &c.
Shall turn out and look like an ass, lilli... Lero...

Now, now de Hereticks all go down, lilli &c.
By Christ and St. Patrick the Nation's our own, lilli... Lero...

Pepys, Ballads, 5: 33

In a mockery of Irish speech, the song is set as a congratulatory dialogue between two Irishmen on the coming triumph of Popery and the Jacobite cause, and it caught the spirit of a nation whose allegiances are still divided. Called a foolish ballad by some, it "made an impression on the army that cannot be imagined by those who saw it not." At the time too dangerous to print, the song circulated orally and became a powerful propaganda weapon for the Protestant Williamite cause. It was said that "all the people were singing it...and perhaps never had so slight a thing so great an effect." Indeed it was one of the last public outbreaks again the King, and he finally fled after only four years on the throne. So many political and topical ballads were set to the tune in the succeeding decades that the very tune title became a slogan of resistance. Naturally a country dance was immediately created for the inflammatory tune and title. It is tempting to speculate that the image of the dancers taking turns leading by couples through couples was a reference to bisexual James II, his mistresses, and his courtiers. Such visual references would be impossible to prove but they cannot be discounted with this particular melody in this period of high political feeling and anti-catholic fervor.

References: Ward, 57; Moss, 2: 319-25; Simpson, 449-55; Chappell, 568-74, 786; Feuillet, *Recuëil* (1706): 70-75; Samuel Lover, *Poems of Ireland* (London: Ward, Lock, & Co., 1858), 254; *Lilliburlero! ...and more Songs of the Orange Tradition* (Lurgan: Ulster Society, 1988), 10

Lilli Burlero.   *Longways for as many as will.*   ⊙⊙⊙⊙
>>>>

The first man lead his Partner down through the 2. cu. and cast up to his own Place, and the 2. cu. lead up through the 1. cu. and cast off into their own places, then the 1. man cross over with the 2. wo. and the 1. wo. with the 2. man, then fall back, and meet and turn S. then cross over and the men back to back, the wo. at the same time doing the like, then the two men right and left, the wo. at the same time doing the like, till the 1. cu. comes into the 2. cu. place.

Courtesy of the Vaughan Williams Memorial Library   *DM I:8 (1690): 216*

63

LOVE'S TRIUMPH

Longways for three couples
3 x AA BB   MM ♩ = 108

Bernard J. Bentley, 1962
DM II: 1710-1728

A1	1-4	1st couple face down and 2nd couple face up, then forward a double and turn single back to place, partners turning **towards** each other.
	5-8	1st and 2nd couples circle four-hands half-way.
A2	1-4	As in A1, 1st and 3rd couples meet, turn single back to places, partners turning **away** from each other.
	5-8	1st and 3rd couples circle four-hands half-way.
B1	1-4	1st couple cast up to middle place.
	5-8	All back-to-back and turn single.
	9-16	1st and 2nd couples circular hey, four changes, beginning with partners.
B2	1-4	1st man turn 3rd woman right-hand once-and-a-quarter **while** 1st woman and 2nd man the same.
	5-8	1st man turn 3rd man left-hand three-quarters **while** 1st and 2nd women the same.
	9-14	1st couple, now improper, lead up through top couple and cast down to middle place, then lead down center to bottom place, 3rd couple moving up.
	15-16	All turn partners left-hand half-way.

Repeat dance twice more.

Catchpenny Prints, #175, 120
Courtesy Dover Publications

LOVE'S TRIUMPH

The Italian opera *La Pastorella*, with music by C. F. Cesarini and others, was rewritten for the London stage by Peter Motteux and premiered in the 1708 season as *Love's Triumph*. This tune is not among the songs in the published score, but the acts were punctuated with scenes of shepherds and shepherdesses dancing, one of which may be the source or inspiration for this lovely country dance which appeared so soon after its premier.

Note : *Each Strain is to be play'd twice over.*

All four meet and turn fingle, then Hands half round ∴ The firft couple meet the third couple and turn fingle, then Hands half round ∴ The firft couple being in the third couples place, caft up into the fecond couples place, then back to back with your Partners, then turn fingle, and Right and Left quite round with the fecond couple ∴ The firft couple being in the fecond couples place, the firft man turn the third woman, and the firft woman the fecond man, then the firft man turn the third man, and the firft woman turn the fecond woman, then back to back with your Partners, then lead through the fecond couple and caft off, and lead through the third couple and caft up ∴

By permission of the Director of Manchester Public Libraries

DM II:1 (1710): 166

64

LULL ME BEYOND THEE

Longways for four couples, 3rd and 4th couples improper

3 x A BB   MM ♩. = 84

Cecil Sharp, 1912

DM I: 1651-1690

Dm F C F Dm Gm A⁷ Dm F B♭ Gm A Dm A⁷ Dm

F C⁷ F C F C⁷ F C⁷ F C Dm Am F Gm A⁷ Dm

Part I

A   1-8   All forward a double to meet and fall back a double. That again.

B1   1-2   Middle men lead neighbors out a double **while** end couples lead in, to form lines of four facing across the hall.

      3-4   Taking hands in line, all fall back a double.

      5-8   All forward a double and turn opposite two-hands once around.

B2   1-2   New middle men lead neighbors out, new end men lead in, to form lines facing up and down the hall.

      3-4   Taking hands in line, all fall back a double.

      5-8   All forward a double and turn opposite {*partner*} two-hands once around.

Part II

A   1-4   Partners side.

      5-8   End couples side with partner **while** middle couples side with neighbor.

B1   1-2   All turn to right to face out, then taking hands in line, lead forward a double.

      3-4   All fall back a double, ends closing in to form a circle.

      5-8   Circle four-hands once around, ending in lines across the set.

B2   1-2   Turning to neighbor to face out, lines of four lead out a double.

      3-4   Fall back a double, ends closing in as in B1.

      5-8   Circle four-hands once around, ending in lines up and down the hall.

Part III

A   1-4   Partners arm right.

      5-8   End couples arm left with partner **while** middle couples arm left with neighbor.

B1   1-2   Middle men lead neighbors out a double, change hands to make an arch and face center of set **while** end couples lead forward to meet.

      3-4   New middles lead opposites out, passing under arches made by ends, who move back to center.

      5-8   All turn current partners two-hands once around, ending in lines across the hall.

B2   1-4   Repeat B1 1-4 from new places.

      5-8   All turn two-hands with partners to original places.

{*This is a rather slow, stately dance.*}

LULL ME BEYOND THEE

A ballad in the Roxburgh collection begins:
I was walking all alone, I heard a youth lamenting,
Under a hollow bush he lay, but sore he did repent him.
   Alas! quoth he, my love is gone,
   Which causes me to wander,
Yet merry will I never be, till I lie lulling beyond her.
Dean Smith adds the subtle comment that, in the sense of this ballad, "beyond" means "athwart" [!].
References: Simpson, 445-46; Dean-Smith, 78; Chappell, 259-60; Roxburgh, 4: 214

DM I:7 (1686): 148
Courtesy of the Vaughan Williams Memorial Library

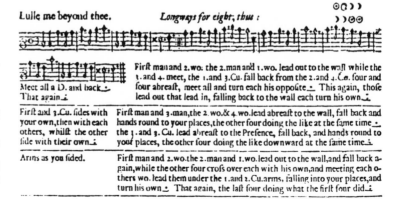

MAD ROBIN

Duple minor longways
AA BB ad lib   MM ♩ = 112

Cecil Sharp, 1922
DM I: 1687-1728

A1   1-8   1st man turn 2nd woman right-hand, then turn 1st woman left-hand and cast down to 2nd place, 2nd man moving up.

A2   1-8   1st woman turn 1st man {*in second place*} left-hand, then turn 2nd man right-hand and cast down to 2nd place, 2nd woman moving up.

B1   1-4   1st woman move up center and cast down to 2nd place **while** 1st man move up outside and down the center to 2nd place.

           5-8   1st couple turn two-hands once around.

B2   1-8   2nd couple repeat B1, woman going down center and casting up to 1st place, her partner moving down outside and returning up the center.

           5-8   2nd couple turn two-hands once around.

MAD ROBIN

John Gay attacks female pride in this song from *Polly* (1729) to the tune of "Mad Robin."

How faultless does the nymph appear,
   When her own hand the picture draws!
But all others only smear,
   Her wrinkles, cracks and flaws.
Self-flattery is our claim and right,
   Let men say what they will;
Sure we may set our good in sight,
   When neighbours set our ill.

Perhaps this is the conceit that Richard Leveridge had in his mind when, in 1731, he advertised that "Tickets to the Tune of Mad Robin" were available for his benefit night at Lincolns Inn Fields (*London Stage*, Part 3, 129).

The tune first appeared without a dance among the "tunes of other country dances" in an appendix to the seventh edition of *The Dancing Master*, then was included in the ninth with dance figures.

Dezais included a version of this dance as "Madame Robin" in his *Recueïl* (Paris: 1712) and in 1716 a scene from a theatrical dance to the same tune was described and depicted in Lambranzi's *New and Curious School of Theatrical Dancing* published in Nuremberg (1: 21).

References: Moss, 3: 10-12; Chappell, 512; Gregorio Lambranzi, *New and Curious School of Theatrical Dancing* (Nuremberg: 1716), reprint, (Brooklyn: Dance Horizons, 1966); Dezais, *Recueïl de Contredanses* (Paris: 1712), reprint, (Farnborough, Gregg International, 1972)

Woodcut from Rollins, Pepys Ballads, 6: 266

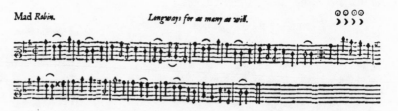

The 1. man turn the 2. wo. with his right hand, and his own Partner with his left, and caſt off below the 2. man ⁝. The 1. wo. turn her Partner with her right hand, and the 2. man with her left, and caſt off below the 2. wo. ⁝ The 1. wo. caſt up above the 2. man and ſlip down the middle, the 1. man go up between, and then caſt off below and turn hands ⁝. The 1.wo go up the middle and caſt off below the 2. wo. the 1. man caſt up above the 2. man, and ſlip down the middle and turn his Partner ⁝

DM I:9 (1695): 185

MAGE ON A CREE

Round for four couples   Cecil Sharp, 1911
12 x A   MM ♩. = 120   DM I: 1651-1716

Part I

A1   1-4   All take hands, forward a double and fall back a double.

       5-8   Face partner, set and turn single.

A2   1-8   Repeat A1.

A3   1-4   Men forward a double to center, face out and circle four-hands once around clockwise
                    {to their right}, slipping.

       5-8   Men turn original corner women two-hands, skipping.

A4   1-4   Women forward a double to center, face out and circle four-hands once around clockwise, slipping.

       5-8   Partners turn two-hands, skipping.

Part II

A1&2   1-16   Partners side, set and turn single. That again.

A3   1-4   Men skip clockwise half-way around the set, passing in front of corner women,
                    and behind next woman to opposite place.

       5-8   Women forward a double, then fall back a double turning single to right.

A4   1-8   Repeat A3, to place.

Part III

A1   1-8   Partners arm right, set and turn single.

A2   1-8   Partners arm left, set and turn single.

A3   1-4   Men turn women on left two-hands once around, skipping. Men leave women in center facing out
                    and move one place to left.

       5-8   Men turn next woman on left two-hands and move another place.

A4   1-8   Continue movement in A3 to original places.

MAGE ON A CREE

This dance is a progressive round, one of the earliest types found in *The Dancing Master*. No one has been able to explain the meaning of the title, and from the entries in old books, it seems that it was not clear then to English-speaking people. It may have been Irish.

At first the term appears to reflect the old meaning of "magpie" with no clear understanding of what "cree" was. By the last edition of the DM the old title had reappeared, explained as a girl named "Margery!" Hyder Rollins suggests that "hone a cre" is an exclamation of sorrow in the Irish language. (*Pepys Ballads*, 150) By implication, this anglicized title then could be read as "Mage hone a cree" or "Madge's lamentation." Such other titles as "Gramacree," "Ben my cree," and "Cushla ma cree" may also be related, cree being the anglicized Irish word *croi* or "heart."

When the title was first used for a ballad in 1633, the tune name was "Magina-cree." Then the dance appeared as "Mage on a Cree" (1651-1665). Then it was changed to "Mage on a Tree" (1670-1686), which sounds fine for a bird. But then it was changed again to "Madge on a Tree" (1690-1716) and finally "Madge on a Tree. or: Margery Cree" (1721-1728), and a new longways dance was substituted. Sharp chose the early dance for his collection.

References: Simpson, 478-49; Dean-Smith, 20; Pepys Ballads, 2: 240-41

DM I:4 (1670): 14

Courtesy of the Vaughan Williams Memorial Library

The first and last verses of a moral song in the Pepys ballad collection follow:

Good Admonition, or To al sorts of people this counsell I sing,
That in each ones affairs, to take heed's a faire thing. to the tune of, Magina-cree.

1. To all christian people, this ditty belongs,
    That have the true sense, of their ears, eyes and tongues:
    If well they doe keepe it 'twill profit them bring,
    I give but this Item: take heed's a faire thing.

7. Let no tempting harlot bewitch or intice,
    To sell that for lust, which did cost such a price,
    As his that died for thee, to heaven thee to bring,
    If thou wilt goe thither: take heed's a faire thing.

Mage on a Tree.   *Round for Eight.*

Hands and meet a D. back again, fet and turn S. ∴ That again ∴ Men meet in the midft, turn back to back, come to your places, and turn the Co. We. ∴ We. meet, turn back to back, come to your Places and turn your own ∴ ∴

Sides all, fet and turn S. ∴ That again ∴ Men go towards the left hand before the Co. We. and behind the next We. meet and turn S ∴ That again to your places ∴ ∴ Then the We. as much ∴ ∴

Arms all, fet and turn S. ∴ That again ∴ Turn all the Co. w. turn all the next we. ∴ Turn all the next, turn all your own ∴ ∴

MAID PEEPED OUT AT THE WINDOW
or, The Friar in the Well

Longways for four to six couples
3 x A BB   MM ♩. = 112

Cecil Sharp, 1922
DM I: 1651-1690

Part I

A   1-8   Partners lead up a double and fall back a double. That again.

B1   1-4   1st man, followed by the other men, cast down to bottom of the set
             while women do the same, reversing the set, top to bottom.

        5-8   Partners set and turn single.

B2   1-8   Repeat B1, casting up to top.

Part II

A   1-8   Partners side twice.

B1   1-4   All face up: Men go four slips right to women's side, passing in front of women
             while women go four slips left to men's side.

        5-8   Still facing up, all forward a double, then face partner, set and turn single.

B2   1-4   All face down. Women slip left in front of partner **while** men slip right.

        5-8   Facing down, all forward a double, then set to partner and turn single, ending in original places.

Part III

A   1-8   Partners arm right, then left.

B1   1-4   All half-poussette clockwise, 1st and 3rd men pushing to start.

        5-8   Partners set and turn single.

B2   1-4   Complete the poussette to original places, 1st and 3rd men pulling.

        5-8   Partners set and turn single.

MAID PEEPED OUT AT THE WINDOW

Although the first title is not reflected in the ballad text, the story is an old one, and one of the many popular songs against monks and friars. D'Urfey included an amusing song in *Wit and Mirth; or, Pills to Purge Melancholy* (1719):

> The Fryer and the Maid.
>
> As I lay musing all alone, a merry tale I thought upon;
>   Now listen a while and I will you tell,
> Of a fryar that lov'd a bonny lass well.
> He came to her when she was going to bed,
>   Desiring to have her maiden-head;
> But she denyed his desire,
>   And said that she did fear hell-fire.
> Tush, tush, quoth the fryer, thou need's not,
>   If thou wert in hell, I could sing thee out.
> Why then, quoth the maid, thou shalt have thy request,
>   The fryer was a glad as a fox in his nest...

[The maid tricks the friar, who winds up falling in a well, she suggests that he can sing himself out of the well, as well as her out of hell. Finally she takes pity on him and helps him out.]

> Quoth the Fryar I never was serv'd so before,
>   Away quoth the Wench, come here no more;
> The Fryer he walk'd along the street,

> As if he had been a new wash'd sheep.
>   Sing hey down a derry, and let's be merry,
>   And from such sin ever keep. *(3: 325-26)*

A C strain was added to the tune in *The Dancing Master* in the fourth edition but the dance was not altered.

References: Simpson, 240-42; Dean-Smith, 36; Chappell, 273-75

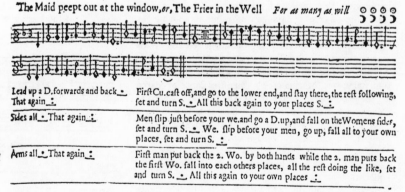

DM I:3 (1665): 65

THE MERRY, MERRY MILKMAIDS

Longways for four couples

3 x AA BB   MM ♩. = 120

Cecil Sharp, 1912

DM I: 1651-1716

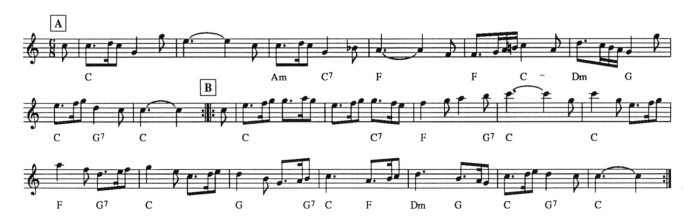

Part I

A1	1-4	Partners lead up a double and fall back a double.
	5-8	Partners set and turn single.
A2	1-8	Repeat A1.
B1	1-2	1st and 3rd couples balance back and forward to partners.
	3-4	1st and 3rd couples take two hands with partner and slip down center one place **while** 2nd and 4th couples slip up outside one place.
	5-8	All fall back a double and move forward a double.
	9-12	1st and 2nd couples right-hands across **while** 3rd and 4th couples the same, once around.
B2	1-12	Repeat B1 to places, 2nd & 4th couples balance back and slip down **while** 1st and 3rd couples slip up outside.

Part II

A1	1-8	Partners side, set and turn single.
A2	1-8	Repeat A1.
B1	1-4	1st man, followed by other men, cast down to left to bottom place, skipping.
	5-8	1st woman, followed by the other women, cast down to right to bottom place, skipping.
	9-12	Partners set and turn single.
B2	1-4	1st man, followed by other men, cast up to right to place.
	5-8	1st woman the same, casting left.
	9-12	Partners set and turn single.

Part III

A1	1-8	Partners arm right, set and turn single.
A2	1-8	Partners arm left, set and turn single.
B1	1-4	Men fall back a double, move forward a double.
	5-12	Men straight hey for four, skipping.
B2	1-12	Women repeat B1.

One of the verses in "The Milkemaid's Life" describes an eighteenth-century May Day custom in which the milkmaids and the sweeps dance in the streets with a garland:

Upon the first of May, with garlands fresh and gay;
With mirth and music sweet, for such a season meet,
  They pass their time away;
They dance away sorrow, and all the day thorow,
  Their legs do never fail;
They nimbley their feet to ply,
  And bravely try the victory,
In honour o' th' milking pail, in honor...   (Chappell, 296)

References: Simpson, 490-93; Dean-Smith, 29; Chappell, 281-82, 295-99, 777

The merry merry Milk maids.   *Longwayes for eight.*

Lead up all a D. forwards and back, fet and turn S. • That again :

Sides all, fet and turn S. • That a-gain :

Arms all, fet and turn S. • That a-gain :

First and 3. Cu. meet your own, flip between the other, take hands acrofs and go round each four • The other four as much :

First man caft off, go to the lower end and ftay, the rest following The We. as much, fet and turn S. .• All that back again :

Men back, and go the S. Hey • Women as much :

Courtesy of the Vaughan Williams Memorial Library

DM I:4 (1670): 71

MISS SAYERS' ALLEMAND

Longways for three couples
3 x AA BB   MM ♩ = 112

Bernard J. Bentley, 1962
Budd, *Six Favourite Minuets* (Rutherford), 1781

A1	1-4	1st couple cast down to bottom of set, then cast back up to 2nd place, 2nd couple moving up on bars 3-4.
	5-8	1st couple turn two-hands three-quarters, 1st woman ending between 2nd couple facing down, 1st man between 3rd couple, facing up.
A2	1-4	Taking hands in lines of three across the hall, step on left foot and swing right across {*step-swing*}, step on right, swing left. Repeat step-swings.
	5-8	1st woman move directly to stand between 2nd and 3rd women, 1st man move between men: take hands in lines facing across the set and repeat step-swings.
B1	1-8	Circle six-hands and back, slipping.
B2	1-4	Partners turn right-hands.
	5-8	1st couple cast down to bottom of set **while** 2nd and 3rd couples turn left-hands, 2nd couple at top, 3rd couple moving up center while turning.

Repeat dance twice more.

MISS SAYERS' ALLEMAND

The allemande was a German couple dance which became fashionable in Europe and England in the late 1760's. It featured a series of hand and arm holds with which partners moved and turned about each other. Several of the allemand movements were incorporated into country dance figures and have been interpreted in various ways, from arms interlaced behind the back to turns under the arms. Bentley interpreted the allemand of this dance as simple hand-turns.

Caft off 2 Cut caft up one and foot. it, the Lady fall in at top, the Gent: at bottom, fet 3 and 3 top and bottom, fet 3 and 3 fideways, Hands 6 quite round, Allemande with the Right and Left Hands.

Budd, Six Favourite Minuets (1781): 19
By permission of the British Library

MISS SPARKS'S MAGGOT

Longways for three couples
6 x AA BB   MM ♩. = 116

Bernard J. Bentley, 1968
Two Hundred Favourite, v. 8 (Johnson), 1753

Part I

A1   1-4   1st couple lead through 2nd couple and cast up to place.

         5-8   1st couple set to each other, twice.

A2   1-8   1st couple lead down center, through 3rd couple, cast up to middle place and set.

B1   1-8   1st and 3rd couples right hands-across, and left back.

B2   1-8   1st and 2nd couples circular hey, four changes, beginning with partner.

Part II

A1   1-4   1st man set to 3rd woman and turn two-hands **while** 1st woman the same to 2nd man.

         5-8   1st couple turn two-hands.

A2   1-8   As in A1, but to the other corners.

B1   1-4   1st man lead 2nd and 3rd woman out a double, change hands and lead back
                 while 1st woman lead the other men out and back.

         5-8   1st couple turn two-hands once-and-a-half.

B2   1-4   1st man lead men out a double, change hands and lead back **while** 1st woman lead the women out
                 and back.

         5-8   1st couple turn two-hands down the center to bottom place
                 while 2nd couple turn two-hands at the top and 3rd couple cast up to middle place.

Repeat dance twice more.

MISS SPARKS'S MAGGOT

   Miss Sparks was the rumored mistress of Rear-Admiral Edward Hawke, who had presided over several well-publicized courts-martial in 1750 shortly before this dance appeared. Her portrait was linked with his, called "Admiral Sternpost," in the *Town and Country Magazine* 10 (1778): 289, with a long satirical essay cloaked in metaphors.

Two Hundred Favourite...vol. 8 (Johnson), [1753]: 6
Courtesy of the Vaughan Williams Memorial Library

Courtesy of the Print Collection
The Lewis Walpole Library, Yale University

71

MR. BEVERIDGE'S MAGGOT

Duple minor longways
AA BB ad lib   MM ♩ = 100

Cecil Sharp, 1922
DM I: 1695-1728

A1   1-2   1st man and 1st woman change places, falling back on last three steps.

      3-4   1st couple face down and back-to-back right shoulder with 2nd couple.

A2   1-2   1st couple turn single to right, then 1st man turn 2nd woman right-hand once around **while** 1st woman the same with 2nd man.

      3-4   1st couple turn left-hand half-way to place.

B1   1-2   1st couple cross and move down outside one place **while** 2nd couple meet and lead up to top.

      3-4   Partners back-to-back; then 1st couple move in between 2nd couple to form line of four facing up.

      5-8   Taking hands, line lead up {*five steps and close*}, fall back, 1st couple ending in first place improper, 2nd couple ending in 2nd place proper. The ending is done thus: 1st couple drop partners hand, then 2nd couple, still holding hands with 1st couple, hand them to first place, 1st man turning right, 1st woman turning left.

B2   1-6   1st couple figure-eight down through 2nd couple with skip or skip-change step, being careful to phrase so as to cross through the second time on measure 5.

      7-8   1st couple cross and move down outside one place, 2nd couple leading up to top.

MR. BEVERIDGE'S MAGGOT

Mr. Beveridge was a dancing master active in London during the first quarter of the eighteenth century. His public dancing school is mentioned in Ned Ward's satirical *A Walk to Islington* of 1704. The author and his consort were watching the activities in the public dancing room and singled out one lady for description.

> Her arms by her side are so formally posted,
> She looks like a pullet truss'd up to be roasted,
> True dancing-school-breeding in her is recorded,
> She shows all she learn'd when at Hackney she boarded...
> The Jills, with their cullies, by this time were prancing,
> Within a large shed, built on purpose for dancing;
> Which stunk so of sweat, pocky breath, and perfume,
> That my mistress and I soon avoided the room,
> And left the lewd herd, to examine new faces
> And practice their buttock-ball capers and graces,
> At Bev'ridges learnt, and at such sort of places."

(66, 73 and 74)

In 1696, John Playford's son, Henry, collected a small group of new dances and added them to the back of the most recent edition of *The Dancing Master* with the following note mentioning Beveridge's contributions:

"To all Gentlemen, Ladies, and others, Lovers of Country Dances. Having lately Printed the Ninth Edition of my Book of Country Dances, which is the Best of that Kind ever yet Published and being thereby Encouraged to set forth a Second Part, containing plain Directions for the Newest and Best Dances, most of them made by Mr. Beveredge, and the rest by other Eminent Masters: 'Tis hoped This will meet with the same Kind Reception that

my former Endeavors have done, and Encourage my farther Care to serve All the Lovers of Musical Diversions and Entertainments. Your humble Servant, H.P."

Whether Beveridge wrote this particular country dance is unclear. The same figures appear in the second volume of *The Dancing Master* with different music, called "Ever Happy" (1710-1728). The music for both "Mr. Beveridge's Magot" and "Mr. Isaac's Magot" (see page 74) share melodic motives and may have been written by the same composer.

The 1. man crofs over and go back to back with the 2. wo. then the 1. wo. crofs over and go back to back with the 2. man at the fame time ⚏. Then meet and turn S. then 1. man turn the 2. wo. with his right hand, and 1. wo. turn the 2. man with her right hand at the fame time, then 1.cu. take left hands and turn into their own places ⚏. The 1 cu. crofs over into the 2. cu. place, and go back to back with their Partner, then all four lead up hands abreaft, then go the Figure through; and caft off into the 2. cu. place ⚏.

Note: *The firft Strain is to be played twice, and the fecond but once.*

DM I:9 (1695): 180
Courtesy of the Vaughan Williams Memorial Library

MR. COSGILL'S DELIGHT

Duple minor longways
AA BB ad lib   MM ♩ = 84

Douglas and Helen Kennedy, 1929
New Country Dancing Master 3d Bk (Walsh), 1728

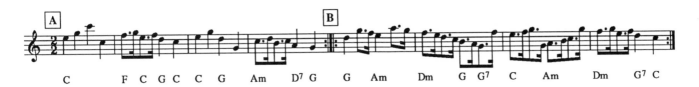

C   F   C   G   C   C   G   Am   D7 G   G   Am   Dm   G   G7   C   Am   Dm   G7   C

A1	1-4	1st and 2nd couples right hands-across.
A2	1-4	1st and 2nd couples left hands-across.
B1	1-2	1st corners change places, then 2nd corners change places.
	3-4	All circle clockwise half-way around without hands.
B2	1-4	Partners face and circular hey, three changes.

{A walking step, two to a measure, is suggested. A catch step (1-2-3) may be used occasionally to maintain the necessary drive and flow.}

MR. COSGILL'S DELIGHT

The walking around figure in B1 is reminiscent of similar movements in Thomas Bray's dances of 1699. This same tune and dance was reprinted in Wright's *Compleat Collection* (1740), 75, there titled "Corelis Gavot."

The music is the final movement "Gavotta" from Archangelo Corelli's Trio Sonata, op. 2, no. 1, dedicated in 1685 to Cardinal Panfilio in Rome.

References: Thomas Bray, *Country Dances* (London: 1699)

from a program "Folk Dance Festival " (New York: 1932)
Courtesy of the Country Dance and Song Society archives

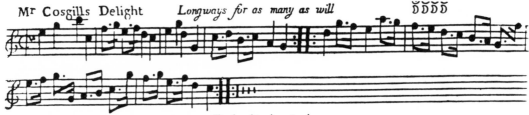

Mr Cosgills Delight   *Longways for as many as will*

Each strain twice
First cu. hands across, with the 2d cu. and go the half round. the same back again. 1st man change places quick with the 2d wo. 1st wo. the same time, with the 2d man and all four go round, into their proper places. right hand and left, with the 2d cu.

New Country-Dancing Master, 3d Bk (1728): 114
By permission of the British Library

MR. ISAAC'S MAGGOT

Duple minor longways
A B ad lib   MM $\quad \downarrow$ = 108

Cecil Sharp, 1916
DM I: 1695-1728

A	1-4	1st man turn 2nd woman right-hand three-quarters, then return to place moving below and around 2nd man.
	5-8	1st woman turn 2nd man left-hand three-quarters, then return to place moving below and around 2nd woman.
B	1-4	Taking inside hands with neighbor, all fall back six steps, come forward three steps, then turn single to right.
	5-8	Face partners and circular hey, three changes, beginning with partner and ending in a line of four facing up. {*1st couple between 2nd man and 2nd woman who are on the ends of the line.*}
	9-10	Taking hands, all lead up a double and fall back a double.
	11-12	All lead up again three steps, then 1st couple drop partner's hand and cast down one place, 2nd couple, now in 1st place, acting as a pivot.

MR. ISAAC
Harvard Theatre Collection

MR. ISAAC'S MAGGOT

Highfill quoted John Essex, from *The Dancing Master* (second edition of 1731), in praise of Isaac: "The late Mr. Isaac 'had the Honour to teach and instruct our late most gracious Queen [Anne] when a young Princess, [in the 1670's], first gained character and afterwards supported that Reputation of being the Prime Master in England for 40 years together; He taught the first quality with Success and Applause and was justly stiled the Court Dancing Master." (xc, Highfill, 104)

Although there is no question of the Royal connections and that Isaac, a patron and colleague of John Weaver, was one of the most important teacher/choreographers of his period, he has defied persistent attempts to discover his name, national origin or details of his life. A dancing master named Isaac instructed the French court in English country dances in 1686 and "Les Folies d'Isac" was printed with diagrams in Feuillet's *Recuëil* of 1706 and is closely related to this dance. Although it seems reasonable to do so, without further proof we cannot confidently link the French references to the London master, especially since another master with a similar name, M. Le Sac, was active in the same period.

References: Marsh, 13-16; Highfill, 8: 103-104; Ralph, 116 and *passim*

Mr. Isaac's Magot.   Longways for as many as will.

The 1. man turn the 2. wo. with his right hand, and cast off below the 2. man, the 1. wo. turn the 2 man with her right hand, and cast off below the 2. wo...: The two men take hands and fall back, the two we. doing the same at the same time, all four meet and turn S. then go the whole Figure through, then all four hands abreast, and then lead through and cast off ...:

Note: *Each Strain is to be play'd twice over.*

DM I:10 (1698): 193
By permission of the British Library

NEWCASTLE

Square for four couples
3 x AA BB   MM ♩ = 112

Cecil Sharp, 1911
DM I: 1651-1690

Part I

A1	1-4	All take hands, forward a double and fall back a double.
	5-8	All set to partners, then to corners.
A2	1-8	Repeat A1.
B1	1-8	Partners arm right (1-2), men left hands-across once around **while** women skip clockwise around outside of set to places (3-8).
B2	1-8	Repeat B1, arming left, women right hands-across **while** men skip counter-clockwise.

Part II

A1	1-8	Partners side once (1-4), slow set and honor right (5-6), then pass each other by left shoulder to meet a new partner.
A2	1-8	With new partner, repeat A1.
B1	1-4	Present side couples lead to center {*inside hands*}, change hands and lead back, then make an arch.
	5-8	Present head couples cast off outside, go through nearest arch and return to place, skipping.
B2	1-8	Repeat B1, head couples leading in and out, side couples casting off.

Part III

A1	1-4	Present partners arm right.
	5-8	Present partners arm left once-and-a-half, then go forward to meet a new partner.
A2	1-4	New partners arm right.
	5-8	New partners arm left once-and-a-half, ending in two lines **up and down** the hall, women to their new partner's left.
B1	1-4	Taking hands along the sides, all fall back a double (1-2) and come forward a double (3-4).
	5-8	All turn single right (5-6), then pass through line changing places with opposite and forming new lines **across** the hall. {*Dancers on the inside of the old line go to the ends of the new line.*}
B2	1-8	Repeat B1, passing through to original places in the set, and honor partner.

NEWCASTLE

Simpson feels that the surviving tune is not the one which had some currency in Elizabethan days. He points out that wrenchings of accent are necessary to accomplish the fit of Playford's dance tune to a curious fragment of text found in the eighteenth-century Percy folio manuscript, a source of dubious authenticity itself.

"Came you not from Newcastle? Came yee not there away? Met yee not my true love, ryding on a bon[n]y bay? Why shold not I love my love? Why shold not my love love me? Why shold not I love my love, gallant hound sedelee?

And I have land att Newcastle, will buy both hose & shoone, and I haue Land att Durham, will feitch my hart to boon. Why shold...&c."

Although the town of Newcastle was an important source of coal for London, it is quite possible that this elegant dance was inspired by William, Duke of Newcastle, a royalist who remained in London and bent his interests towards the theatre during the interregnum.

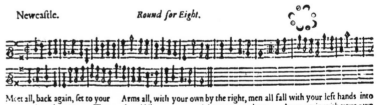

Newcastle.   *Round for Eight.*

Meet all, back again, set to your own, and to the next ∴ That again ∴

Arms all, with your own by the right, men all fall with your left hands into the middle, we. go roond then to your places ∴ Arms again with your own and we. left hands in, men go about them towards the left to your places ∴

Sides all with your own, and change places with them ∴ Sides with the next, and change places with them ∴

The first man and 3. Wo. take hands and meet, the first Wo. and 3. man lead out again, then holding up your hands, the other four cast off and come under your arms to their places ∴ the other four the like ∴

Arms all with your we. and change places ∴ Arms with the next and change places ∴ Now every man is with his own Wo. in the Co. place.

Fall back from each other, four and four a breft to each wall, turn and change places with your opposites ∴ Fall back from each other four and and four along the Room, turn S change places with your oppofite ∴ So each falls into his place as at first.

Courtesy of the Vaughan Williams Memorial Library

DM I:4 (1670): 16

References: Mendham and Cook, *Newcastle and Newcastle II*, (London: 1985); Simpson, 82-83; Dean-Smith, 65; Chappell, 339-40, 779

NONESUCH; or, A LA MODE DE FRANCE

Longways for four couples
9 x AB plus A   MM ♩= 108

Cecil Sharp, 1911
DM I: 1651-1728

Part I

A   1-8   Partners lead up a double and fall back a double. That again.

B   1-8   Partners set and turn single. That again.

Part II

A   1-4   With a light spring 1st couple set forward to meet (1), join hands, slip down between 2nd couple (2), then 1st man turn out to right to face 2nd man, **while** 1st woman turn to left to face 2nd woman (3-4).

         5-8   Taking both hands, 1st man push 2nd man up and out obliquely a double and draw back, **then** open out to face across the set, 1st man ending in second place and 2nd man in first place. **Meanwhile** 1st and 2nd women do the same.

B   1-8   The same four, now facing partners, fall back a double and move forward a double (1-4) and turn partners two-hands (5-8).

AB x 4   Repeat II four more times, the couple in top place joining in when the leading couple starts from third place. The original bottom couple ends in top place and becomes 1st couple.

Part III

A   1-4   Partners half side {*left shoulder*} across the set, then turn single right.

         5-8   Partners half side {*right shoulder*} back to place and turn single right.

B   1   In top place, the new 1st man, with a light spring, move to the center of the set facing down.

         2   His partner, the new 1st woman, do the same, ending facing up, facing partner.

         3-8   In sequence, each couple do the same, first the man, then the woman.

Part IV

A   1-8   Partners arm right, then left.

B   1-4   Partners facing, all go four slips out to right and back into line.

         5-8   Continuing the movement, all go four slips out to left and back.

Part V

A   1-8   First man move out to place on the side of the set with a light spring (1). His partner the same (2), and the rest the same, in sequence as in Part III, B 3-8.

BA   1-16   Progressive hey with hands: 1st couple begin by taking right hands, everyone else face up and begin when 1st man or woman reaches them. All move completely around the set to finish where they began the hey.

THE PALACE OF THE KING OF ENGLAND, CALLED NONESUCH

Hoefnagel's engraving of 1582, illustrated in *Shakespeare's England,* 1: 207

None such   *Longwayes for eight*   ♪♪♪♪

Lead up forwards and back _∙_. That again, set and turn single, that again _∙_. First Cu. flip just between the 2. Cu. turn your faces to them, put them back by both hands, and halfe turn them, put them back, and set them as they were, turn your own in the 2. place _∶_. Do thus to the last. _∙_

Sides all that again, set and turn S. that again _∙_. First man flip before, and stand with his face downwards, the Wo. flip before him and stand faces to your own, the 2. Cu. as much, the third Cu. as much, the last Cu. as much _∶_.

Arms all as you stand, that again, flip all to the left hand, and back to your places, then as much to the right hand _∙_. first man flip to the left hand, and stand, the Wo. as much to her left hand, the 2. Cu. as much, third as much, fourth as much, _∶_. Then the single Hey, all handing down, and come up on your own side.

All a Mode de France   *Longwayes for as many as will*   ♪♪♪♪

Lead up all a D. and back, this again _∶_. Set and turn singl, this again _∶_.

First Cu. meet, take both hands, and fall in between the 2. Cu. each of you turn your face towards them, and put them back, you meet the two men and We. all four fall back, and turn your Woman, so to all.

Sides all to the right and left, set and turn S. this again _∙_. Then fall all into one File, each Wo. behind her own man ○) ○) ○) ○ _∙_) _∶_. Then armes all with your own by the right and left, and remain in the same Figure, then men fall off to the right, and We. to the left hand, fall back into the same Figure, then men to the left, and We. to the right, and back again into the same Figure, then the first man fall into his first place, and his Wo. the like, so the rest one after another, then the first man takes his Wo. by the hand, his left hand to the 2. Woman, the right to the 3. and so forward, his Woman doing the like on the other side, untill you all meet again in your places.

DM I:2 (1662): 71, 3
By permission of The Huntington Library, San Marino, California

NONESUCH and A LA MODE DE FRANCE

This dance is described twice in *The Dancing Master*, once as "Nonesuch" (1651-1665) and again as "A la Mode de France" with virtually the same tune (1651-1728).

The second title was derived from a ballad probably written in 1642-3 while the Queen was in Holland raising money and troops to support Charles I. Called "The French Report" it is set in the conventionalized "foreigner's accent" as is the song to "Lilli Burlero." (See page 63) The first verse is:

Me have of late been in England, vere me have seen much sport
De raising of de Parliament, have quite pull'd down de Court.
De King and Queen dey seperate, and rule in Ignorance,
Pray judge ye Gentlemen, if dis, be *a la mode de France*. *(Rump (1662), I: 27)*

Since torn down itself, Nonesuch was built in 1538 by Henry VIII, over the demolished property of the village of Cuddington, near Epsom Wells in Sussex, to be the most ostentatious hunting lodge ever made. At the very end of her life, Elizabeth I visited Nonesuch, as a guest of Lord Lumley, son-in-law of the Earl of Arundel, and it was reported that "there is much dancing of country dances in the privy chamber at Nonesuch, before the Queen's majesty, who is exceedingly pleased there with."

The pages shown here are both from the second edition of *The Dancing Master* (1662), both utilise the old violin clef, with G on the bottom line. With the exception of a few passing notes, the tunes are identical, written on the same keynote of D. It appears that the editors simply were not sure how the tune should sound. In the first two editions (1651-1652), "Nonesuch" has no key signature, but in the third edition (1665), "Nonesuch" was barred, rescored with the modern G clef and and two sharps added, converting the tune to the major mode. Then it was dropped. "A La Mode" was in the major from the beginning, but avoids the third note of the scale and has only one sharp. This was not caught until the seventeenth edition (1721), when C# was finally added to conform to proper music notation.

Although described differently, the dance figures are the same.

References: Charles W. Warren, "Music at Nonesuch," *Musical Quarterly* 54/1 (1968): 47-57; Simpson, 516-17; Dean-Smith, 27, 42; Chappell, 444-45

THE NORTHDOWN WALTZ

Duple minor longways
AA B C ad lib   MM ♩ = 120

A. Simons, 1971
Goulding & Cos. Collection (Goulding), 1820

A1   1-4   1st corners join right hands, balance forward and back, then change places.
      5-8   2nd corners the same.
A2   1-8   Repeat A1 to places.
B   1-8   1st couple take inside hands, lead down center and lead back to 2nd place, 2nd couple moving up.
C   1-8   In ballroom position, 1st and 2nd couples waltz completely around each other counter-clockwise, ending in progressed places.

THE NORTHDOWN WALTZ

The North Downs are a long ridge of hills running southwest from Rochester to Dover in Kent.

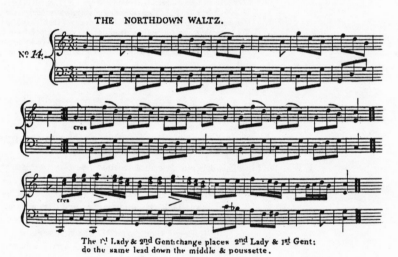

THE NORTHDOWN WALTZ.

Nº 14.

The 1st Lady & 2nd Gent: change places 2nd Lady & 1st Gent:
do the same lead down the middle & poussette.

Goulding & Cos. Collection (Goulding), 1820, no. 14
Courtesy of the Kidson Collection, Mitchell Library, Glasgow

THE OLD MOLE
{See opposite page}

The "old mole" probably refers an old artificial harbor created from massive stone piers. Pepys noted on February 1, 1661 that "by a great storm and tempest the mole of Algiers is broken down, and many of their ships sunk into the mole." However, the image and connotation of a grey, earth-burrowing creature may also have been intended, referring to some current political intrigue.

THE OLD MOLE

The Old Mole.   *Longways for six.*   ⊙⊙⊙
                                                      〉〉〉

Lead up a D. forwards and back, set and turn S. ፡ That again ፡ All a D. to the left hand, back again, set and turn S. ፡ As much to the right ፡ First man and last wo. meet a D. back again, meet again and change places ፡ First wo. and last man as much ፡ The second man as much with his own ፡

The two first we. hands, and the two last men hands, lead forwards and back to the odd one against them, let the odd ones go under your arms. Do this Change ፡ Over to the place where you began it ፡ Then first and last change as before to your places ፡

All the men hands, and all the we. hands, meet all forwards and back the first and last, last on each side turn each other, the 2. turning his own. Sides where you turned, and turn your own ፡ Men the S, Hey ፡ we. as much ፡ The D. Hey thrice over ፡ Cast off all and come to your places. That again.

DM I:7 (1686): 77
Courtesy of the Vaughan Williams Memorial Library

References: Dean-Smith, 15

THE OLD MOLE

Longways for three couples

22 x A   MM ♩. = 120

Cecil Sharp, 1912
DM I: 1651-1686

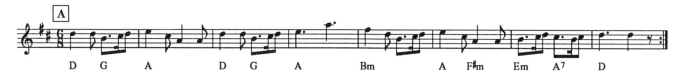

Part I

A1   1-4   Partners lead up a double and fall back a double.

       5-8   Set and turn single.

A2   1-8   Repeat A1.

A3   1-4   All face men's wall, forward a double, fall back a double and face partner.

       5-8   Partners set and turn single.

A4   1-8   Repeat A3 towards the women's wall.

Part II

A1   1-8   1st man and 3rd woman forward a double to meet, fall back to place (1-4),
              then change places, passing right shoulders (5-8).

A2   1-8   1st woman and 3rd man the same.

A3   1-8   2nd couple the same.

Part III

A1   1-4   2nd and 3rd women take inside hands, forward a double towards 3rd man,
              and fall back **while** 1st and 2nd men do the same toward the 1st woman.

       5-8   2nd and 3rd women make an arch and cross to the women's side, 3rd man crossing to the men's side
              through the arch **while** the 1st and 2nd men make an arch and cross, 1st woman crossing through
              their arch.

A2   1-8   Repeat A1, 2nd and 3rd men and 1st and 2nd women making arches, 3rd woman and 1st man going
              through them.

A3&4   Repeat A1 and 2 back to places at beginning of Part III.

Part IV

A1   1-8   Repeating Part II, 1st man and 3rd woman forward a double to meet and fall back (1-4),
              then change places, passing right shoulders (5-8).

A2   1-8   1st woman and 3rd man the same.

A3   1-8   2nd couple the same. {*All now in original places.*}

Part V

A1   1-2   Men take hands and forward a double **while** women the same.

       3-4   1st and 3rd men, 1st and 3rd women fall back a double.

       5-8   1st and 3rd men turn two-hands **while** 1st and 3rd women the same **and** 2nd couple the same.

A2   1-4   1st and 3rd men side **while** 1st and 3rd women side **and** 2nd couple side with each other.

       5-8   Partners turn two-hands.

Part VI   {*Use a skip step throughout this section.*}

A1   1-8   Men hey for three, 1st man passing right shoulder to start.

A2   1-8   Women the same.

A3&4   Circular hey for six twice around, 1st couple passing right shoulder to begin.

A5   1-4   1st man cast down to the bottom of set, followed by the 2nd and 3rd men
              while 1st woman the same followed by 2nd and 3rd women.

       5-8   Repeat 1-4, 1st couple casting back to top, followed by others.

A6   1-8   Repeat A5.

ONCE A NIGHT
to the tune of YE SOCIAL POWERS

Longways for three couples

3 x AA BB C   MM ♩. = 116

W. S. Porter, 1931

Twenty Four Country Dances (Thompson), d: 1774, m: 1778

A1   1-4   1st couple cast down to middle place, 2nd couple moving up on bars 3-4.

        5-8   1st and 3rd couples circle four-hands once around.

A2   1-4   1st couple cast up to the top, 2nd couple moving down on bars 3-4.

        5-8   1st and 2nd couple circle four-hands once around.

B1   1-8   Hey on opposite side, skipping.

B2   1-8   Hey on own side, skipping.

C   1-8   1st couple lead down center to the bottom, and cast up around 3rd couple into middle place
           2nd couple moving up; then 1st couple lead to the top and cast down to bottom,
           3rd couple moving up.

Repeat dance twice more.

YE SOCIAL POWERS

This chorus is the finale of Charles Dibdin's dialogue opera, *Lionel and Clarissa (1768)*.

Come now all ye Social Pow'rs, Shed your influence o'er us;
Crown with bliss the present hour, Enliven those before us:
  Bring the flask, the music bring, Joys shall quickly find us;
  Come let's laugh, and drink, and sing, and cast our cares behind us.

Friendship with thy Pow'r divine, brighten all our features;
What but friendship, love, and wine, can make us happy creatures.
  Bring the flask, the music bring...

Love, thy Godhead we adore, source of generous passion;
Nor will we ever bow before, those idols wealth and fashion.
  Bring the flask, the music bring...

Why should we be dull or sad, since on earth we moulder.
The grave, the gay, the good, the bad, they every day grow older.
  Bring the flask, the music bring...

Then since time will steal away, spite of all our sorrow;
Heighten every joy today, and never mind tomorrow.
  Bring the flask, the music bring...

From a songsheet in the Marshall Collection, at the Houghton Library, Harvard University.

Thompson's Compleat Collection, vol. 4 (1780): 16, 68
By permission of the British Library

Caft off & hands 4 round with the 3.d Cu: .;. caft up & hands 4 round at top .;. figure down contrary fides then on your own fides .;. lead down 2 Cu. & caft up lead thro' the top & caft up .;.

Caft off 2.d Cu: and fet caft off 3.d Cu: & fet .;. fame up again .;. crofs over two Cu: lead up to the top, caft off & hands 4 round at bottom .;. fet contrary Corners Right and Left at top .;.

ORANGES AND LEMONS

Square for four couples
3 x AA BB   MM ♩ = 88

Cecil Sharp, 1911
DM I: 1665-1690

Part I

AA	1-8	All forward a double and fall back a double. That again.
B1	1-2	Men: honor partners (1), honor corners (2).
	3-6	Men circle four-hands clockwise half-way and fall into opposite place.
	7-8	Women: honor men on left (7), honor men on right (8);
	9-12	Women circle four-hands clockwise half-way and fall into opposite place beside partner.
B2	1-12	Repeat B1, but with circles going counter-clockwise.

Part II

AA	1-8	Partners side twice.
B1	1	Partners take right hands, raise them and release with a slow set to the right.
	2	Partners take left hands, raise them and release with a slow set to the left.
	3-6	Right-and-left, two changes, beginning with partners.
	7-12	Repeat B1, 1-6.
B2	1-12	Repeat B1 to place.

Part III

AA	1-8	Partners arm right, then arm left, ending in diagonal lines with head couples facing couples on their left. {*Head men and side women will be on the ends of the lines.*}
B1	1-2	All honor opposite (1); honor partner (2).
	3-6	With opposite couple, circle four-hands half-way; head men drop hands with side women to open in a line on the other diagonal, facing line formed by the other couples.
	7-12	Repeat 1-6.
B2	1-12	Repeat B1 to place.

{*This is a stately dance.*}

ORANGES AND LEMONS

The nursery rhyme now associated with this title does not fit the sophisticated tune which accompanies this courtly dance, but the two may share common ancestry in the old singing game.

'Oranges and lemons,' say the bells of St. Clements.
'You owe me five farthings,' say the bells of St. Martin's.
'When will you pay me?' say the bells of Old Bailey.
'When I grow rich,' say the bells of Shoreditch.
'When will that be?' say the bells of Stepney.
'I'm sure I don't know,' says the great bell at Bow.
　　Here comes a candle to light you to bed,
　　Here comes a chopper to chop off your head.
The game is played in a fashion similar to "London Bridge." The makers of the arch determine in secret which shall be an 'orange' and which a 'lemon.' Each captive chooses a side, and when all sides are chosen, a tug of war ensues. Both St. Clement Eastcheap and St. Clement Danes claim to be the first church in question, both then near the docks where Spanish fruit was sold.

References: Iona and Peter Opie, ed. *The Oxford Dictionary of Nursery Rhymes* (London: Oxford University Press, 1951), 337-39; *Michelin "Green Guide" London* (London: Michelin Tyre, 1985): 53, 144

Oranges and Limons.　　*A Figure Dance for eight, thus:*

Meet all and fall back, that again ⁞ ⁞ Men honour all to your own we. then honour to the contrary, men meet in & take hands an I go half round and fall into your co. places ⁞ Then we. honour to your left hand, and then to your right, we. meet in & take hands and go half round & fall into your co. places by your men ⁞ do all this back again till you come all into your own places.

Sides all with your own ⁞ That again ⁞ Men and we give right hands to your own, and then left, change places with your own then change with the next ⁞ And then give right hands to the next, and then left, then change places, and then change with the next, and meet your own ⁞ Do this back again till you come into your places.

Arms all with your own ⁞ That again ⁞ The first and second cu. and the third and last cu. honour to each other, then honour to your own, the first and second cu. take hands and go half round, and the third and last cu. take hands and go half round ⁞ Then the first and last cu. honour, and the second and third cu. honour to each other, and then honour to your own, the first and last cu. take hands and go half round, and second and third cu. take hands and go half round all at one time ⁞ Do this back again till you come into your own places.

DM I:7 (1686): 155
Courtesy of the Vaughan Williams Memorial Library

ORLEANS BAFFLED

Triple minor longways
A ad lib   MM $\downarrow$ = 108

Cecil Sharp, 1916
DM II: 1710-1728

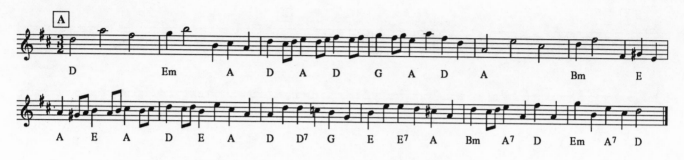

A   1-2   1st couple cast down to second place, 2nd couple moving up.
     3-4   1st and 3rd couples poussette half-way clockwise, 1st man pushing.
     5-6   1st couple cast up to second place, 3rd couple moving down.
     7-8   1st and 2nd couples poussette half-way clockwise, 1st man pulling.
     9   1st corners change places.
     10   2nd corners change places.
     11-12 1st couple face up, 2nd couple down: circular hey, three changes.

ORLEANS BAFFLED

In the first decade of the eighteenth century, the French royal family was the house of Orleans and England and all Europe was deeply involved in the War of Spanish Succession. Philippe, Duc d'Orleans (1674-1723), held military command in Spain in 1707 and 1708. In 1715 he became the powerful regent of France during the minority of Louis XV. A patron of the arts and of women, one of the Duke's most notable contributions to the welfare of Paris was to establish public balls at the Opera. This dance title may refer to him.

The shuttling movement of the pousette is a graphic image of a "baffle" in the title, although the reference may have been to indecision or impotence of action.

Note : *The first Strain is to be play'd twice, and the last but once.*

The first couple cast off and draw Hands below the third couple, then cast up again and draw Hands above the second couple, then the first man change places with the second woman, and the first woman do the same with the second man, then Right and Left till the first couple comes into the second couples place.

DM II:1 (1710): 113
By permission of the Director of Manchester Public Libraries

PARSON'S FAREWELL

{See oppposite page}

This tune was an instrumental piece known as *Bourrée* in Europe in the first half of the seventeenth century. No conclusive identification of the English title has yet been made, except the explanation that a "farewell" was often associated with a death, natural or otherwise, and took the form of a song, "...being the last will and testament" of the deceased. These farewells also appeared as didactic or sensationalist broadsides sold at the time of public executions. (See page 49)

References: Dean-Smith, 9

Meet all, four flips to the left hand ⁚   Men rise once, we. once, rise all 4 times, turn each others wo. ⁚
Back all, four flips to the right hand ⁚   we. rise once, men once, rise all 3 times, turn each others wo. ⁚

Meet all, lead each others wo. a D. to the left hand ⁚ Change hands, meet again, take your own we. and to your places ⁚   Men meet, cross right hands, then left pass over, turn each others wo. with your right hand, cross to your place again, and turn your own ⁚ We. as much with the Co. hands ⁚

Take your own by both hands, and meet with four flips, take the co. we. four flips to the left hand ⁚ Meet again, take ur own, and to your places ⁚   Turn your own with your right hands, men cross and go all the S. Hay to the Co. fide, and turn your own ⁚ Turn your own with the left hand, we. cross, go the S. Hay to your places, and turn your own ⁚

DM I:7 (1686): 21
Courtesy of the Vaughan Williams Memorial Library

PARSON'S FAREWELL

Cecil Sharp, 1911
DM I: 1651-1690

Two couples, facing
3 x A BB   MM ♩ = 116

Part I

A   1-4   All forward a double to meet (1-2), four slips to their own left (3-4).

   5-8   All fall back a double (5-6), and four slips right to places (7-8).

B1   1-2   Men nod to each other with a little rise on halftoe (1); women the same (2).

   3-4   All rise and nod to opposite, opposite's partner, own partner in sequence.

   5-8   Turn opposite two-hands, skipping.

B2   1-8   Repeat B1, women rising first.

Part II

A   1-4   All forward a double to meet (1-2), men lead opposites away from set (3-4).

   5-8   Changing hands, opposites lead back (5-6); taking right hands, partners fall back a double to places (7-8).

B1   1   All of B skipping: men forward to meet and take right hands.

   2   Men change hands.

   3-4   Men pull by the left, and turn opposite women right-hand once around.

   5-8   Men repeat 1-4 back to place.

B2   1   Women forward to meet and take left hands.

   2   Women change hands.

   3-4   Women pull by the right and turn opposite men left-hand once around.

   5-8   Women repeat 1-4 back to place.

Part III

A   1-2   Partners take two-hands and go four slips to center.

   3-6   Opposites take two-hands and go four slips away from set and four slips back.

   7-8   Men take partners by right-hand and fall back a double.

B1   1-2   All of B skipping: Partners turn right-hand once around.

   3-4   Men change places by right shoulder and turn to the right to face partner across the set.

   5-6   All circular hey, two changes, beginning with partner.

   7-8   Partners turn two-hands half-way.

B2   1-2   Partners turn left-hand once around.

   3-4   Women change places by left shoulder and turn to the left to face partner across the set.

   5-6   All circular hey, two changes, beginning with partner.

   7-8   Partners turn two-hands half-way.

"The Duke of Albemarle's Farewell"
Woodcut from Rollins, Pepys Ballads, 3: 308

THE PHOENIX

Longways for four couples
8 x AA BB   MM ♩ = 116

Cecil Sharp, 1912
d: DM I: 1670-1698

Part I *{Use running step throughout the dance.}*
AA   Partners lead up a double and fall back a double. That again.
BB   Partners set and turn single. That again.

Part II
A   1st man, followed by other men, cross over and go down the set behind the women, stopping to
     stand behind the 4th woman, the others behind the other women, the women turning to face
     them on bar 4.
A   Each man take the woman in front of him two-hands, put her back a double towards the men's
     wall, and pull her forward a double to place.
BB   All balance back and forward (1-2), then change places with opposite (3-4). That again.
AABB   Repeat AABB above, women crossing behind the men, and women pushing and pulling men.

Part III
A   4th couple, now at top of set, cross by right shoulder and move down center to bottom place.
     Meanwhile the others move up sides to the top and go down center following 4th couple and
     invert the set: 3rd couple do not cross, 2nd couple cross, 1st couple do not cross.
A   Circle eight-hands once around.
BB   Partners set and turn single. That again.

Part IV
A   Each man turn woman on his right two-hands.
A   Men circle four-hands once around, clockwise.
B1   Women forward a double to center (1-2), fall
     back a double turning single (3-4).
B2   Men the same.
A   Partners turn two-hands.
A   Women circle four-hands once around,
     clockwise.
BB   Repeat Part IV, B1&2, men forward
     a double to center first.

Part V
AA   Each line straight hey for four.
BB   Partners set and turn single. That again.

Part VI
A   4th couple, now at the bottom of the set,
     cross and, followed by 3rd couple
     not crossing, 2nd couple crossing,
     and 1st couple not crossing, move up
     the center to top place.
A   4th couple cast to the bottom,
     followed by the other couples,
     inverting the set.
BB   Partners set and turn single. That again.

THE PHOENIX

The great fire of London destroyed most of the old city in 1666. Surely
this title is related to that catastrophe. Ships were named and several
plays were written on the theme of "The Phoenix," the mythical bird which
arose recreated from its own ashes.

The Phœnix.   *Longways for eight.*

Lead up all a D. forwards and back .•. That again ·¦·   Set and turn S. •. That again ·¦·
First man go down on the outside of the wo. to the laſt, the reſt following.   Back all, change places .•. That again ·¦·
Take every man a wo. by both hands .•. Put the we, a D. backward and
forward ·¦·
Womens go down and do as the men did ·¦·   Back and change places as before.
Firſt Cu. croſs over and go to the lower end, the ſecond Cu. following and   Set and turn S. •. That again ·¦·
not croſs, the third Cu. croſs and follow, the fourth not croſs, take hands
all in a ring .•. Go all round ·¦·
Turn the contrary wo, .•. men hands and go round ·¦·   We. meet and turn S. •. men as much ·¦·
Turn your own .•. We. hands and go round ·¦·   Men meet and turn S. •. We. as much ·¦·
Four on each ſide the ſingle Hey ·¦·   Set and turn S. •. That again ·¦·
As before, four croſs, and four not croſs .•. Lead up, caſt off, and come   Set and turn S. •. That again ·¦·
to your places ·¦·

Courtesy of the Vaughan Williams Memorial Library   *DM I:7 (1686): 113*

84

PICKING UP STICKS
to the tune of LAVENA

Longways for three couples
17 X A   MM ♩.= 120

Cecil Sharp, 1916
d: DM I: 1651-1698, m: DM: I: 1651

Dm   A⁷   Dm   B♭   A⁷   Dm   Gm   C⁷   F   C   Dm   Gm   A⁷   Dm

Part I

A1   1-8   Partners lead up a double and fall back a double. That again.

A2   1-4   1st man change places with middle dancer opposite, then with last dancer on his own side.

      5-8   All lead up a double and fall back a double.

A3   1-8   1st woman change twice as 1st man did, then all lead up a double and fall back a double.

A4   1-8   2nd woman, now at top, the same.

A5   1-8   2nd man, now at top, the same.

A6   1-8   3rd man, now at top, the same.

A7   1-8   3rd woman, now at top, the same, ending with all in original place.

Part II

A1   1-8   Partners side twice.

A2   1-2   1st couple take both hands and go four slips down between 2nd couple
           while they move four slips up outside to the top.

      3-4   Repeat 1-2, 2nd couple slipping down inside, 1st up outside.

      5-8   Repeat 1-4.
           Meanwhile 3rd couple face, cross and skip around outside of set, cross again at the top
           and back down to place (A2 1-8).

A3   1-8   3rd and 2nd couples repeat movement, 3rd couple slipping up inside, 2nd couple down outside **while**
           1st couple cross and skip around set.

Part III

A1   1-8   Partners arm right, then left.

A2-4   1-24   Men's sheepskin hey.

A5-7   1-24   Women's sheepskin hey.

PICKING UP STICKS

Dean-Smith notes that "Picking of sticks" is a variant of an older tune called "Whoop, do me no harm," a salacious song which Chappell could not bring himself to print. Except for the opening measures, the concordance is hard to see. Sharp changed the dance title to the more graphic "Picking up sticks," and changed the music to "Lavena" for this dance. Elsie Whiteman of the Benacre Band introduced the tune of "Kitty Magee" (O'Neill #716, 133), which Phil Merrill used to play for the third part of the dance.

Sharp's version of "Lavena" is from *The English Dancing Master* (1651). All later editions have a distinct variant as can be seen in the illustration on the right. The B strain may be an ancestor of the traditional American children's singing game, "Pop goes the Weasel."

Although it is quite different from the hey described in "The Three Sheepskins" (DM I: 1698-1728), the movement in the last figure, which is described in detail in the glossary has become known as the "sheepskin hey."

References: Simpson, 777-80; Dean-Smith, 14, 51; Chappell, 208

Picking of Sticks   *Longways for six.*   ⊙⊙⊙ ⟩⟩⟩

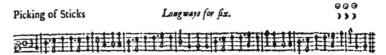

Lead up a D. forwards and back ⁞. That again ⁞. First man change places with the 2. wo. then with the last man ⁞. Lead up as before, then the wo. change as the man did, every co. doing thus.

Sides all ⁞. That again ⁞. First cu. flip down between the 2. they flipping up, then the 2. flip down and the first up ⁞. All this again, the last cu. crossing over below, go up and cross above, fall to your places ⁞. Then the four last flip, and first cu. cross about ⁞.

Arms all ⁞. That again ⁞. The we. standing still, men going the Hey between them, the last man going about the middle wo. Do this three times over, then go quite round all the we. to your places ⁞. We. as much ⁞.

DM I:8 (1690): 89

Lavena, or (The Passionate Lover.)   *Longways for as many as will.*   ⊙⊙⊙⊙ ⟩⟩⟩⟩

Lead up all a D. forwards and back, set and turn S. ⁞. That again ⁞. The first Cu. go down between the 2. cast off and come to your places on the outside of the 2. turn your own, fall into the 2. place again ⁞. As much to the 3. place, and so to the last, the rest following.

Sides all, set and turn S. ⁞. That again ⁞. First Cu. go down on the outside each on the 2. back again, fall into the 2 place, and turn your own ⁞. Do this to the last the rest following and doing the like.

Arms all, set and turn S. ⁞. That again ⁞. First Cu. cast off, fall into the 2. place come up between the 2. cast off again, fall into the 2. place, turn your own ⁞. Do this to the last the rest following.

PORTSMOUTH

Duple minor longways
AA B ad lib   MM $\downarrow$ = 100

Cecil Sharp, 1922
DM I: 1670-1698

G   C   G C D D⁷ G   C   G D⁷ G

G D⁷ G   Em Am   Am D⁷ G   C   G D⁷ G

A1   1-8   1st man cross diagonally down center and hey for three with the two women, passing 2nd woman right shoulder, and ending in his original place.

A2   1-8   1st woman the same with the two men, passing 2nd man left shoulder and ending in her original place.

B   1-4   1st couple half figure-eight through 2nd couple, then change places, passing right shoulder.

    5-8   All circular hey, three changes, beginning with partner.

PORTSMOUTH

This dance was probably originally named in honor of the city of Portsmouth which, from the 1540's, was the home of the Royal Navy. It was continually in the news with arrivals and departures of the fleet and of prominent political figures, royalty, and official shipping. In the 1660's, Charles II strengthened the fortress at the harbor mouth, making it the strongest in Britain.

Shortly after the dance was published, however, the title may have taken on a new meaning. Louise Renée de Kéroualle came to London in 1670 as maid of honour to Charles II's sister. Soon established as the King's mistress, she was naturalized and created Duchess of Portsmouth in 1673. Over the next two decades, both she and their son, made Duke of Richmond as an infant (see page 91), earned considerable dislike from the English people.

Several street ballads about the Duchess of Portsmouth were in circulation, one representing dialogue between her and Nell Gwyn, another of the King's favorites, on the supposed intention of the former to retire to France with the jewels and other treasures she had acquired. It is written to the tune of "Tom the Taylor" which we have not been able to find, but fits the tune of "Portsmouth" well. Chappell quotes the first verse:

> I prithee, Portsmouth, tell me plain
>   Without dissimulation,
> When dost thou home return again,
>   And leave this English naton?
> Your youthful days are past and gone,
>   You plainly may perceive it,
> Winter of age is coming on,
>   'Tis true - you may believe it.

Reference: Chappell, 325, 605

DM I:14 (1709): 243
Courtesy of the Vaughan Williams Memorial Library

Louise, Duchess of Portsmouth

Courtesy of the Print Collection, The Lewis Walpole Library, Yale University

The first men Hey with the first and second woman, the first woman do the same with the first and second man; then the first couple cross over and Figure In; then right and left quite round.

PRINCE WILLIAM

Longways for three couples
6 x AA BB   MM ♩= 108

Pat Shaw, 1960
Compleat Country Dancing-Master (Walsh), 1731

Part I

A1	1-8	Hey on opposite side, 1st couple crossing through the middle place to begin.
A2	1-8	Hey on own side, 1st couple crossing again through middle place.
B1	1-4	1st couple cross and go down outside to middle place, 2nd couple moving up on bars 3-4.
	5-8	1st couple turn two-hands once-and-a-half.
B2	1-8	2nd couple repeat B1, 1st couple moving up.

Part II

A1	1-4	1st man move down center ahead of his partner and turn 3rd woman right-hand **while** 1st woman turn 2nd man right-hand **and** 2nd woman move up to top place.
	5-8	1st couple turn left-hand in center.
A2	1-4	1st man turn 2nd woman right-hand, 1st woman turn 3rd man right-hand.
	5-8	1st couple turn left-hand in center and end facing women's wall, woman on partner's right.
B1	1-8	1st couple lead between women, cast around and back to middle place and turn two-hands, opening to face men's wall, woman on partner's right.
B2	1-8	1st couple lead between the men, cast around and back to middle, turn two-hands while moving down into bottom place, 3rd couple casting up.

Repeat dance twice more.

PRINCE WILLIAM

Prince William, A New Dance for his Majesty's Birthday, a ballroom dance for a couple, was choreographed in 1721 by L'Abbé, and probably named in honor of William Augustus, Duke of Cumberland, the infant son of George II, then Prince of Wales. The tune was called "Rigodon" and soon appeared with a country dance which was reprinted several times.

William Hogarth's portrait of the youthful Duke (1721-1765) was painted in 1732. Identified by his sash, he stands with his sisters before the fireplace, watching his playmates enact Dryden's *The Conquest of Mexico*. This martial subject was certainly suitable for a young man who was to gain fame and notoriety as "the butcher" in his zealous management of the defeat and disarming of the Scottish Jacobites in the rebellion of 1745-1746!

Compleat Country Dancing Master (Walsh, 1731): 2
By permission of The Colonial Williamsburg Foundation

Courtesy of the Print Collection, The Lewis Walpole Library, Yale University

87

PRINCE WILLIAM OF GLO'S'TER'S WALTZ

Duple minor longways

AA B C ad lib   MM ♩ = 120

Pat Woods, 1958

Preston's Twenty Four Country Dances (Preston), 1801

A1	1-8	1st corners set forward right and left, turn single to right back to places, then change places passing right shoulders.
A2	1-8	2nd corners the same.
B	1-8	Taking ballroom position, couples waltz around each other counter-clockwise, ending in lines, proper.
C	1-8	1st and 2nd couples right hands-across once around, and left hands-across back.

THE FAIR PRINCE   HIS CONSORT

Prince Wm of Glos'ter's Waltz.

1st Lady set to the 2d Gent: & change places
1st Gent: set to the 2d Lady & change places
1st & 2d Cu: Poussette right & left quite round

Preston's Twenty Four Country Dances (Preston, 1801): 192

Courtesy of William Litchman, Dance-Away Library, Albuquerque, New Mexico

William IV, Prince William Frederick of Gloucester (1765-1837), was the third son of George III. He succeeded George IV in 1830, and in turn was succeeded in 1837 by Victoria, the daughter of his brother, Edward, Duke of Kent (see page 30).

Courtesy of the Print Collection, The Lewis Walpole Library, Yale University

THE QUEEN'S JIG

Duple minor longways
AA BB ad lib   MM ♩. = 104

Cecil Sharp, 1922
DM I: 1701-1728

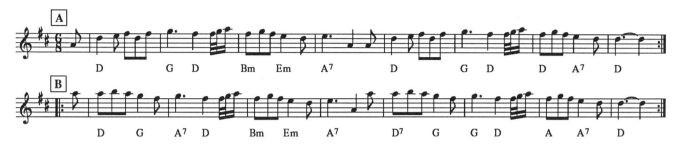

D		G	D	Bm	Em	A⁷		D		G	D	D	A⁷	D

D		G	A⁷	D	Bm	Em	A⁷		D⁷	G	G	D	A	A⁷	D

A1	1-8	1st corners side, then set and turn single.
A2	1-8	2nd corners repeat A1.
B1	1-2	1st corners change places.
	3-4	2nd corners change places.
	5-8	Partners face, balance back, and change places.
B2	1-6	All right hands-across.
	7-8	All turn single.

THE QUEEN'S JIG

It is not clear which Queen this title refers to as Mary died in 1694 and Anne did not succeed until 1702. The tune is closely related to John Jackson's catch, "Begone, old care, I prithee be gone from me."

This woodcut, and another using the same design, appears on several of the ballads in Pepys' collection. It is usually intended to be Queen Mary, wife of William III.

The fairly simple longways dance reappeared with the same tune as "Princess of Hesse's Jigg" in a mid-century publication of John Walsh, and as "London Bridge" and "The Foxhunter's Jig" with different tunes.

References: Chappell, 689-90; Rollins, *Pepys Ballads*, 5: 134

DM I:11 (1701): 260
Dundee District Libraries, Wighton Collection

RAMSGATE ASSEMBLY

Longways for three couples

3 x AA BB CC   MM ♩ = 120

A. Simons, 1972
Budd, *Twenty-fifth Book* (Preston), 1795

A1	1-8	1st and 2nd couples set twice, then half right-and-left.
A2	1-8	Repeat A1, facing neighbors.
B1	1-8	1st couple lead down center and back, then cast down to second place, 2nd couple moving up.
B2	1-4	All take right hands with partner, balance forward, back and change places.
	5-8	Repeat B2, 1-4 with left hands.
C1	1-4	1st man turn 3rd woman right-hand **while** 1st woman turn 2nd man right-hand
	5-8	1st couple turn left-hand.
C2	1-8	1st man turn 2nd woman right-hand **while** 1st woman turn 3rd man right-hand, then 1st couple turn two-hands moving down center to bottom place, 3rd couple casting up to middle place.

Repeat dance twice more.

RAMSGATE ASSEMBLY

Kentish towns lying on the point of land north of Dover, Ramsgate and Margate developed as resorts with the vogue for sea bathing at the very end of the eighteenth century. Enterprising dancing masters, innkeepers, or others who could obtain large halls sponsored commercial public dances or assemblies for daytime and evening entertainment during the holiday season.

1st & 2d Cu: fet & half right & left ∺ fet & half right & left back again ∺ lead down the middle up again ∺ Allemande ∺ turn opposite corners ∺

Budd, Twenty-fifth Book (Preston), 1795: 8-9

MR. LANE'S MAGGOT

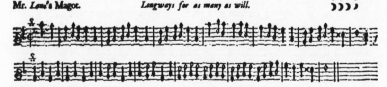

Mr. *Lane's Magot.*   *Longways for as many as will.*   ◔◔◔◔ 〉〉〉〉

A SONG made by Mr. Tho. D'Urfey upon a new Country Dance at Richmond called, Mr. Lane's Magot, and sung to the foregoing tune.

The 1. cu. caſt off and lead through the 3. cu. then caſt off and leap up through both cu and caſt off into the 2. cu. place; the 1. man being in the 2. man's place turn the 1. wo. with the right hand, and fall into their own places, the 1. wo. being in the 2. wo. place turn the 1. man, and ſo fall into their own places, then all four lead up abreaſt, and caſt off into the 2. cu. place.

S Trike up drowſie Gut-Scrapers ;
Gallants, be ready
Each with his Lady ;
Foot it about
Till the Night be run out ;
Let no one's Humour pall :
Brisk Lads, now cut your Capers ;
Put your Legs to't,
And ſhew you can do't ;
Frisk, frisk it away
Till break of Day,
And hey for *Richmond* Ball !
Fortune-biters,
Hags, Bum-fighters,

Nymphs of the Woods,
And ſtale City-Goods ;
Ye Cherubins
And Seraphins,
Ye Caravans
And Haradans,
In Order all advance :
Twittenham Loobies,
Thiſtleworth Boobies,
Wits of the Town,
And Beaus that have none ;
Ye *Jacobites* as ſharp as Finn,
Ye *Monſieurs*, and ye *Sooterkins* ;
I'll teach you all the Dance.

Note : *Each Strain is to be played twice over ; likewiſe in the following SONG, which was made to this Tune, each Strain is alſo to be ſung twice over.*

All by permission of the British Library

DM I: 10 (1698): 194-96 Continued opposite.

THE ROUND
to the tune of MR. LANE'S MAGGOT

Duple minor longways
AA BB ad lib   MM ♩ = 116

Cecil Sharp, 1922
d: DM I: 1701-1728; m: DM I: 1695-1728

A1	1-4	1st couple turn two-hands down the center to second place skipping
		while 2nd couple cast up to top {*not skipping*}.
	5-8	Repeat movement, 2nd couple turn, 1st couple cast up.
A2	1-4	Men's line and women's line move four slips to left and four slips back {*without hands*}.
	5-8	Partners arm right.
B1	1-6	All fall back a double, forward a double, then turn single.
	7-8	1st couple take both hands and move four slips down center to second place
		while 2nd couple slip up outside to first place.
B2	1-4	All circular hey, four changes, beginning with partner, skipping.
	5-8	Partners arm right.

THE ROUND and MR. LANE'S MAGGOT

Sharp discarded the original tune of "The Round," which is not a round in either the musical or dance sense, and substituted "Mr. Lane's Magot," which had been added to *The Dancing Master* at the very end of the ninth edition (1695) immediately following "Mr. Isaac's Magot." Here, and in the following edition, the lyrics of a new satirical song describing the dancers and amplifying the dance directions were printed on the following pages.

The lyrics were expanded and published with the tune on a broadside now in the Pepys collection, entitled: *A new Song, call'd, The Richmond Recreation: or, The Royal Dance of Delight. to an excellent new Play-house Tune.* After 1698, the dance continued to appear in *The Dancing Master* without the song, and in 1718 the title was changed to "Richmond Ball: or, Mr. Lane's Magot." Only one other such song appears in the DM, "The Quakers Dance, Danc'd in the Play-House" (DM II: 1710-1728).

"Richmond" in this case refers to Charles Lennox, Duke of Richmond, illegitimate son of Charles II by the Duchess of Portsmouth (see page 86). A controversial figure, he served Louis XIV, William III and Queen Anne, taking his seat in the House of Lords in 1693. It was for his wife that Mr. Isaac choreographed "The Richmond," a lovely duet for a couple, which was transcribed and published by John Weaver in 1706.

George Lane was a dancer and dancing master who performed at court and on the stage in the last quarter of the seventeenth century. Other dances in the DM associated with him are "Lane's Minuet" (DM I: 1695-1728) and "Lane's Trumpet Minuet" (DM I: 1698-1728).

References: Highfill, 9: 143-44; Rollins, *Pepys Ballads*, 5: 408; Ralph, *Life and Works*, 289-94; Simpson, 494; Durfey, *Wit and Mirth* vol. 2 (London, 1719), 218-19

The D A N C E.

Caſt off, *Bœ*, behind *Johnny*,
  Do the ſame, *Nanny*,
  Eyes are upon ye ;
  Trip in between
  Little *Dicky* and *Jœs*,
  And ſet in the ſecond Row :
Then, then caſt back you muſt too,
  And up the firſt Row,
  Nimbly thruſt through ;
  Then, then turn about
  To the left, or you're out,
And meet with your Love below.

  Paſs, then croſs,
  Then *Jack's* pretty Laſs,
  Then turn her about, about and about;
And, *Jack*, if you can do ſo too
With *Betty*, whilſt the Time is true,
  We'll all your Ear commend :
    Still there's more
    To lead all four ;
    Two by *Nancy* ſtand,
    And give her your Hand,
Then caſt her quickly down below,
And meet her in the ſecond Row :
  The D A N C E is at an End.

The Round.   *Longways for as many as will.*

The 1ſt man and woman turn both hands down between the 2d. couple, the 2d. man and woman turn down below the firſt couple, the 1ſt. and 2d. man ſlide up, the 1ſt. and 2d. woman down and come in their own places, then Arms round with their own Partners; *The firſt Strain twice.*
The 1ſt. and 2d. man fall back and meet up, the 1ſt. and 2d. woman do the ſame at the ſame time, and all 4 turn ſingle, the 1ſt. couple ſlide down the middle, and 2d. couple up at the ſame time, then right and left a whole round, and arms round till done. *The ſecond Strain twice.*

DM I:12 (1703): 282

Courtesy of the Vaughan Williams Memorial Library

91

RUFTY TUFTY

Two couples facing

3 x A B CC   MM ♩ = 124

Cecil Sharp, 1911
DM I: 1651

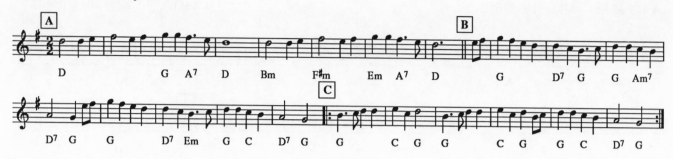

Part I

A	1-8	All forward a double and fall back a double. That again.
B	1-8	Partners set and turn single. That again.
C1	1-4	Men lead partners away from set, change hands and lead back.
	5-6	All turn single.
C2	1-4	Men lead opposite women away from set, change hands and lead back.
	5-6	All turn single.

Part II

A	1-8	Partners side, twice
B	1-8	Partners set and turn single. That again.
CC	1-12	Repeat C1 and C2 of Part I.

Part III

A	1-8	Partners arm right, then left.
B	1-8	Partners set and turn single. That again.
CC	1-12	Repeat C1 and C2 of Part I.

RUFTY TUFTY

This dance appeared only once. The title means swaggering, casual or helter-skelter, and no song connections can be found. In form the dance is derived from Italian models and the idea of layout of the dance on the page, the figures directly under the music to which they are danced, is similar to that in Arbeau.

In this rare early photograph, Cecil Sharp seems to be emulating the title of this dance, his casual pose adding piquancy to his formal attire.

References: Dean-Smith, 59

CECIL J. SHARP
The English Dancing Master

The English Dancing Master (1651): 70

SAINT MARGARET'S HILL

Longways for three couples

3 x A BB   MM ♩ = 116

Bernard J. Bentley, 1962

DM II: 1710-1728

A	1-4	1st couple cast down the outside into second place {*2nd couple moving up*}, and turn two-hands three-quarters, so that the 1st woman ends between the 2nd couple, 1st man between the 3rd couple, in two lines, facing.
	5-8	Taking hands, lines fall back a double, forward a double and circle six-hands around half-way.
B1	1-2	1st man turn 3rd woman right-hand **while** 1st woman the same with 2nd man.
	3-4	1st couple turn left-hand three-quarters.
	5-8	1st couple {*improper*} lead down through couple at bottom, cast up to middle place and turn two-hands half-way to end proper.
B2	1-2	1st man and 2nd woman, 1st woman and 3rd man, turn left-hand.
	3-4	1st couple turn right-hand three-quarters, to end in middle place improper.
	5-6	1st couple lead up through top couple and cast down to middle place.
	7-8	All turn two-hands half-way to end proper.

Repeat dance twice more.

SAINT MARGARET'S HILL

St. Margaret's Hill is in Southwark, across the Thames from the old city and was the site of the Southwark Fair.

DM II:1 (1710): 27
By permission of the Director of Manchester Public Libraries

SAINT MARTIN'S

Two couples facing
3 x AA BB   MM ♩ = 116

Cecil Sharp, 1911
DM I: 1651-1686

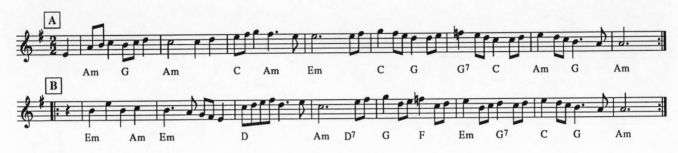

Part I

A1	1-4	All forward a double, then two slips to left and back.
	5-8	All turn single twice:, first men to left, women to right; then men right, women left.
A2	1-8	All change places with opposite (1-4), with partner (5-6), then all turn single (7-8).
B1	1-2	Men fall back a double **while** women turn single.
	3-4	Men meet, take left-hands and turn half-way.
	5-8	Men turn opposite women right-hand once-and-a-half, skipping.
B2	1-2	Women fall back a double **while** men turn single.
	3-4	Women meet, take left-hands and turn half-way.
	5-8	Partners turn right-hand once-and-a-half, skipping, to end facing opposite.

Part II

A1	1-4	All balance back, forward, and change places with opposite.
	5-8	Partners set and turn single.
A2	1-8	Repeat A1.
B1	1-2	Men meet and stand face-to-face.
	3-4	Women the same.
	5-8	Circle four-hands around half-way, slipping (5-6), and all turn single (7-8).
B2	1-8	Repeat B1, women meeting first.

Part III

A1	1-2	All forward a double to meet, take opposite two-hands.
	3-4	All two slips away from partner and back.
	5-8	Men cast down to left followed by partner and return up center to place, skipping.
A2	1-4	All fall back a double (1-2), then partners change places by right shoulder.
	5-8	Men back-to-back **left** shoulder and fall back into original place.
		Immediately after men pass left, women back-to-back right shoulder and fall into original place.
B1	1-4	Men honor partners (1-2), women honor partners (3-4).
	5-8	All right hands-across once around.
B2	1-4	Women honor partners, men honor partners.
	5-6	All left hands-across half-way;
		end in a line facing up,
		1st couple on right,
	7-8	All lead forward a double,
		and honor the Presence.

SAINT MARTIN'S

The old church of St. Martin, Ludgate, named for the patron Saint of the Vintners, described as "a proper church and lately new-built," was destroyed in the Great Fire and rebuilt in 1673-1684 from the designs of Sir Christopher Wren.

Saint Martain.   *For four.*

Meet all, two slips to the left hand, and two to the right, men turn single to the left hand and back again, while the We. turn the Co. way ⁙ Meet again, change places, then change with your own and turn S. ⁚

Meet all a D change places, set and turn S. ⁙ That again ⁚

Meet all, take each others We. by both hands, two slips to the left, and two to the right, men caſt off to yours, come to your places, We. following ⁙ Back all, change places with your own, men croſs aboue each other, and fall back to your firſt places, We. doing the like: not turn your faces ⁚

Men back a D. We. turn S, men croſs over, taking left hands, turn the Co. We. with the right, and ſtay there ⁙ We go back men turn S. We croſs over, handing right hands, turn your own with the left ⁚

Men meet & ſtand, We. as much, hands all, four ſlips half round and turn S. ⁙ we. meet, men meet, and four ſlips to your places and turn S. ⁚

Men honour, We. honour, right hands acroſs and go round ⁙ We. honour, men honour; left hands acroſs and go half round ⁚ I all a lectft to the preſence.

DM I:4 (1670): 22

Courtesy of the Vaughan Williams Memorial Library

94

SCOTCH CAP

Longways for three couples
3 x A BB   MM ♩.= 112

Cecil Sharp, 1916
DM I: 1651-1698

Part I

A   1-8   Partners lead up a double and fall back a double. That again.

B1   1-4   1st and 2nd women face 2nd and 3rd men. They balance back,
            then move forward diagonally across set to change places.

     5-8   1st man and 3rd woman change places.

B2   1-8   Repeat B1 to place.

Part II

A   1-8   Partners side twice.

B1   1-4   Taking hands along the sides, lines fall back a double and forward a double.

     5-8   1st and 3rd men, 1st and 3rd women, 2nd couple: arm right and fall back to place.

B2   1-4   Lines fall back as in B1, 1-4.

     5-8   Partners turn two-hands.

Part III

A   1-8   Partners arm right, then arm left.

B1   1-2   Men four slips up, women four slips down, ending in a line in the middle of the set,
            3rd man facing 1st woman.

     3-8   3rd man and 1st woman take right hands and begin a progressive hey with hands back to places.

B2   1-8   Repeat B1, men slip down, women up, and 1st man and 3rd woman begin the hey with left hands.

SCOTCH CAP

In 1633 Charles I made his first visit to Edinburgh to be crowned in Scotland by the Archbishop of Canterbury. His insistance on full Anglican rites was part of his futile attempt to bring the Scottish church into line with the Church of England, and it infuriated the Scots and their many supporters in London. The title, "Scotch Cap or Edinburgh Castle," may have been a sly reference to that crown, although the extension was not added until the 4th edition (1670). Dean-Smith noted a connection in title and tune to "Blue Cap" (DM: 1651-1690) which would also refer to the Scots bonnet.

Scotch Cap, *or* Edinburgh Caftle.   *Longways for fix.*

Lead up, back again :
That again :   The two upper we. fall back, and the two lowermoft men fall back, crofs over, then the firft man and the lower wo. crofs over, then the two upper men fall back, and the two lower we. crofs over, then the other crofs over as before, thefe three times over :

Sides : That again :   Three men and three we. joyning hands, fall all back and meet all, men turn your faces one towards another, we. doing the like, the two ends on each fide arms, while the middle with his own, then fall back, then turn your backs together, and every one turn his own.

Arms : That again :   Three men flip up, and three we. flip down, then the lower man gives his right hand to the 1. wo. and fo go into your places by hands, then the we. flip up and the men flip down, and the firft and laft give hands to your places as before :

DM I:10 (1698): 17
By permission of the British Library

References: Dean-Smith, 83.

SELLENGER'S ROUND; or, THE BEGINNING OF THE WORLD

Round for as many as will
5 x A BB   MM ♩. = 116

Cecil Sharp, 1916
d: DM I: 1670-1690; m: *Fitzwilliam Virginal Book* (1609)

G G7 C Dm G7 C G G7 C Am Dm G7 C

Am Dm G Dm F G7 F G7 Am D7 G

Part I

A   1-8   All take hands and circle eight slips
           to the left and eight back.

B1   1-2   All set forward to center {no hands}.

     3-4   Fall back a double to place.

     5-8   Partners set and turn single.

B2   1-8   Repeat B1.

Part II

A   1-8   With hands, all forward a double
           to center {*not setting*}
           and fall back a double.
           That again.

BB   1-16 As in Part I.

Part III

A   1-8   Partners side twice.

BB   1-16 As in Part I.

Part IV

A   1-8   Partners arm right, then arm left.

BB   1-16 As in Part I.

Part V

ABB   Repeat Part I.

SELLENGER'S ROUND

"Sellenger's Round" first appeared on the last page of
dances in the third edition of the first volume of the DM.
The figure was simpler and the formation "either round,
or longways for six." The round for as many as will was
substituted in the fourth edition in 1670. An opening
"circle, set and turn single" figure was added to the early
figures and the dance was printed on the first page,
retitled "Sellenger's Round; or, The beginning of the
World." (See the 1607 reference to this title on page iv
above.) By 1695, it was dropped from the DM.

Rather than using the tune as it appeared in the DM,
Sharp selected a version used for a set of variations by
William Byrd, which he found in the *Fitzwilliam Virginal
Book*. Sharp edited the Byrd version and omitted the
repetition of the last four bars when he published the
music in *Country Dance Tunes, Book 7* (London: Novello,
1916), 4.

References: Ward, 72-73; Simpson, 643-46; Chappell, 69-
71; Francis Tregian, compiler, "Fitzwilliam Virginal Book"
[1609-1619] (New York: Dover Publications, 1963), 1: 248
(LXIV); Pepys Ballads, 4: 232

The Great Boobee.

To a pleasant New Tune; Or, *Sellengers Round.*

M͞r Friend, if you will understand
  my Fortune what they are,
I once had Cattle, House, and Land,
  but now I am never the near,
My Father left a good estate,
  as I may tell to thee,
I cousned was of all I had,
  like a great Boobee.

I went to School with a good intent
  and for to learn my Book,
And all the day I went to play,
  in it I never did look,
Full seven years, or very nigh,
  as I may tell to thee
I could hardly say my Christ-Cross Row,
  like a great Boobee.

My Father then in all the hast,
  did set me to the Plow,
And for to lash the Horse about,
  indeed I knew not how:
My Father took his Whip in hand,
  and soundly lashed me,
He call'd me fool and Country Clown,
  like a great Boobee.

But I did from my Father run,
  for I will Plow no more,
Because he had so slashed me,
  and made my sides so sore:
But I will go to London Town,
  some Fashions for to see,
When I came there they call'd me clown,
  and great Boobee.

But as I went along the street,
  I carried my hat in my hand,
And to every one that I did meet,
  I bravely bust my hand:
Some did laugh, and some did scoff,
  and some did mock at me,
And some did say I was a Wood co.
  and a great Boobee.

Then I did walk in hast to Pauls,
  the Steeple for to view,
Because I heard some people say,
  it should be builded new,
Then I got up unto the top,
  the City for to see,
It was so high it made me err,
  like a great Boobee.

Broadside of 1656 from the Pepys collection
Courtesy of Boydell & Brewer

Sellengers Round, or The begining of the World. *Round for as many as will.*

Take Hands and go round twice, Back again.   All set and turn S. that again.

Lead all in a D. forward
and back. That again.

Two fingles and a D. back.
Set and turn fingle. That again.

Sides all. That again.   As before.

Arms all. That again   As before.

DM I: 4 (1670): 1

Courtesy of the Vaughan Williams Memorial Library

SHEPHERD'S HOLIDAY; or, LABOUR IN VAIN

Longways for three couples
3 x AA BB   MM ♩.= 104

Cecil Sharp, 1912
DM I: 1651-1686

Part I

A1	1-4	Partners lead up a double and fall back a double.
	5-6	Partners change places.
A2	1-6	Repeat A1, leading down a double.
B1	1-2	1st couple slip down and stand between 2nd couple, all facing in.
	3-4	3rd couple slip up to stand outside 2nd couple.
	5-8	1st man followed by 2nd and 3rd men, cast down to left in a small circle track back to places **while** women cast down to right, skipping.
B2	1-8	Repeat B1, 3rd couple slipping inside, 1st couple outside, and 3rd man casting to right, 3rd woman to left.

Part II

A1	1-6	Partners side (1-4), then change places (5-6).
A2	1-6	Repeat A1.
B1	1-4	Taking hands along the sides, lines fall back a double, then forward a double.
	5-8	Each line circle three-hands around.
B2	1-8	Repeat B1, circles facing out.

Part III

A1	1-6	Partners arm right (1-4), then change places (5-6).
A2	1-6	Partners arm left, then change places.
B1	1-4	1st man and 2nd woman change places (1-2), 2nd man and 1st woman change places (3-4).
	5-8	3rd couple cross and move up outside to top of set, skipping **while** 1st and 2nd couples move down.
B2	1-4	3rd woman and 2nd man change places. 3rd man and 2nd woman change places.
	5-8	1st couple cross and move up outside to top of set, skipping **while** 2nd and 3rd couples move down.

SHEPHERD'S HOLIDAY

Evelyn Wells suggests that the following ballad by Martin Parker was set to this tune:

Labour in Vaine, or An imperfect description of Love...to a dainty new tune, called Jenkinson.

Fie upon love! fond love! false love!
  Great are the torments that Lovers endure:
It is a snare - brings care - bones bare -
  None can a remedy for it procure.
Of all the afflictions that are incident
  To us while we march under Time's regimènt,
There's nothing to man brings so much discontent
  As love unbelovèd againe
It breaketh our sleep; it distracteth the wit;
  It makes us doe things that for men are unfit:
If I may but give a true censure on it,
  It shall be call'd *Labour in vaine.*

(Roxburghe, 1: 593)

References: Dean-Smith, 85; Wells, 271

(18)

Shepherd's Holiday, *or* Labour in vain.   *Longways for six.*   ☉☉☉ ❯❯❯

Lead up all a D. back, crofs over-: Lead down, back again, crofs over-:

The firft man flip before the 2. man while his r. wo. before the 2. wo. then the laft man flip behind the 2. man while his wo. behind the 2. wo. then all fix turn round about to the left hand into their places, then the laft cu. do as the firft, and the firft as the laft-:

Sides, back again, crofs over-: That again-:

Three men and three we. back, joyning hands, meet, three men hands and go round, we. doing the like, men and we. back as before and meet, hands backward and go round as before.

Arms as you fided-:

The r. man crofs into the 2. wo. place, and his wo. into the 2. man's place, &c.

DM I:10 (1698): 18
By permission of the British Library

THE SHREWSBURY LASSES

Longways for three couples

3 x AA BB   MM ♩ = 108

W. S. Porter, 1931
Twenty-four Country Dances (Thompson), 1765

A1	1-4	1st man slow set and honor, right, then left, to 2nd woman.
	5-8	1st man turn 2nd woman two-hands.
A2	1-8	1st woman the same to 2nd man.
B1	1-2	1st couple cast down to middle place, 2nd couple moving up.
	3-6	1st and 3rd couples circle four-hands once around.
	7-10	1st man skip up outside and around top couple, to end in middle place improper
		while 1st woman skip down outside and around bottom couple, to end in middle place, improper.
	11-12	1st couple turn two-hands half-way.
B2	1-2	3rd couple cast up to middle place, 1st couple moving down.
	3-6	3rd and 2nd couples {*at top*} circle four-hands once around.
	7-10	3rd man skip up outside and around top couple, to end in middle place, improper
		while 3rd woman skip down outside and around bottom couple, to end in middle place, improper.
	11-12	3rd couple turn two-hands half-way.

Repeat dance twice more.

THE SHREWSBURY LASSES

Celebrated in dance for its cakes, rakes, and lasses, the old town of Shrewsbury (pronounced "shrozebree") was home to the renowned dancing master, choreographer and scholar, John Weaver.

Charles Burney returned to Shrewsbury between 1742 and 1744 and studied with him. "The old friend of my father, Mr. Weaver, now near 90 [actually 70], still continued to keep open his boarding school wth the assistance of the beautiful Mrs. Weaver & his daughters; taught dance, & had an Annual Ball, at wch his Scholars, besides [the] Minuet, Rigadon, and L'Ouvre, performed figure & pantomime dances such as at the beginning of the century he had invented as Ballet Master in London. In remembrance of my father he gave me lessons, & alloted me a part in a Wooden shoe dance at one of his balls."

Reference: Burney MS, quoted in Ralph, *The Life and Works of John Weaver*, 36

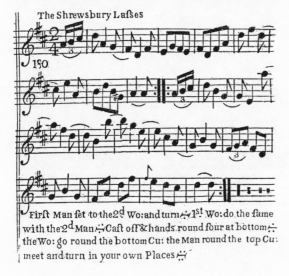

Thompson's Compleat Collection, vol. 4 (1780): 90
By permission of the British Library

The Wooden Shoe Dancers.

Catchpenny Prints, no. 30, 18
Courtesy Dover Publications

SPRING GARDEN

Longways for four couples

3 x A BBBB   MM ♩. = 88

Cecil Sharp, 1912
DM I: 1665-1728

repeat 4 times

Part I

A	1-8	Partners lead up a double and fall back a double. That again.
B1	1	All balance back.
	2-4	1st and 2nd couples, 3rd and 4th couples, circle four-hands around half-way.
	5-6	In lines, balance back and move forward.
	7-8	Partners at top and bottom change places **while** middle men change places, as do middle women.
B2-4		Repeat B1 three times until all are in original places.

Part II

A	1-2	1st and 2nd men move backward into each other's places, passing right shoulders, **while** 3rd and 4th men, 1st and 2nd women, 3rd and 4th women, do the same.
	3-4	Partners change places.
	5-8	Repeat A 1-4.
B1	1-4	1st couple cast down to middle place, meet and face down, 2nd couple follow to stand outside them in a line of four **across** the hall. **Meanwhile** 4th couple cast up to middle place followed by 3rd couple to form a line facing the other line.
	5-8	All set and change with opposite, turning right into lines across the hall again.
B2	1-4	Ends of the lines cast to middle, new ends follow to make lines **up and down** the hall.
	5-8	Partners set and change places.
B3&4		Repeat B1 & 2, ends cast to middle, middles follow to end of lines. All set and change with opposite.

Part III

A	1-4	All face men's wall, forward a double, then partners face and change places.
	5-8	All face women's wall, forward a double, then partners face and change places.
B1	1-2	All balance back and move forward.
	3-4	1st and 4th couples face and forward a double **while** 2nd couple slip up to top and 3rd couple slip to bottom.
	5-8	Partners at top and bottom arm right once-and-a-half **while** 1st man arm with 4th woman and 1st woman arm with 4th man, once-and-a-half.
B2-4		Repeat B1 three times: balance back and move forward, then ends meet, middles slip to ends, then arm left, then right, then left, each time once-and-a-half.

SPRING GARDEN

Because this dance appears first in 1665, the reference must be to the new Spring Garden at Lambeth, later to be called Vauxhall. Samuel Pepys visited May 28, 1667.

"I by water to Foxhall, and there walked in Spring Garden. A great deal of company, and the weather and garden pleasant: and it is very...cheap going thither, for a man may go to spend what he will, or nothing, all is one. But to hear the nightingale and other birds, and hear fiddles and there a harp, and here a Jew's trump, and here laughing and there fine people walking is mighty divertising."

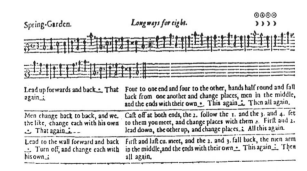

DM I:8 (1690): 118

STEP STATELY
to the tune of JACK PUDDING

Longways for three couples
15 x A B   MM ♪. = 116

Cecil Sharp, 1916
DM I: 1651-1690

Part I

A1	1-2	Partners lead up a double.
	3-4	All face up: men go four slips to right behind partners **while** women go four slips to left.
	5-8	Men join hands in line facing out, women same: 1st man lead men down to the bottom of the set, **while** 1st woman lead women the same, to form a straight line across the hall facing up, 1st couple in the center.
B1	1-4	With hands, all lead forward a double and fall back a double.
	5-8	The women's line move to the right in front of the men and lead up to place **while** men move left and lead up.
AB	1-16	Repeat Part I.

Part II

A1	1-4	1st couple lead up a double, change hands, lead down a double to meet 2nd couple.
	5-6	1st and 2nd couple circle four-hands around half-way.
	7-8	1st man and 2nd woman change places.
B1	1-4	Taking left hands, 2nd woman lead 1st woman up the middle and hand her across to fall behind 2nd man, 2nd woman falling back to stand behind 1st man.
	5-8	1st and 2nd man take right hands, pass by, and turn partners by the left, 1st couple ending in second place, 2nd couple in first place, both proper.
AB2-6		1st couple repeat Part II AB1 with 3rd couple. 2nd couple then lead the figures of Part II AB1, and then 3rd couple. {*All end in original places.*}

Part III

A1	1-4	1st couple cross and move down outside to second place, 2nd couple moving up. 1st couple change places passing right shoulder and end facing in, taking hands in lines of three on sides.
	5-6	Lines fall back a double and move forward a double.
	7-8	1st couple meet **while** 2nd and 3rd couples cross by right shoulders and turn around to face partners, women to the left, men to the right.
B1	1-4	1st couple lead to the top; 2nd couple move in behind them, 3rd couple behind 2nd. 1st couple cast down to bottom, 2nd couple follow but cast down into second place **while** 3rd couple lead straight up the center to top place and turn inward to take hands in a ring with 2nd couple.
	5-8	2nd and 3rd couples hands-four around half-way **while** 1st couple arm right.
AB2-6		Part III is then repeated twice, led by 2nd, then 3rd couple. All will end in original places.

Part IV

A	1-8	Repeat Part A1.
B	1-4	With hands, all lead forward a double and fall back a double.
	5-8	Women's line pass in front of the men's, which goes behind, again forming line of six across the hall. All lead forward a double and honor the Presence.

{*Use running step throughout. This dance is very theatrical and should be performed with verve, using plenty of space.*}

STEP STATELY and JACK PUDDING

Miſs Sicamore

Step Stately. *A long Dance for 3, 5, 7, or 9 Couple.*

[musical notation]

Lead up all a D. change places each with his own, keeping your faces ſtill to the preſence, the men ſlipping behind the We. and the We. before the man, face all to the wall ● Men hands, and We. hands, firſt man and ſecond Wo. lead all the reſt round to the bottom, facing all to the preſence ∴

The firſt Cu. lead up a D change hands, and lead down a D. ● Take hands with the 2. Cu. and all four half round, firſt man and 2. Wo. change places ∴

Firſt Cu. croſs over, meet in the ſecond place, change places ● The three uppermoſt men, and the three We. hands, taII a D. back 2. and 3. Cu. change each with his own, while the firſt Cu. meet, then fall 2 D. back again three and three ∴

The firſt man and Wo. being in the middle, lead up all a breſt a D and back ● We. ſlip before the men to the right, and men behind the We. to the left, going a compaſs to their places as at firſt ∴

The 2. We. lead up between the ſecond, then croſſing over the firſt Wo. go behind the 2. man, and the 2. behind the firſt ● Men change over by the right hands, then giving left hands to their own We. turn the firſt Cu. in the 2. place, and the 2. in the firſt ∴

Now ſtanding as in Greenwood, the firſt man between the 2. and 3. Wo. and the firſt Wo. between the 2. and 3. man, the firſt Cu. lead up, caſt off and meet below, whileſt the 2. and 3 We. and the 2. and 3. men change places ● The firſt Cu. being in the 3. place, arms whilſt the other four take hands and go half round to the left ∴

DM I:4 (1670): 97

Sharp paired this unique and complex dance with an unexpected tune. As Dean-Smith delicately puts it, "Jack Pudding or Merry Andrew" [is]...frequently associated with harvest supper songs, swearing-in songs admitting an apprentice or other to the fellowship of a calling or society, and with ribald songs of the "barley" type. (See page 60.)

Although the concordance is distant, "Jack Pudding" is related to the tune called "The Budgeon it is a delicate trade," best known from the late eighteenth century to today with the lyric beginning: "There was a jolly miller once, liv'd on the River Dee."

An earlier lyric to the tune is in a canting dialect and promotes the trade of thievery.

The budgeon it is a delicate trade, and a delicate trade of fame,
    For when that we have bit the blow, we carry away the game.
But if the cully nab us, and the lurries from us take,
    O then he rubs us to the whit, though we are not worth a make.
        from the Triumph of Wit (1725), quoted in Chappell, 666

The only lyric known to a tune entitled "Step Stately" is a rather grim story in the *Westminster-Drollery* in which Anthony takes revenge on his wife by blinding her. The full title and first verse follows:

A late and true story of a furious Scold, served in her kind.

The tune, Step Stately.

Was ever man so vex'd with a Trull,
    As I poor Anthony since I was wed,
For I never can get my belly full,
    Before I have supp'd, I must hasten to bed.
Or else she'l begin to scold and to brawl,
    And call me Puppy and Cuckold and all
Yet she with her Cronies must trole it about,
    Whilst I in my Kennel must snore it out.

Despite the tune indication, the lyrics do not appear to fit the DM music.

References: Dean-Smith, 48, 84; Simpson, 685-86; Dean-Smith, *Guide*, 120; Chappell, 666-68; *Westminster-Drollery. or a choice Collection of the newest Songs & Poems both at Court and Theaters by a Person of Quality with Additions* (London: H. Brome, 1672), 37

Merry Andrew

Jack Pudding, or (Merry Andrew.) *Longwayes for ſix.*

[musical notation]

Firſt and 2. Cu. lead up a D. and fall back, whilſt the third Cu. lead up to the top between the other, firſt and 2. Cu. lead up again and back, whileſt the 3. lead down.

Sides all ● That again ∴

Arms all ● That again ∴

Third Cu. lead up between the other, and caſting off, go on the outſide under their arms croſs over and under their arms, and fall to the bottom as at firſt, then the firſt 4. hands and round, and ſit whileſt the third do as much.

Men round and hold up their hands, We. under their arms, and turn their own, We. go round, and each man turn his own.

The third Cu. lead under the firſt Cu. arms, and come face to the We. hands you four and round, the firſt Cu. fall into the 2. place, the 3. Cu. lead under the 2. Cu. arms, and hands round the 3. Cu. fall into the 2. and the 2. into the firſt place ●

DM I:4 (1670): 97, 62

Catchpenny Prints, #40, 27

SUN ASSEMBLY

Ken Sheffield, 1982
Thompson's Compleat Collection, v. 1 (Thompson), 1757

Duple minor longways
A B ad lib   MM ♩ = 108

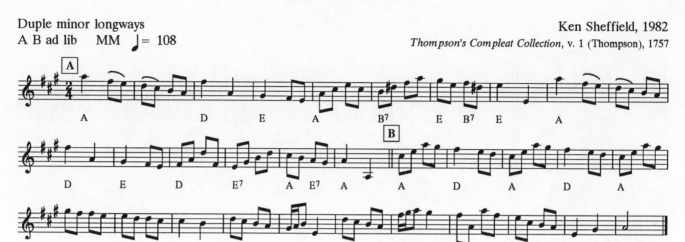

A   1-4   1st and 2nd couples circle four-hands around half-way and fall back.

       5-8   1st couple, holding neighbor's hand, move up center and cast down one place, 2nd couple acting as a pivot.

     9-12   1st couple half figure-eight through the couple above, who change places after 1st couple goes through.

   13-16   All set and turn single.

B   1-4   1st couple right hands-across with couple **below**.

       5-8   1st couple left hands-across with couple **above**.

     9-12   1st couple lead through couple below and cast up to progressed place.

   13-16   Partners turn two-hands.

SUN ASSEMBLY

A Sun Tavern was located near the intersection of Gray's Inn Road and High Holborn, near the corner of Brook Street. Daniel Wright, musical instrument seller and dance book publisher, had his shop next door. Perhaps the establishment had a large room for dancing parties. This title may refer to a subscription series at the Sun.

The title page of the volume in which the dance was printed gives a good picture of a dancing party at mid-century.

Thompson's Compleat Collection, vol. 1 (1757): tp and 5
Courtesy of the Forbes Library, Northampton, Massachusetts

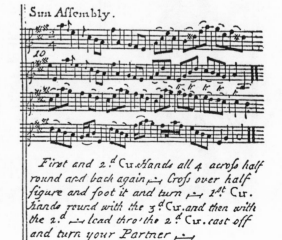

THE TOUCHSTONE

Longways for three couples
3 x AA BB   MM ♩ = 112

W. S. Porter, 1931
Twenty Four Country Dances (Thompson), 1780

A1 1-8 1st couple cross at the top and hey on opposite side with skip-change step,
         passing **outside** 2nd couple to begin.

A2 1-8 1st couple cross back and hey on own side, again passing **outside** 2nd couple to begin.

B1 1-4 1st couple lead down center through bottom, and cast up to middle place, skipping,
         2nd couple moving up on bars 3-4.

    5-8 1st couple turn two-hands.

B2 1-4 1st couple lead up through 2nd couple and cast down the
         outside to bottom, 3rd couple moving up on bars 3-4.

    5-8 1st couple turn two-hands in bottom place.

Repeat dance twice more.

THE TOUCHSTONE

Charles Dibdin's popular operatical pantomime *The Touchstone; or, Harlequin Traveller* played nearly every night when it first opened at Covent Garden in January of 1779. This tune is not in the score published by S. and A. Thompson (London: 1779). Nonetheless, with its sailor's hornpipe rhythm it certainly reflects the nautical theme of the play and may have been inspired by it.

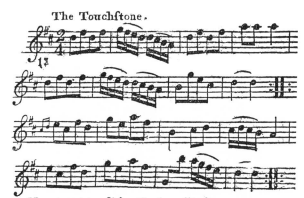

Hey contrary fides ⁒ then the fame on your own
fides ⁒ Hands 6 quite round ⁒ Lead thro' the 3d
Cu. and caft up one Lead thro' the top and caft
off ⁒

Sailor and his Lafs

Thompson's Compleat Collection, vol. 4 (1780): 8
By permission of the British Library

Catchpenny Prints, no. 139, 88
Courtesy of Dover Publications

A TRIP TO PARIS

Duple minor longways
A B ad lib   MM ♩ = 120

Douglas and Helen Kennedy, 1929
New Country Dancing Master, Book 2d (Walsh), 1711

A	1-4	Partners set and change places as they turn single moving forward and revolving clockwise around each other, keeping to the left.
	5-8	All that again to places.
B	1-8	1st couple cross, go down outside, cross again below 2nd couple and go up outside to 1st place, skipping.
	9-10	1st couple turn single.
	11-14	1st corners change places, 2nd corners change places.
	15-16	Circle four-hands around half-way.
	17-18	1st couple cast down one place **while** 2nd couple lead up.

A TRIP TO PARIS

"A passion for travel swept England in the late eighteenth century. The grand tour of the Continent was considered a must for young men of means, and less ambitious trips to various corners of the British Isles were also the rage.   Books on travel proliferated... Part of this eagerness to explore the homeland was attributable to improved highways and more comfortable coaches..."

> Jonathan Norton Leonard, *The World of Gainsborough*
> (New York, Time-Life Books, 1969), 154

Naturally, eighteenth-century English dancers danced "trips" to everywhere as well, to spas, cities, colonies and taverns, from Bath to Tunbridge, Abbotsbury to York, Georgia to Jamaica, and from the Bell to the Oaks.

An amusing song on the subject of trips is quoted by Chappell from *Wit and Drollery* (1656), 60. It was set to the tune of "The New Exchange." (See page 3 above for tune.)

> We'll go no more to Tunbridge Wells, the journey is too far;
>   Nor ride in Epsom waggon, where our bodies jumbled are.
> But we will all to the westward waters go, the best that e'er you saw,
>   And we will have them henceforth call'd,
>   The Kentish new-found Spa.
>
> Then go, lords and ladies, whate'er you ail; go thither all
>   that pleases;
> For it will cure you without fail, of old and new diseases.
>   *Chappell, Popular Music, 317*

New Country-Dancing Master, 3d book (1711): 115

A TRIP TO TUNBRIDGE

Longways for three couples
3 x AA BB   MM ♩ = 116

A. Simons, 1961
Preston's Twenty four Country Dances (Preston), 1793

A1	1-8	1st couple cast down to bottom of set, "take a peek," and cast up to top.
A2	1-8	1st couple lead down center (1-4), then, skipping, lead back and cast down to middle place (5-8), 2nd couple moving up on bars 7-8.
B1	1-4	1st couple pass right shoulder, then 1st man turn 3rd woman right-hand **while** 1st woman turn 2nd man right-hand.
	5-8	Passing partner by right shoulder again, 1st man turn 2nd woman right-hand **while** 1st woman turn 3rd man right-hand.
B2	1-4	1st couple cross by right shoulder, all face out on own side, then 1st man lead 2nd and 3rd men out a double and fall back **while** 1st woman lead 2nd and 3rd women out a double and fall back, then all face partners.
	5-8	1st couple cast down to bottom **while** 2nd couple turn two-hands **and** 3rd couple lead up to second place.

Repeat dance twice more.

A TRIP TO TUNBRIDGE

In 1606 Lord North found that a sample of water from a spring in Kent contained iron and other minerals thought to be valuable for health restoration. Thus the Spa of Tunbridge Wells was born. The "King of Bath," Beau Nash, presided over its social activities occasionally in the early eighteenth century, and being only thirty-four miles south of London, Tunbridge was so often visited by royalty that in 1909 it was granted the prefix "Royal" to its name.

The tune used for this country dance of 1793 is "Green Grows the Rashes, O" which can be found in seventeenth-century manuscript books. Robert Burns revised an old lyric and published it in the *Scots Musical Museum* (Edinburgh: 1787, 1:78), perhaps giving the old tune new popularity.

VIEW OF TUNBRIDGE WELLS, BATHS, LIBRARY

illustration from Melville, Society, opp. 218
Courtesy of the Print Room, The Lewis-Walpole Library, Yale University

> There's naught but care on every han'.
>   In every hour that passes, O;
> What signifies the life o'man,
>   And 'twere na for the lasses, O?
> Green grow the rashes, O!
>   Green grow the rashes' O!
> The sweetest hours that e'er I spent,
>   Are spent amang the lasses, O!

James Morrison spotted the similarity of the eighteenth-century figures of "A Trip to Tunbridge" to a version of "Chorus Jig" danced by the Ed Larkin Dancers of Tunbridge, Vermont, a nice footnote to the 1793 title.

References: A. Barbeau, *Life & Letters at Bath in the xviijth Century* (London: William Hernemann, 1944); James Morrison, cover notes for *By Popular Demand* (recording) (New York: Country Dance and Song Society, 1978); Lewis Melville, *Society at Royal Tunbridge Wells in the Eighteenth Century - and After* (London: Eveleigh Nash, 1912)

Preston's Twenty four Country Dances (1793): 95
Courtesy of the Vaughan Williams Memorial Library

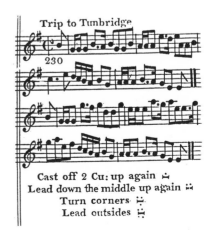

Trip to Tunbridge

230

Cast off 2 Cu: up again :||:
Lead down the middle up again :||:
Turn corners :||:
Lead outsides :||:

UP WITH AILY
to the tune of THE HARE'S MAGGOT

Duple minor longways
AA B ad lib   MM ♩ = 100

Cecil Sharp, 1922
d:DM I: 1651-1690; m:DM I: 1701-1728

A1	1	1st woman and 2nd man move a double to stand on either side of 1st man and face 2nd woman.
	2-3	Taking hands, all three move forward a double to 2nd woman and fall back.
	4	2nd man and 1st woman return to places.
	5-6	1st man cast down to 2nd place **while** 2nd man move up turning single left **and** two women turn single right.
A2	1	2nd man {*now in top place*} and 2nd woman move a double to stand on either side of 1st woman and face 1st man.
	2-3	Taking hands, all three move forward a double to 1st man and fall back.
	4	2nd man and 2nd woman return to places.
	5-6	1st woman cast down to 2nd place **while** 2nd woman move up to 1st place turning single to right **and** two men turn single to right.
B	1-2	1st couple back-to-back.
	3-4	1st couple cast up into 1st place **while** 2nd couple lead down center and turn single to face up, man to right, woman to left.
	5-7	Circle four-hands once around.
	8	1st couple cast down one place **while** 2nd couple move up, turning single, man to left and woman to right.

UP WITH AILY

"Up goes Ely," which Sharp had reconstructed in 1916, is a different dance, but the tunes are very similar, perhaps prompting him to select an alternate for this dance of 1922. A theme of celebration runs throughout the ballads set to this tune, implying the archaic use of the term "aley," for "Ely" and "Aily," to mean "ale."

A "maggot" was an idea or whim. This tune may have been named for Constantia Hare, whose portrait, illustrated on the page opposite, was published in a beautiful mezzotint. A copy is preserved in the Bliss collection, an album of portraits of "court ladies" now at the Lewis Walpole Library. Miss Hare was the daughter of Henry, second Baron of Coleraine.

She may also have been the London beauty to whom Kit-Cat Club member Lord Lonsdowne's toast was given:

"Love is enjoyn'd to make his favourite toast,
And HARE'S the goddess that delights him most."
(Ashton, *Social Life in the Reign of Queen Anne*, 21-22)

References: Simpson, 728-30; Ward, 78
See also illustration on page 17 above.

DM 1:12 (1703): 343; DM 1:14 (1709): 255
Courtesy of the Vaughan Williams Memorial Library

UPON A SUMMER'S DAY

Longways for three couples
3 x AA BBB   MM ♩.= 116

Cecil Sharp, 1912
DM I: 1651-1690

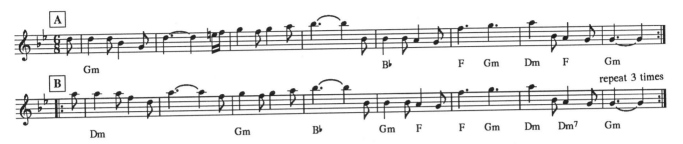

Part I

A1	1-4	Partners lead up a double and fall back a double.
	5-8	Partners set and turn single.
A2	1-8	Repeat A1.
B1	1-4	Taking hands along the sides, all go forward a double and back a double.
	5-8	2nd and 3rd men make an arch **while** 2nd and 3rd women the same; 1st couple lead down center, and separate, 1st man going out through men's arch to bottom place **while** 1st woman go out through women's arch to bottom place, 2nd and 3rd couples moving up on bars 7-8.
BB		As in B1, led by 2nd, then 3rd couple.

Part II

A1	1-4	Partners side.
	5-8	Partners set and turn single.
A2	1-8	Repeat A1.
BBB		Repeat B1-B3 in Part I.

Part III

A1	1-4	Partners arm right.
	5-8	Partners set and turn single.
A2	1-8	Repeat A1, arming left.
BBB		Repeat B1-B3 in Part I.

UPON A SUMMER'S DAY

This dance occupies a prestigious place in the canon of English country dance, appearing as it does as the first dance in the first edition of *The English Dancing Master*. In the second and third it was dropped to page 104 and in the fourth the title became "The Garland or A Summer's Day," perhaps in reference to a contemporary song.

The title and first verse of an early song set to this tune follows:

The Discourse betweene A Souldier and his Love. Shewing that she did beare a faithfull minde, for Land nor Sea could make her stay behinde, to the tune of Upon a Summer time.

Souldier: My dearest deare adue, since that I needs must goe,
             my fortunes to pursue against some Forraine Foe.
             Being that it is so, I pray thee patient be,
             and doe not kilt thy Coat, to goe along with me.

Pegge: Alas my dearest heart, if that thou leave me here,
             Death kills me with his dart, as plainly may appeare.
             For sorrow griefe and smart, will quickly make me dye,
             Therefore Ile kilt my Coat, and goe along with thee.

Pepys, Ballads, I, 296.

References: Simpson, 730-31; Dean-Smith, 6; Ashton, *Humour*, 159-64; Chappell, 254-55

CONSTANTIA HARE
Courtesy of the Print Collection
The Lewis Walpole Library, Yale University

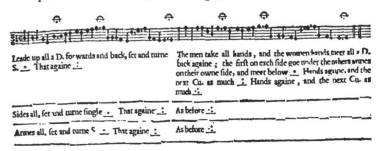

The English Dancing Master (1651): 1
Courtesy of the Vaughan Williams Memorial Library

WELL HALL

Duple minor longways
AA BB ad lib   MM ♩ = 108

Frank Van Cleef, 1982
DM I: 1679-1728

A1   1-4   1st couple turn right-hand once-and-a-half.
      5-6   1st couple cast down one place, 2nd couple moving up.
      7-8   1st couple change places, falling back on last three steps.
A2   1-8   2nd couple repeat A1.
B1   1-2   1st corners change places.
      3-4   2nd corners change places.
      5-6   Circle four-hands around half-way.
      7-8   All turn single, 1st couple turning up and away from each other, 2nd couple turning down and away.
B2   1-2   2nd corners change places.
      3-4   1st corners change places.
      5-6   Circle four-hands around half-way.
      7-8   1st couple cast down one place **while** 2nd couple lead up.

The Fiddle plays: they Dance and gaze

WELL HALL

The only "Well Hall" we have been able to find is in the late medieval records of the *Domesday Book*, where a Well Hall is located in Gayton (Freebridge) in Norfolk.

"Belgia Retriev'd," which Tom Cook reconstructed in 1979, is based on a dance published in 1710 to a different tune but with similar figures worded slightly differently.

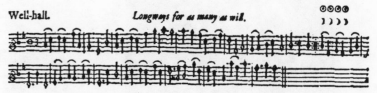

Well-hall.   *Longways for as many as will.*

Honour to the Prefence, then to your women. Lead up all forward and back, that again.

The firft man turns his own wo. once and a half, and fo they go into the fecond place and crofs over, the fecond man and wo. being in the firft places do the fame, then the firft man and the fecond wo. changing places, the firft wo. and fecond man do the fame. Hands all together, and go half round into your own places, and turn S. then the firft wo. and the fecond man crofs over, and the firft man and the fecond wo. do the fame; then all take hands, and go half round into their own places, then the firft Cu. caft off into the fecond place: And fo on to the end.

Illustration from Catchpenny Prints, no. 111, 76.
Courtesy of Dover Publications

DM I:7 (1686): 171
Courtesy of the Vaughan Williams Memorial Library

ZEPHYRS AND FLORA

Duple minor longways
AA BB ad lib   MM ♩= 116

Bernard J. Bentley, 1965
Twenty Four Country Dances (Walsh), 1715

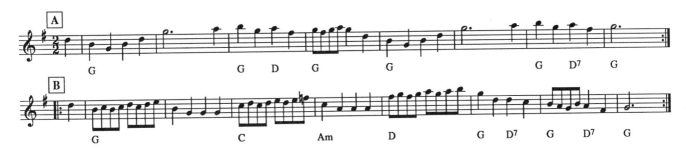

A1   1-4   1st corners back-to-back.

       5-8   1st corners join right hands (5), then left hands (6) and with crossed hands, turn half-way (7-8).

A2   1-8   2nd corners repeat A1.

B1   1-8   1st couple cast up one place, 2nd couple moving down,
             then 1st couple half figure-eight down through 2nd couple.

B2   1-8   2nd couple cast up, 1st couple moving down,
             then 2nd couple half figure-eight down through 1st couple.

ZEPHYRS AND FLORA

Queen Anne was affectionately known as Flora to her subjects. Her death in 1714 may have inspired this title. In Greek mythology "Zephyrus" was the personification of the west wind and "Flora" the goddess of the spring.

Illustration from Catchpenny Prints, no. 189, 134
Courtesy of Dover Publications

Second Book of the Compleat Country Dancing Master (1719): 319
Courtesy of the Library of Congress

Siding in 1930

Although there is no breeze blowing, skirts are fluttering as the dancers turn to face their partners after siding across the set. Elsie Avril, violin, and (left to right) Marjorie Sinclair, Maud Karpeles, and May Gadd perform a demonstration of a three-couple set dance at the summer school in Amherst, Massachusetts.

Courtesy of the Country Dance and Song Society archives

110

MODERN COUNTRY DANCE TECHNIQUE

Over the years, modifications have altered some of Cecil Sharp's dicta on how to perform certain steps and figures. Yet his fundamental philosophy is still valid. He was committed to making the dances appropriate for an informal setting: not for display, but for recreation. He chose a style adapted to suit the average man in the street rather than the dance expert primarily interested in the authenticity of interpretation and steps. Sharp repeatedly spoke of the "gay simplicity" of the country dance, a term he found in an early nineteenth-century dancing manual. "Every movement should...be executed quietly, easily, and with an economy of motion, and in a simple unaffected manner ... The spirit of merriment, however, although never wholly absent from the dance, is not always equally obvious." (*ECD, Gr.Ser.*, 3: 10)

This restrained, almost inhibiting description does not really fit today's dancers. Perhaps the most marked change since 1915 is in the social aspect of the dance. Here in the United States particularly, dancers now enjoy the interplay between partners to the full. Their eye-contact is sometimes carried to extremes, and the physical pleasure found in hand-turns or swings is open and unfettered. Energy and exuberance are more obvious than in the early days and there may well be less elegance and refinement. Today's dancers let their enthusiasm and enjoyment create a wonderful community spirit.

The way in which a country dancer moves and uses the body has also undergone some modification over the years. Changing footwear has had the biggest impact. Until World War II, dancers wore sneakers or gym shoes. The rubber soles gripped the dance floor and permitted the dancer to lean, indeed to swoop into figures such as siding over and back or weaving the figures of a hey.

In addition, in the early days the music was occasionally played faster than it is today. The opening turns and circles in "Jacob Hall's Jig," and the skip around the outside in the opening of "Newcastle," for example, were much easier to sustain at a faster pace with a good grip on the floor than they would be today in leather-soled shoes.

A New Style for the Post-War Period

The change came about in the late 1940's - when a "new look" was urged by the then director of the English society, Douglas Kennedy, and by May Gadd, his counter-part in America. Concerned that GI's and others were coming to dances without "dancing shoes" in hand, they urged a re-focus of the dance as an artistic expression. "Walking on Air" was Kennedy's term for the new attitude toward the physical aspects of the dance. Erect posture was encouraged. "Lift the egg from the egg cup" was the picturesque metaphor for the torso lift from the hips. In street shoes, dancers lost the prop of rubber soles. They had to control their balance in a different way. The whole look of the dancing changed.

But still, by contrast with the robust, driving energy of the average American square or contra dance, English country dance as Sharp constructed and his followers have promoted it has very special qualities, hard to define or to put into words. There is more lightness to it, the feeling of moving above the floor rather than sliding over it. There is a lilting to the step, never a march, dancing on the ball of the foot rather than coming down on the heels, though never dancing on the toes. The poise of the body is vitally important, relaxed yet standing tall. The dancer carries the head up and should be able to feel a movement spread through arms that are neither rigid nor limp, but serve an integral part in the balance of the body.

There is a buoyant quality to English country dancing which comes from the ability to prepare oneself ahead of time and to appreciate the all-essential up-beat that launches the dancer from inaction into movement. It is always the body that moves ahead of the feet, not a step that pulls the body forward. The style offers tremendous opportunity for the dancer to make the most of his body, to appreciate the difference it makes when legs are relaxed and the ankles flexible.

In summary, one of Cecil Sharp's demonstration dancers spoke with deep appreciation of his work: "Sharp made no attempt to give an exact reproduction of the style of dancing that may have been current in the seventeenth century, but allowed the style to be gradually evolved. The re-creation which was thus effected was a thing of great beauty: lovely to behold and completely satisfying to the dancers." (Karpeles, 104)

The first of these engravings was used on the title page of the seventh edition of the first volume of *The Dancing Master* (1686), when Henry Playford took the series over from his father. It replaced the formal picture of a gentleman making his honors to a lady which John Playford has used on all editions before, a design which was not originally related to dancing at all. (See page xvi above and Dean-Smith, *Playford's English Dancing Master*, xiv-xvi, 1.) Still based somewhat on Wenceslas Holler's original design for the *Academy of Love* (London: Humphry Blunden, 1641), the new engraving suggested that a dancing school is in progress. Musicians play on either side and a admiring audience is in the background. A sensitive owner clipped the naked figure of Cupid from the copy at the Vaughan Williams Memorial Library! This version of the print from the eighth edition (1690) appears to be printed from the same block.

Courtesy of the Vaughan Williams Memorial Library

The prominence of the headdresses imply that the second print was probably designed in the 1690's. They are called *fontanges*, a style which enjoyed wide popularity between 1690-1710. The earliest known copy of this print is on John Walsh's *New Country Dancing Master, 2d book* of 1711 as well with the collection of twenty four dances for that year. It was usually used as a frontispiece, rather than part of the title page. Again, four couples are depicted, this time standing as couples. The music is playing and the end couple has turned around to face the other three. The Walsh firm apparently used this design with almost every country dance collection they published to 1730. It was re-engraved a number of times, and ranged from fine work to crude reversed copies.

Courtesy of the British Library

For the last edition (1728) of the first volume of *The Dancing Master*, John Young commissioned a new engraving, one which was apparently used only with this volume. Although it is clearly derived from the Walsh design, the dancers are now shown actively dancing. The men's backs are to the viewer, and one couple is turning two-hands. This type of active picture was used for the remainder of the century.

Courtesy of the Vaughan Williams Memorial Library

GLOSSARY OF FORMATIONS, FIGURES, AND STEPS

FORMATIONS

Almost all of the dances in this book are performed by couples, men with their partners standing to their right in squares, circles, and two-couple dances, or, in longways dances, opposite in lines of men and women facing. In the seventeenth and eighteenth centuries, the top of the set was placed nearest the King or honored person, the "Presence." Today, the music and the dance leader are the Presence.

The Longways Set

The longways set is formed by making two lines, the men in one line facing their partners in the other. If the dance is a duple minor longways for an indefinite number of couples, to identify the subsets the dancers can join hands in groups of two couples, starting at the top, the modern command being "hands-four from the top." If it is a triple minor, the dancers join hands in groups of three couples or "hands-six". This numbers the couples "one," "two," (and "three") from the top of each minor set. (See diagrams below.)

While the dance is in progress, the 1st couples move down one place with each repetition of the dance. They keep their number designation until they reach the bottom of the set. In a triple minor when there is only one couple below them, they should dance with an imaginary 3rd couple to effect the final progression. The 1st couple then waits out one turn of the dance before becoming a 3rd couple and progressing up the set.

The twos and threes move up one place and change their numbers from two to three, then three to two, with each repetition of the dance. When a 2nd couple reaches the top, they wait out two turns of the dance, until there are two inactive couples to dance with. They then become a 1st couple, and start their progress down the set. The twos and threes have to be especially alert as the roles they play in the dance change each time the dance starts again.

DIAGRAMS OF FORMATIONS

GENERAL GUIDELINES FOR DANCING

Listen carefully to the music. Each figure starts and ends perfectly on each phrase and the dancers usually begin and end in their original or progressed positions at the side of the set. Steps should fall on the beat and all the dancers in a set must move together so that all parts of the figures occur at the same time. In 3/2 and 3/4 time, take three steps in each bar; in 6/8, 2/2, 2/4 or cut time, take two steps in each bar; in 4/4 or common time, take four steps in each bar.

Each dancer should **pay attention** to what is going on around himself, even when not active. In crowded rooms, dancers may need to give space to accommodate the other dancers as they go through their movements. It is vital to be ready when becoming active.

Dance with partner and the other people in the set, not just solo on a track. "Eye contact" is the modern term for looking at other dancers during the execution of the figures. Ogling is not necessary, just friendly acknowledgement of each dancer's presence and participation.

Stand tall and keep weight over the feet. Use the weight of the body to move through the figures using a light dance step. This is different from walking where the feet lead and pull the body along. Good dancers appear to float across the floor and besides looking and moving well, they use a minimum of energy.

Taking hands requires a firm hand grasp, the man (or lower number) palms up and the woman's down. In any turning movement, there should be a feeling of equal tension between the dancers. By the gentle giving of weight, the dancers support each other during the movement. This feeling of support should also be present in circles, hands-across, and similar movements.

The dances should be performed **without effort and without affectation,** but they are not as casual and loose as the modern contra dance. They are a group activity and each dancer must match his or her movement carefully to fit in with the whole pattern of the dance.

FIGURES AND STEPS

Unless otherwise directed, all movements begin and end from home position on the sides of the set. Movements usually begin with the right foot.

Active, inactive: Active dancers are in motion according to the instructions of the dance. Inactive dancers remain in their places on the side of the set until included in the figures of the dance. Inactives may occasionally find it necessary to move to one side or the other to allow active dancers to pass between or around them.

Arm right, left: Dancers link right arms at elbow, turn once around clockwise, and fall back to places. **Arm left** is counter-clockwise. The arms should be firmly linked, dancers giving each other support in the turn.

Back to back: Dancers face and move forward to pass right shoulders, step to the right behind each other, and move backwards to place passing left shoulders.

Balance forward and back: To balance forward, step forward onto the right foot, bring the left forward to close beside the right, then step backward on the left. To balance back, step backward onto the left foot, bring the right to close beside the left, then step forward onto the left. This is a simple forward and back body movement, as used in waltzes such as "The Northdown Waltz" in A1: 1-4.

Balance back and move forward: This movement differs from those above in that there is a definite *change of weight*. Step back on the right foot, bring the left back beside it, then step forward on the **right** foot. Stepping forward in this case usually leads right into a travelling figure such as the change places in "Spring Garden," Part I, B1: 5-8.

Cast: Partners turn away from each other and move outside the set to a new position, the other dancers usually moving up or down as indicated on the last four beats. To **cast down** in a progressive longways dance, the 1st (or active) couple face up, separate, and move down outside one place. To **cast up,** 1st couple face down, separate and move up outside one place.

Change places: Dancers exchange places by moving across the set passing right shoulders unless otherwise directed, turn around to the right and end facing each other as before. This movement uses an entire phrase. In some triple time dances such as "The Hole in the Wall" and "Well Hall" as noted, the first part of the change is danced like a half-gipsy, the dancers backing into new places on the last three steps.

Circle three-hands, four-hands, &c: Dancers form a ring by joining hands, a little above waist level, and circle to the left once around. Three-hands involves 3 dancers

114

(actually six hands); four-hands is for 4 dancers, six-hands for six, and so on. If the directions specify "and back," dancers then circle an equal number of steps to the right, back to places.

Circular hey: see **Hey**

Corner: In duple minor formation, **first corners** are the 1st man and 2nd woman. **Second corners** are the 1st woman and 2nd man. In a square or round, the **corner** is on the man's left or woman's right.

Cross: The actives simply go directly across the set to the other side, passing right shoulders unless otherwise directed. This is usually followed by a movement down the outside, or a hey on the opposite side.

Double: Three steps and close in duple time; two steps and close in triple time.

Fall back: Move backward as directed.

Figure-eight: In a longways progressive dance, the active dancer pass between the couple below (or above), around the dancer on the opposite side of the set, pass between the same couple, around the other dancer and return to place. This figure is frequently danced by a couple simultaneously, the woman moving ahead of her partner. If a **half figure-eight** is directed, the active couple will end in partner's place in the set.

Forward a double, fall back a double: Starting on right foot, take three steps forward and close (no weight); to **fall back,** start with the left, take three steps backward and close. In triple time, take two steps and close.

Gipsy: Dancers face each other and move clockwise (keeping to the left) completely around one another, facing inward. The movement may be compared to a two-hand turn without hands. This figure sometimes leads to exaggeration! Avoid eyeball to eyeball contact or "airplane" arms.

HEYS

Hey: A weaving figure for 3, 4, 6, or 8 dancers without hands unless otherwise specified.

Hey for three: This figure is danced up and down, or across the set. The dancers, moving simultaneously, describe a figure-eight. No. 1 faces Nos. 2 and 3; moving slightly to the left, No. 1 passes No. 2 by the right shoulder, then No. 3 by the left shoulder. Turning left, No. 1 re-enters the set to complete the figure-eight with the other dancers. This weaving figure is best performed when the figure-eight is made as wide as possible.

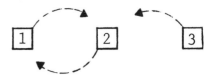

Track of the Hey for Three

Half-hey: Here only half the figure is danced, the ends will have changed places, the middle dancer will dance through an end position and back to the middle.

Hey on opposite side, hey on own side: In this variation of the **hey for three,** the 1st couple hey on the opposite side while the 2nd and 3rd couples hey on their own: 1st woman cross down center to pass 3rd man by the left, 1st man cross down center to pass 3rd woman by the right. 1st couple finish the hey in top place, improper.

To **hey on own side** they cross again down the center to their own side while 2nd and 3rd couples do as they did in the first part. Note that for the 2nd and 3rd couples, the pattern of the hey is a continuous meeting and separating from partner as in mirror hey below.

In a variation of this hey, the 1st couple change places across the top of the set, and begin the hey from the outside, 1st man passing 2nd woman right, 3rd woman left, and 1st woman passing 2nd man left, and 3rd man right, as in "The Touchstone" (see page 103).

Mirror hey: When both sides hey together, the figure is often in mirror image: 1st and 2nd men pass right shoulders, 1st and 2nd women pass left shoulders to start. In this case the 1st couple begins the hey leading down the middle, the 2nd couple facing up and separating outside 1st couple, the 3rd leading up the center, the 1st couple separating around them. This figure became known as the "Grimstock" hey because of Sharp's use of it in that early dance.

Straight hey for four: Nos. 1 and 2 face, Nos. 3 and 4 face. All begin by passing right shoulders, reversing direction at both ends of the hey, turning right and passing right on reentering the figure.

Circular hey for four: This is danced like a right-and-left (see page 116), except that the dancers do not take hands to pass and they weave in a circular track rather than a square.

Circular hey for six: In this weaving figure, the 1st couple face each other, the 2nd couple face the 3rd who face up. All begin by passing right shoulders and continue all around the set to places.

Progressive hey: In this variation, the movement is initiated by two dancers as directed, who face each other, take right hands, pass by, give left hands to the next, right to the next, and so on, eventually bringing all dancers into the hey which is continued until all dancers reach their ending places.

Sheepskin Hey: This is not a true hey, but rather a weaving track figure around standing dancers and occurs only in "Picking up Sticks." Using a skip step, 1st man, followed by 2nd and 3rd men, crosses above the 1st woman and begins to weave around the standing women. 1st man passes 2nd woman left and 3rd woman right, 2nd and 3rd men following. When the 3rd man (who is at the end of the line) has passed the 2nd woman, he reverses direction by going completely around her and weaves back, leading the hey up the line, followed by the 1st and 2nd man. When the 2nd man (now at the end of the line) reaches the 2nd woman, he does the same, dancing completely around her and reversing the direction of the hey, followed by the 3rd and the 1st man. When the 1st man becomes the end of the line and reaches the 2nd woman, he does the same, weaves back up to the top and leads the line in a cast off to his right, around behind the women, across the bottom of the set and up to original place. Then the women do the mirror image.

. . .

Honor: A courtesy movement. A man bows, simply dropping the torso with the arms relaxed at the sides; a woman brings one foot behind and bends and straightens her knees in a simple curtsey. Theatrical flourishes and held-out skirts are inappropriate.

Improper: see **Proper, improper**

Lead: Partners or actives take hands, the man or lower number dancer offering palms up, and they move together. Current practice is to take inside hands rather than right-to-right as Sharp originally indicated. Both are acceptable, remembering that all movements **begin and end in place** at the side of the set.

Neighbor: In a longways dance, the neighbor is the person beside the active dancer.

Poussette: Men take both hands with partners, arms straight and nearly shoulder high. 1st man take four steps obliquely forward, pushing partner out of set, then fall back four steps pulling partner into other couple's place. Simultaneously, 2nd man fall back four steps, pulling partner, then forward into 1st man's place. For a half-poussette, stop here. For a full poussette, continue the movement until all are in original places.

Presence: Top of the room, usually where the music is.

Proper, improper: When all are on their own side, they are **proper**. If the woman is standing on the men's side, or a man on the women's side, they are **improper**.

Right-and-left: This figure is usually danced by two couples. Begin by giving right hand to partner, pass by and turn towards neighbor, give left hand to neighbor and pass by *, right hand to partner, pass, left hand to neighbor and pass. Each dancer will pass through the places of each of the other dancers in turn. Move directly from place to place without extra loops or turns. This figure is usually phrased with four beats for each pass but can occasionally be in three, and less frequently, a quick two. Each pass is called a "change." **Half right-and-left** is the same up to the *. **Grand right-and-left** is the same, but involves a larger number of dancers.

Right hands-across, left hands-across: Diagonally opposite dancers join right or left hands in a shake-hands position, two pairs making a star. Giving some support, the dancers then move around in the direction they are facing, usually for eight steps.

SET

Set: Setting steps are done either in place or advancing toward or retiring from another person. One "set" is to the right *and* the left and usually takes two bars. Dancer springs lightly onto right foot, usually to the side, steps onto the left briefly and back onto the right, with a quick change of weight. The movement is then repeated with a spring onto the left foot.

Slow set: A step to the right or left and a close, taking one bar. **Slow set and honor right** (or left) is a step to the right (or left) followed by an honor.

. . .

Siding: As defined by Sharp in 1911, siding is danced thus: Partners face and change places, each moving slightly to the right diagonally, starting with the right (outside) foot and passing left shoulders. Take two steps forward, turn counter-clockwise to face on the third, bringing the feet together on the fourth step. Returning, start with the left foot, take two steps to pass, turn clockwise to face, and bring feet together. If partners look at each other while dancing the figure, it is almost impossible to turn the wrong way.

Historically more accurate, **side-by-side siding** was described by Sharp (*CDB* 6, 10-11) but disregarded by his disciples. This interpretation of siding was re-introduced in the 1970's by Pat Shaw and now is widely practiced: partners face, move forward a double bringing right shoulder to right shoulder, fall back a double, and repeat to left shoulders. While leaving the final choice of which siding to use to the leader, the preferred method for the dances in this collection is Cecil Sharp's 1911 interpretation.

Single: A single is a step and a close, from weight on one foot to weight on two feet.

STEPS

Running step is used most frequently when ground has to be covered in a limited amount of time and to add excitement and verve to a movement, as in "The Phoenix" or "Step Stately." The dancer springs lightly from foot to foot, quietly and easily, knees loose but not bent, feet under the body.

Walking step is a modification of the running step in which the spring is scarcely noticeable. The general effect is of a lilting movement which should be sustained even in slow dances such as "Oranges and Lemons" or "Hunsdon House."

Skipping step is a step-hop on alternate feet. The hop should be small, legs relaxed, no kicking up the heels or prancing! This step is often used for a hey for three as in "The Fandango" or "The Old Mole."

Skip-change step is a variation of the skipping step. Step forward on the right foot, bring the left to close beside the right, step-hop on the right foot. Repeat beginning left foot.

Slipping step is a sideways spring to the right or left. The trailing foot is brought up to the leading foot, takes the weight and the spring is repeated. It is used frequently in circle movements, such as those in "Gathering Peascods."

Waltz step: In ballroom position, partners use the regular waltz step (step, step, close) to dance around another couple. For traveling in movements such as lead, cast, turn single, cross over, and right-and-left, use a "long, short, short" lilting walking step. The feet should pass each other, but not come to a close, as this would interrupt the flow of the movement.

. . .

Turn: Two dancers join right, left, or both hands as indicated, and, giving a little weight, move around one-another, usually clockwise in a two-hand turn.

Turn single: A solo turn for one person, usually clockwise. This takes four walking steps, and should trace a small circle on the floor, and not be a pivot in place.

Drawing by Genevieve Shimer
for Pat Shaw's Pinewoods
(Plymouth, Mass.: Pinewoods Camp, 1985), 25

Courtesy of Pinewoods Camp, Inc.

INDEX OF TUNE TITLES, FIRST LINES, AND SUBJECTS